EPHESUS

The New Guide

Edited by

PETER SCHERRER

authorised by

ÖSTERREICHISCHES ARCHÄOLOGISCHES INSTITUT

and

EFES MÜZESI SELÇUK

English translation by

LIONEL BIER and **GEORGE M. LUXON**

revised edition 2000

EPHESUS - THE NEW GUIDE

edited by PETER SCHERRER in cooperation with many professional colleagues

Typeset and layout: Zero Prod. Ltd.

Printed and entirely produced by: Graphis Ltd.

Printed in Turkey

ISBN 975-807-036-3

Front cover picture: Artemis Ephesia, copy of the cult-statue from the time of Hadrian, so-called "Beautiful Artemis".

Rear cover pictures: golden statue of Artemis and votive offerings to the goddess, 7th century BC

Aerial photos, right: Ephesus - Ayasoluk - Selçuk: an invitation to 5000 years of history

PREFACE

Ever since JOSEF KEIL wrote the first guide to Ephesus in 1915 (subsequently reissued in five editions through 1964), it has been a tradition to present the results of archaeological research in the ruined city in a concise and readable form both for visitors and members of the academic community. Thus, when in 1995 the Österreichisches Archäologisches Institut commemorated 100 years of Austrian research at Ephesus, it seemed appropriate to make a summary of our present knowledge available to the public in a new guide book which has now been revised in an English translation. This is a handy and useful book to conduct the visitor on a tour of the excavations. It not only introduces the ancient city of Ephesus and its monuments, but also offers the most recent information on academic research, and allows the reader to share in the fruits of the work of Austrian and Turkish archaeologists.

We have indeed been fortunate that SELAHATTİN ERDEMGİL, Director of the Ephesus Museum in Selçuk, and his colleagues have agreed to contribute to this work in a modern spirit of international cooperation. It is the pleasant duty of the directorate of the Österreichisches Archäologisches Institut to thank them warmly for their help, and, at the same time, to hope for further success in this partnership.

The directorate's thanks are extended to all the authors whose contributions have made the guide book into a reflection of the Ephesian team and particularly to PETER SCHERRER who has undertaken the task of bringing this work to publication. The Austrian BUNDESMINISTERIUM FÜR WISSENSCHAFT UND VERKEHR is also to be thanked for making our work possible within the framework of the statutory contract and for guaranteeing the necessary funding for the publication of this book.

In November 1963, FRITZ EICHLER ended his preface to the last edition of the KEIL guide book with a wish that the undersigned would like to repeat here, as it has lost none of its relevance:

May the new guide book to Ephesus convey to the reader a vivid picture of the rise and fall of this ancient metropolis and win new friends and sponsors for this great Austrian undertaking.

FRITZ KRINZINGER
Director of the Österreichisches
Archäologisches Institut
Vienna, in January 2000

PREFACE

Ephesus, one of the very few ancient cities which has been continuously inhabited for more than three thousand years up into the present era, has asserted itself in each epoch as a centre of civilisation and the focal point of a rich and flourishing cultural life. True to the importance of this glorious past, the Österreichisches Archäologisches Institut has carried out excavations in Ephesus for more than a hundred years, and provided for the conservation and restoration of the archaeological finds and the re-erection of architectural monuments. It is hoped that the work of recovery and restoration, carried out jointly with the Ephesus Museum Selçuk, under the auspices of the Ministry of Culture of the Republic of Turkey, will serve as a model of co-operation for similar undertakings in the future.

Looking back, it is clear that the labours of the Österreichisches Archäologisches Institut over the years has not been in vain, and that all the effort taken to restore this place to its former magic and splendour has born fruit. Ever since the year 1895, countless academic specialists and workers have put themselves, with great patience and devotion, in the service of Ephesus. We are very much obliged and our heartfelt thanks go to all of them. It is only through their activities that we have again become aware that Ephesus is a substantial part of the cultural heritage of mankind.

Ephesus, one of the most important centres of ancient civilization, has also paved the way for the culture of the west. As in antiquity, Ephesus is today again a centre of cultural life. Those who seek to broaden their minds must linger for a while at Ephesus. In such a way will Ephesus continue to live in the future as an important and integral part of the world cultural heritage.

The excavations which have continued over 100 years have led, each year, to important results which have opened new horizons in academic research into the civilizations of Anatolia. The decisive thing is, however, that the results of this research have been submitted, without delay, to the international scientific community. The German version of this book was prepared and printed by the Österreichisches Archäologisches Institut on the occasion of the hundred-year jubilee of the excavations at Ephesus by experts of outstanding merit who have given their special attention to that ancient city. May the revised English edition also give valuable service to those who are interested in Ephesus, academic specialists and lay people alike.

Selahattin Erdemgil
Director of the Ephesus Museum,
Selçuk, in January 2000

AGATHE TYCHE

May all go well

Many ephesian inscriptions commend themselves to the reader with this wish. The team of authors of the New Guide to Ephesus, all of them colleagues of long-standing at the excavations of the Österreichisches Archäologisches Institut and at the Ephesus Museum in Selçuk, hope that the following introduction to the history and the ruins of the metropolis will be of use to you, and that during your visit to Ephesus, all may indeed go well.

A few tips may help you to find your way through this guide book. Each building or monument is given a [number] by which it can be identified in the numerical list of monuments and on the plan of the ruins included at the end of the book. The signposts at the ruins also bear the same numbers.

The coloured illustrations show the condition of the monuments at the time of printing, black-and-white drawings give some idea as to excavation sites, plans and reconstructions of monuments which are no longer visible or open to the public. The coloured backgrounds to the descriptions of the illustrations give information on the various criteria of accessibility or visibility of the historic material.

GREEN marks the usual tour of easily reached, mainly well-preserved or comprehensively restored monuments.

BLUE indicates that a monument is off the tourist track or lies outside the fenced-off areas of ruins. To see them, additional time is necessary together with suitable clothing and a sufficient level of physical fitness. In some cases a special permit is required.

YELLOW marks monuments which have been re-buried, which no longer exist or are not accessible.

Where several criteria apply, the colour appropriate to the main category has been chosen. The length of text and the headings are based, on the one hand, on the historical importance and, on the other, on the state of preservation of the items described.

An insert box contains a choice, in shortened form, of selected academic literature (mainly excavation reports) about the monument concerned.

A glossary defining technical terms and a list of references at the end of the book serve to make the information more readily understandable.

SUMMARY OF CONTENTS

INTRODUCTION TO THE HISTORICAL TOPOGRAPHY OF EPHESUS

Ephesus lies on the Aegean coast of Turkey some 70 km south of Izmir at the mouth of the river Caystros (Küçük Menderes) and slightly north of the island of Samos. In Greek antiquity this was the centre of the Ionian countryside which was incorporated into the Roman Province of Asia in 133 BC.

The silting up of the deep inlet of the sea by the Caystros and mountain streams originating in the south, on the one hand, and changes to the coastline caused by eustatic and climatic fluctuations together with seismic disturbances on the other, led in ancient times to several relocations of the city site. By the later Middle Ages Ephesus was completely cut off from the sea, and new harbour installations were constructed at *Scalanuova* (modern Kuşadası), founded by the Genoese.

Around the Byzantine-Turkish fortress [151] on the Ayasoluk, with its broad panoramic view, there was, at the beginning of the 20th century, merely a small settlement with the same name which incorporated the nucleus of Ephesus dating back to the bronze age. Renamed *Selçuk*, it has now grown to be the district capital. A straight regional road leads from the western edge of the town, past the ruins of the Hellenistic-Roman city to the beach at Pamucak, some 6 km away.

On a promontory jutting out from the south west of the Ayasoluk lies the famous shrine [1] of Artemis, equated by the Greeks with Ephesia who gave her name to the city. Up into Greek times the shoreline extended from here southward (up into the 20th century the lowland was marshy), and along it ran the road to Magnesia and Tralleis (Aydın) in the valley of the Meander.

The opposite shore of this inlet is bordered by the twin-peaked Panayırdağ. At least the higher southern part (height, 155 m), on the south- west flank of which lies the present day "Upper Entrance" [115] to the ruins, bore the name Pion in antiquity. The east flank of the northern hill (height, 133 m), outside the Hellenistic city wall and deeply eaten away by ravines, was known as Tracheia and here lay the harbour area [3] called Coressus.

Around this and the small cape which once jutted out far into the sea, with the so-called Crevice Temple [103] on its outer tip, lay the settlement founded by the first Greeks under the leadership of the legendary Athenian Androclus. Another village of the archaic-classical period, probably the Smyrna of ancient

Fig. 1: Satellite picture of the Ephesian bay (top is east): the meandering course of the old Caystrus can be clearly seen in the alluvial area; to the south lies the Hellenistic-Roman city with its two hills, Bülbüldağ and Panayırdağ. The semicircle of the theatre and Arcadiane street leading to the harbour are clearly recognisable. In the east (top) lies the Ayasoluk and the present day town of Selçuk.

N

tradition, lay a little to the west, roughly under the Hellenistic-Roman Tetragonos Agora [61]. Just as Croesus, for political reasons, had forced the resettlement of the Coressians in the area of the Artemis Temple in the 6th century BC, so some 250 years later king Lysimachus moved his new city to the edge of the Ephesian bay. The new city wall [77] enclosed an area of settlement which included the entire sea-side slope of the Bülbüldağ (height, 358 m), known in antiquity as Lepre Acte and later Preon, as well as all of the Pion.

The still largely un-excavated Hellenistic city presumably covered only the part of this enormous area near to the harbour. The built-up urban area only expanded under (or in the decades immediately preceding) the first Roman Emperor Augustus, who raised Ephesus to the status of capital of the Province of Asia. The administrative quarter was built in Roman times on the saddle between the two city hills and the next generation experienced the transformation of the ravine leading down to the harbour plain (Embolos, or so-called Curetes Street [36]). From the end of the first century AD, the marshy land north-west of the great theatre was reclaimed by infilling, and large public buildings such as the Harbour Baths [92-94] and the Temple of Zeus Olympios Hadrianus [Olympeion 98], founded around 129 AD, were erected.

FiE I 9 - 110; ZPE 89, 1991, 275-295; Kraft - Kayan - Brückner, in: Steine und Wege, Festschrift D. Knibbe (1999) 91 - 100.
The following section on the history of Ephesus contains further information on the historical topography.

It is no doubt through the generous building activities of the Vedius family in the 2nd century that Coressus was again included to an ever increasing extent in the area of urban development and, with the construction of the Stoa of Damianus [7], a direct land connection to the Temple of Artemis was created over the marshy lagoon.

The city remained in the location chosen by Lysimachus for more than a thousand years - up into the 7th - 8th centuries AD - although it gradually receded into the area around Coressus which was protected by the new city wall.

The spiritual and physical centre during the early Christian period was the bishop's Church of Mary [95], consecrated to the Mother of God, near the present day "Lower Entrance" [116] to the ruins. At the same time a place of pilgrimage came into existence - in the 5th century at the latest - on the oldest area of settlement, the Ayasoluk (from *Hagios Theologos*), where a basilica (and affiliated cloister ?) with its own defensive walls [152] grew up around the grave of *John the Theologian*, already equated at the time with the apostle and evangelist. Up until the final flight of the last inhabitants of the Hellenistic-Roman city to the Ayasoluk, two settlements existed side by side, the western one trying to maintain its connection to the sea for as long as possible. From late Roman times, however, the commercial harbour was on the bay at the outlet of the Arvalia valley, in which Ortygia, the mythical place of birth of Artemis, was built up as a sacred precinct. The crusaders may still have called at Panormos, this last harbour of Ephesus.

The ancient coastal road, on which, early in 1995 near the Magnesian Gate [10], possibly the oldest remains currently known from the Ephesus area were discovered, connected the birthplace of Artemis Ephesia with her temple. On this road, every year on the 6th of May, a festive procession celebrated the birthday of the goddess. The road also served into Roman times as the highway linking the settlements mentioned above. The annual procession thus came into contact with all the inhabitants as well as with the cemeteries which lined its route. For this reason, the road is called today the *Processional Road*, and its stretches which lie within the city (according to ancient inscriptions), *Plateia*. PS

Chronological Table of Ephesus

Before the birth of Christ

5th - 3rd millennia	Oldest places of settlement in the area around Ephesus.
2nd half of 14th century	King Mursilis II. of the Hittites marches against King Uhhazitis of Arzawa and Apaša which he destroys. Mycenaean grave on the Ayasoluk.
11th century	During the Ionic migrations, the Athenian Prince Androclus leads settlers into the gulf of Caystrus where Coressus, a place where Carians lived, was occupied.
9th century	Certain existence of a holy precinct in the area of the Sanctuary of Artemis.
2nd half of 8th century	Establishment of the village settlement called Smyrna near Ephesus
645	Invasion of the Cimmerians under their chieftain Lygdamis.
7th century	The poet Callinus, the oldest known elegist, works in Ephesus.
2nd half of 7th century	The tyrant Pythagoras founds a temple of Artemis.
around 600	Beginning of local minting of coins (small pieces of electrum bearing the image of a lion's paw) under the second tyrant Melas, the son-in-law of Alyattes, king of the Lydians.
around 560	Croesus gains influence in Ephesus: building of the archaic shrine of Artemis, new layout of the city in the surrounding area.
around 550	A certain Aristarchus of Athens introduces democracy for a brief time in Ephesus.
546	The Median general Harpagus takes Ephesus.
2nd half of 6th century	Ephesus under Persian supremacy. Hipponax is the world's first sarcast.
around 480	Of all the Greek temples in Asia Minor, Xerxes spares only the shrine of Artemis. Death of Heraclitus "the obscure".
466	Cimonian peace between Athens and the Persians, Ephesus joins the Attic sea alliance.
431 - 404	Ephesus fights on the side of Sparta-Persia against Athens in the Peloponnesian War.
356	Fire in the Temple of Artemis, allegedly the act of a madman - a certain Herostratus.
334	Alexander the Great in Ephesus: his army paraded in honour of Artemis but the Ephesians diplomatically refuse his offer of help in rebuilding the temple.
323	A certain Hegesias, the last tyrant of Ephesus, murdered by three Ephesians.

319 - 281	Ephesus changes its ruler several times during the Diadochian wars. The city is re-founded under the name Arsinoëia by King Lysimachus.
281	Death of Lysimachus at the battle of Corupedium. Ephesus under the rule of the Seleucids.
around 260	Ptolemy II Philadelphus captures Ephesus.
197	The Seleucid king Antiochus III ends Ptolemaic rule in Ephesus.
195 - 190	Hannibal flees to Antiochus in Ephesus.
191	Antiochus' governor Polyxenidas suffers defeat at sea after which the Roman admiral C. Livius blockades the harbour of Ephesus.
188/187	After the departure of Antiochus, Scipio Asiagenus winters in Ephesus which was annexed as a military district of the kingdom of Pergamum. Introduction of the royal coinage of the Cistophors.
133	In his will, Attalus III bequeaths the kingdom of Pergamum to the Romans. Establishment of the Province of Asia.
around 100	The geographer Artemidorus works in Ephesus.
89/88	The Ephesians welcome the king of Pontus, Mithridates VI Eupator, as liberator. All the Italics murdered (*Ephesian Vespers*).
84	L. Cornelius Sulla holds a trial of the people guilty in 88 BC and orders compensations.
74	First visit of M. Tullius Cicero to Ephesus which he views as a Roman supply centre.
73	L. Licinius Lucullus governor of Ephesus.
51	On the way to his province of Cecilia, Cicero makes a grandiose entry into Ephesus where he meets with renowned Romans.
48	C. Julius Caesar lands at Ephesus and prevents the former proconsul T. Amplius Balbus from robbing the Temple of Artemis. New regulation of the system of taxation.
47/6	A hero cult established in Ephesus for the proconsul P. Servilius Vatia Isauricus.
44	Caesar's murderers, M. Junius Brutus and C. Cassius Longinus, received in Ephesus.
41	Mark Antony enters Ephesus with Cleopatra of Egypt with great pomp as the New Dionysus. Murder of Cleopatra's sister Arsinoë IV, who had sought asylum in the sanctuary of Artemis.
30/29	Octavianus, the victor of the civil wars, reorganizes the East in Ephesus.
29	The geographer Strabo journeys through Ephesus.

After the birth of Christ:

23	An earthquake shakes the city and causes much damage; reconstruction partly with imperial help.
52 (?)	St. Paul comes to Ephesus with Aquila and Priscilla at the end of his second journey. After his departure the preacher Apollus appears.
53 - 55	Return of St. Paul who installs a Christian Centre in the "School" of a tyrant. The silversmith Demetrius instigates a demonstration against St. Paul. St. Luke, the evangelist, in Ephesus.
62	Definition of the customs law for the Province of Asia.
82	1st temple guardianship (Neokoros), the Imperial Temple of the Flavian dynasty erected.

96, Sept. 18th,	Apollonius of Tyana has a vision in Ephesus of the murder of Domitian whose temple was rededicated to Vespasian.
End of 1st century	Timothy, the first bishop of Ephesus, martyred.
around 110	Pliny the younger journeys via Ephesus to Bithynia.
113/114	Emperor Trajan visits Ephesus.
124, Aug. 29th	Emperor Hadrian's first visit to Ephesus.
129/130	Emperor Hadrian's second visit to Ephesus together with Antinoos; 2nd temple guardianship, building of the Olympieion started.
135/136	Antoninus Pius, subsequently emperor, proconsul in Ephesus.
140 - 144	Emperor Antoninus Pius sends an admonition to the Ephesians concerning their obsession with titles.
2nd quarter of 2nd century	Activities of the sophist T. Claudius Flavianus Dionysius, who was buried next to the Agora.
162/163	Emperor Lucius Verus in Ephesus: campaign against the Parthians.
166/167	Verus' troops wait in Ephesus for embarkation to Rome and spread the plague.
210/211	Establishment of the 3rd temple guardianship for Caracalla and Geta.
219	Emperor Elagabalus may have visited Ephesus on his way to Rome. Establishment of the 4th temple guardianship.
262	A major earthquake hits Ephesus. The Temple of Artemis destroyed attracting plundering bands of Goths. End of the minting of coins and the temple guardianships.
351/352	Prince Flavius Claudius Julianus introduced to the Chaldean mysteries in Ephesus by Theurgen Maximus.
3rd quarter of 4th century	A series of strong earthquakes causes more damage.
381	The archbishop of Ephesus becomes Patriarch.
End of 4th century	Extensive new building in the city.
from 391	An edict of Emperor Theodosius makes Christianity the state religion and the Christians begin to destroy or christianize pagan buildings.
431	The Fourth Ecumenical Council convened in Ephesus in cooperation with the local patriarch Memnon. The dogma of Mary as Theotokos (she who gives birth to god) promulgated.
449	Another synod meets in Ephesus and is named Latrocinium (the robber synod) because of its evil doings.
451	The orthodox John is created archbishop of Ephesus with the new title Exarch.
around 530	The pilgrims guide of Theodosius mentions the Seven Sleepers sanctuary.
Mid 6th century	Archbishop John III transfers part of the administration to the Church of St. John, newly built under Justinian.
after 610	Ephesus becomes the capital of the new military district of Thracesion.
654/655	First Arab attack under Muawija. Thereafter, the removal of the seat of the bishop to the Church of St. John.

HISTORY AND RESEARCH HISTORY OF EPHESUS

Prehistory

The history of the Caystros and the valley of the Meander, as it is ascertainable through archaeology, begin with the late chalcolithic around 5000 BC. Finds (implements of pottery or obsidian) which came to light in 1995 some 400 m south of the Magnesian Gate [10] are evidence of the settlement of the Ephesian area at least by the end of this period.

Later than this material are extensive finds of ceramics from the middle bronze age (2nd half of the 3rd millennium BC) which were discovered in 1990 on the north-east flank of the Ayasoluk hill [155] and below the Byzantine-Turkish Fortress.

This history becomes clearer in the late bronze age from the 2nd half of the 2nd millennium BC when Minoan settlements came into existence. These later became Mycenaean bases when the Greeks took over the power and culture of the Minoans around 1450 BC. Such a base existed on the Ayasoluk as is shown by a grave [153] of the 14th century BC (LH III A2). A wall of large rectangular stone blocks may also belong to this period in the middle bronze age. The name *Ephesus* is very probably the hellenized form of *Apaša*, named in Hittite sources as the main place of any size in a country called *Arzawa*, which is placed by modern scholarship (although not without dispute) somewhere in western Asia Minor. This *"Arzawa-land"* seems to have been a buffer zone between the Hittite empire and the Mycenaean settlements on the coast. We hear from the sources of a natural upheaval whose precise nature is unclear, and an outbreak of plague which accompanied the ill-fated campaign of the Hittite king Mursilis (II.) against *Apaša* intended to bring back refugees who had fled to *Arzawa* and to gain or restore Hittite supremacy over this country. SE

The Greek settlement up to Alexander the Great

The Mycenaean world collapsed with the catastrophe of the migrations of the so-called Sea Peoples around 1200 BC, while the Hittite empire fell to the Phrygians who entered Asia Minor from Thrace in the wake of these wide-spread disturbances.

After 1220, Greeks speaking Ionian or Aeolian dialect, fleeing from the Dorians moving southwards out of north-west Greece, began to fill the power vacuum resulting from the collapse of Hittite and Mycenaean authority.

While the Ionians established themselves on the west coast, from the area south of the Hermos to the land beyond Caria, the Aeolians settled to the north of this river (today called Gediz çayı). The Dorians, having taken over the Peloponnese, flocked into Asia Minor via the Dodecanese, before settling in the south-west of the peninsula.

When the Greeks arrived, they met an autochthonic non-Greek people which the geographer Strabo, writing around the time of Christ, called *Carians and Lelegans*. Even then, a cult precinct for a tree, spring and fertility goddess, later worshipped as Artemis, existed at the south-west foot of the Ayasoluk. As they were coming to terms with the people who lived around this shrine, the Carian settlement was destroyed and a strong cantonment established seven stadia (about 1300 m) west of the Artemision. "Ionic" Ephesus, as yet incompletely studied, lay on a shallow inlet of the sea which, in ancient times, reached far to the east beyond the harbour of Coressus (already silted up in Hellenistic times), extending up the slopes of the Panayırdağ, east and west of the spot now occupied by the stadium. Androclus (son of the fabled Athenian king Codros), later to fall in battle against neighbouring Priene, is said to have founded Ephesus and, according to the foundation legend, was shown the way there by an oracle.

Like almost all Greek city states, Ephesus experienced several forms of rule. First ruled by the *Basilids*, descendants of Androclus, the city later saw oligarchies and tyrannical dictatorships. Around 700 BC Ephesus, a member of the Ionian League, wished to extend its influence to the south and took part in the destruction of the city of Melie at the north foot of the Mycale headland. Then, in successful battles with neighboring Magnesia to the south-east, it consolidated its position on the Meander. Inspired to fight by the singer Callinos, the city withstood the invasion of the barbaric Cimmerians, an asiatic tribe of horsemen related to the Scythians (and driven by them out of their homeland in south Russia), who spread like a whirlwind over Asia Minor in the 7th century BC leaving behind them death and destruction. Votive offerings connected with the Cimmerians have been found in the cult precinct at the south-west foot of the Ayasoluk.

It was the inevitable fate of the Greek cities on the east coast of the Aegean to fall under the control of the barbarian kingdoms east of the small coastal strip occupied by Hellenic settlements. This happened to Ephesus before the middle of the 6th century BC when the fabulously rich and powerful king Croesus, lord of the Lydians and covetous of the coastal land, successfully laid seige to the city. Croesus, imposed his suzerainty upon the inhabitants but in general, treated them well. Nevertheless the beginning of Lydian hegemony can be seen as the first major break in the long history of Ephesus. The Greeks had brought with them their supreme god Zeus, common to all Hellenes, and Athena as municipal goddess of their city of origin. The area which they settled, however, was originally the domain of the Phrygian mother goddess Cybele. Croesus wanted to unite the region under a single deity as a counterbalance to the mighty shrines of the oracular Apollo at Didyma and Hera at Samos.

For this reason he raised to a position of supreme importance the fertility goddess of the Ayasoluk who, from her genealogical connection with the Hellenic pantheon as daughter of Zeus and the goddess Leto, was more likely to be accepted as an integral religious figure by the Greek and non-Greek autochthonic peoples alike than the papently un-Hellenized Cybele of the Panayırdağ. This became amply clear when Croesus donated money for the Artemision which was begun as a great marble temple during his reign. At the same time, evidently to do away with the Greek/non-Greek dualism, he forced the Ionians to leave their higher settlement and join in synoicism the inhabitants of the city around the Artemision. An intermediary agent by the name of Aristarchus, allegedly summoned from Athens and invested with unlimited power by the king, is said to have carried out the resettlement and the political reorganization necessary for the establishment of the new Ephesus (the so-called Greek city) which was completed in less than five years.

The Lydian hegemony over Ephesus did not last long. With the defeat of Croesus at the battle of the river Halys (today called Kızıl Irmak) in the year 546 BC, the city, along with the entire Lydian realm, passed under the control of the Achaemenid Persian great king Cyrus I. and found itself part of a world empire which already stretched from the Indus to the lower reaches of the Danube and would soon include Egypt. Like Croesus, Cyrus treated the Greeks well and, from the magnanimity of truly powerful sovereignty, allowed them their individuality, recognizing what he had in this clever and enterprising people.

To the end of the 6th century belongs perhaps the greatest of the sons of Ephesus, Heraclitus "the obscure one" (*skoteinos*), who made a weighty contribution to Greek natural philosophy. His teaching that all things are in a state of balanced, measured change, no longer asking about a permanent, imperishable entity as the older natural philosophers had done, but about the entity of Being as such and its movements and changes, belongs to the great achievements of the early philosophical theory of insight and ontology. Heraclitus stood in diametrical opposition to Parmenides and the Eleans who claimed that Being thrust against Being and that movement is therefore not possible as every apparent movement rests upon a figment of the imagination.

During the Ionian revolt, which began in Miletus and ended in 494 BC with the extraordinary punishment of that city, it seems that the sly Ephesians were neutral and got off scot-free. This did not deter them, after the great sea victories of the Greeks over the Persian fleet in the strait between Attica and the island of Salamis (480 BC), Platea, and the peninsula of Mycale (479 BC) (jutting far out into the sea to the south at the front door of Ephesus, as it were) from joining the Attic Sea Alliance (479 BC) under the leadership of Athens, which in the course of events, developed into an exploitative Athenian tyranny. As the scales moved in favour of Sparta in the course of the great Hellenic fratricidal conflict which we call the Peloponnesian War (431 - 406 BC), the Ephesians entered on the side of the Spartans and helped their new comrades- in- arms to destroy the fleet upon which the power of Athens depended in the last and all-deciding battle of this war near Aegospotami.

For some time afterwards, Ephesus played a major role as an important place of anchorage and as arms-depot for the Spartans in the fight against Persia, but came again under Persian suzerainty after Antalcidas negotiated the so-called King's Peace (386 BC) which was, in fact, dictated by the Persian great king.

This was to end when the Macedonian king Alexander the Great went to war for revenge against Persia and, as commander-in-chief of the forces of the pan-Hellenic (Corinthian) League, was victorious at the river Granicus in the year 334 BC. On his triumphal march after the battle, Alexander passed through Ephesus which had again been won back for a short time for the Persian great king by Memnon of Rhodes. Alexander restored democracy which was thankfully accepted. In the year 356 BC, the Temple of Artemis burnt down. The fire was allegedly caused by the burning torch of the mad *Herostratus* but in fact, he was probably put up to it by the priesthood with the aim of replacing the old Croesus building which was slowly sinking in the ground water. The cautious Ephesians, fearing for their independence and that of their shrine, refused Alexander's offer to rebuild the temple with the polite excuse that it would be unseemly for one god to donate a temple to another god.

Hellenistic times

Ephesus was drawn, like Alexander's entire empire with the early death of its founder (323 BC), into the struggle for power amongst the generals and intimate friends of Alexander. These individuals considered themselves the rightful successors (Diadochi) in the formation of the Hellenistic kingdoms - the Seleucids in Asia, the Ptolemies in Egypt, and the Antigonids in Macedonia- which resulted from the eventual break-up of Alexander's realm. As grants of citizenship in surviving inscriptions show, the Ephesians attempted to come to terms with the individual powers-that-be or their plenipotentiaries in the quickly changing power constellation of the early "Age of the Diadochi". Order and continuity first returned when Ephesus found itself in 300 BC under the control of Lysimachus who, in the meantime had, like all the Diadochi, taken the title of king. Lysimachus caused the second major break in the history of Ephesus when, next to the town founded by Croesus around the Temple of Artemis, he founded a new city named after his wife Arsinoë. This was not to be a new Ephesus but much more a modern city in the Hellenistic style developing at that time. It was laid out rationally with a grid pattern of streets meeting at right angles, as dictated by the principles of urban development later named after Hippodamus of Miletus, and provided with all the facilities appropriate to a Hellenistic city.

Impressive even today are the imposing remains of the city wall, several kilometres long, which Lysimachus erected on the crest of the Bülbüldağ and, to a lesser extent, on the heights of the Panayırdağ. There were two significant reasons for the king's actions, apart from his wish that the foremost city of the region should no longer be subject to the powerful hierarchy of the Temple of Artemis. On the one hand there was the need to replace the old silted-up Coressus harbour at the north foot of the Panayırdağ by a deep water anchorage at the north foot of the Bülbüldağ not far from the village of Smyrna. On the other hand, the rise in the ground water table was not only slowly flooding the Temple of Artemis but also making the old residential quarter inconvenient. The story handed down to us about the resistance of the Ephesians against the move to Lysimachus' new city, which the king is said to have broken by having the drains blocked during heavy rain and thereby causing extensive flooding, is

Distinguished Ephesians

Fig. 1: Heraclitus, founder of the teaching of the continuous changing of all things; portrait in Herakleion from Roman times

Fig. 2: Hellenistic head of a ruler from Ephesus described as Lysimachus. This king who died in 281 BC relocated the city and called it Arsinoeia

Fig. 3: The Athenian king's son Androclus, mythical leader of the Greeks in the colonization of Ephesus, killed the wild boar, according to the founding oracle, and fought against enemies of the new settlement; relief from a cycle of Ephesian local myths on the so-called Temple of Hadrian

Fig. 4: Emperor Augustus; portrait from the ruler cult area east of the Prytaneion (soon after 27 BC)

Fig. 5: Otto Benndorf, professor of classical archaeology at the University of Vienna, initiator of the Austrian excavations at Ephesus in the year 1895 and founder of the Austrian Archaeological Institute

1

2

3

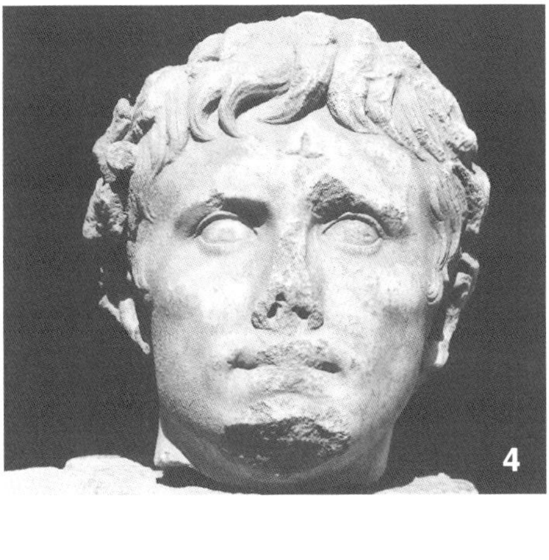

4

5

only half true. In view of the high water level, there was no need to resort to artificial means of preventing the rain water from flowing away. One reason for the refusal to move may well have been that the ancient necropolis around the Panayırdağ ran right through the new city. In addition, Lysimachus forced the inhabitants of the small neighbouring communities of Teos, Lebedos and Colophon to move to the new city. The time of the independent Greek "Poleis", whether large or small, was over. It could not survive in a Hellenism in which the old idea of the city state was sacrificed to the principle of the extensive territorial nation. Lysimachus' measures were therefore - apart from the need to fill the new Arsinoeia with people - a sort of reparcelling of the land in the entire region.

Lysimachus' rule lasted until 281 BC and ended with the defeat of the king by a Seleucid-Ptolomaic coalition at the battle of Corupedium (not far from Magnesia on the Sipylos hill, now called Magnesa). As a result, his realm, with the exception of several small areas in south-west Asia Minor which became part of the Ptolomaic possessions outside Egypt, merged with the Seleucid kingdom. Arsinoeia did not survive Lysimachus; the city which he founded became "New Ephesus" next to the "Old Ephesus", still extant in some form around the Temple of Artemis.

Soon afterwards the city came under the rule of the Egyptian Ptolemies and remained so until the Seleucid Antiochus III did away with the Ptolemaic possessions outside Egypt before he himself was defeated in 190 BC by the Romans at the battle of Magnesia on the Sipylos hill. The peace of Apamea, imposed upon the Seleucids by Rome in the year 188 BC, forced Antiochus to move out of all of Asia Minor as far as the Taurus. The beneficiary of this "inheritance" was the small Hellenistic kingdom of Pergamum whose ruler, Eumenes II, took the side of Rome in the conflict with the Seleucids and now reaped his reward with the grant of large areas of western Asia Minor which included Ephesus. The last king of Pergamum, Attalos III, realized correctly that, sooner or later, all the Hellenistic monarchies would fall into the hands of the Roman Republic which, after the final destruction of Carthage, the humiliation of the Seleucid kingdom and the conquest of Macedon and its transformation into a province of the same name, had now also become all-powerful in the Hellenistic East. When he died in 133 BC (without issue but not before he had bequeathed his kingdom *to the Roman people* in his will), Pergamum was, like Ephesus, merely one of two cities in the Province of Asia that was set up in 129 BC after the brief interlude of a pretender and usurper by the name of Aristonicus. The Romans acted in accordance with the will of Attalos III and the situation as they found it in the kingdom of Pergamum. The sacred *land*, the properties of the gods and temples remained sacrosanct - so also the Temple of Artemis. The *royal land*, which belonged to the king, and was in general let out on long-term leases, became the property of Rome and the tenants now payed their dues to the aerarium of the Roman people (*aerarium populi Romani*) which had taken the place of the royal treasury. The old cities like Ephesus, which were also "free" in the kingdom of Pergamum, were granted tax-free status as *civitates liberae et immunes*, as distinct from the more numerous *civitates foederatae et stipendiariae* which did not enjoy this privilege. The Romans allowed the cities to govern themselves as city-states so long as Roman interests did not suffer. The hands of the Roman tax-farmers (*publicani*) rested heavily on the land. With the purchase by payment at public auction of five-year lease-periods, they acquired the right to thoroughly exploit the province in all matters of taxation. The management of the former royal mines (*metalla*), the grazing dues (*scriptura*), the tithes on all proceeds of the land (*decuma*), the property levy and a poll tax (*tributum capitis*) brought in extrordinary sums. But the most lucrative business by far concerned the customs duties (*portorium Asiae*) which were imposed at all sea and land frontiers of the province, whereby a 2.5% duty was charged on the value of goods as assessed by the customs officer - a murky grey zone of unbridled arbitrariness. The unrestrained exploitation of the rich province was one of the reasons why the half-barbarian king of Pontus, Mithridates VI, was received by the provincials with open arms and greeted almost as a *saviour and rescuer* when he tried to take over Asia in the year 89 BC.

The Roman commander Cornelius Sulla, charged with conducting the war against Mithridates, cruelly punished Ephesus, where in the year 88 BC, the sentence of death was pronounced in the notorious *Ephesian vesper* on all Italic nationals living in the province, and deprived the city of its freedom which it only regained decades later.

The reorganization of Augustus

In the first century BC, Ephesus was at times the scene of turbulent events which sounded the death-knell of the Roman Republic, already in its twilight. Only a few weeks after the battle of Pharsalus in the year 48 BC, Julius Caesar, victorious over Pompey, came to Ephesus where he granted the provincials generous relief from tax revenues. Less generous was the next prominent Roman to visit Ephesus, the triumvir Mark Antony who, in 33 BC, not only revoked this relief but imposed even more exorbitant demands, which could hardly be met. Antony returned in the year 33 with the Egyptian queen Cleopatra, whom he had in the meantime "married", to winter here and prepare for the inevitable showdown with Octavian, subsequently the Emperor Augustus, his arch enemy and rival for the sole and absolute rule of the Roman empire. Real Roman history was made in Ephesus when, in 32 BC, the consuls and 300 senators, driven from Rome by Octavian, established a short-lived opposition senate-in-exile which, however, never achieved any political importance. Octavian's victories, at the sea-battle of Actium in the autumn of 31 BC and in a land-battle in the following year before the gates of Alexandria, put an end to the turmoil of nearly twenty years of bloody Roman civil war. The Republic, which had long outlived itself, having proved incapable of properly administrating a world empire, was dead. A new form of government, the proprietor state founded by Octavian-Augustus, took its place and was to last for the next 300 years.

The victor of Actium and Alexandria had, by 29 BC, wisely and generously reformed the shattered relationships in Asia. Ephesus was, from then on, to be the permanent seat of the Roman governor in place of Pergamum, where the cramped setting of the castle hill was less convenient for the reorganization; the broad territory of Ephesus as laid out by Lysimachus, with its direct access to the sea, was better able than the old residence of the Attalids to receive a new "Roman face", less burdened, as it was, by its Hellenistic past. Under Octavian-Augustus a powerful, and deliberately planned entity was established according to the political intentions of the *princeps*, which cleverly, cautiously, used Roman architectural elements to turn Ephesus into a Hellenistic-Roman city.

We have seen that Artemis took over the new city founded by Lysimachus when the king died. If the new "Roman" Ephesus was to be truly free and independent of the Artemision, its relationships with the Temple of Artemis, in particular the question of ownership of property which had become unclear and muddled in the confusion of the Roman civil war, had to be redefined. In true Roman *Pietas*, Octavian-Augustus gave back to Artemis all the lands which had, from time immemorial, belonged to the goddess but at the same time, cut back the right of asylum, which had increased under Mithridates VI of Pontus and then again under Mark Antony, to the standard radius of one stadium (about 185 metres). Early in the year 27 BC, Octavian shared the provinces of the empire with the Senate. Soon after he was promoted to the rank of Augustus for his services in reimposing governmental normalcy. The emperor was to take under *his* administration those provinces in which legionary forces under the command of his legates (*legati Augusti pro praetore*) were stationed. The other so-called unarmed provinces (*provinciae inermes*), which had long been pacified and needed no military supervision, were to remain in the formal administration of the senate under the direction of proconsuls (*proconsules pro praetore*). So it was with Asia, whose governorship, one of the highest offices in a senatorial career, was reserved for particularly-well qualified men who enjoyed the emperor's favour. The governor, in the tradition of the Roman republic, had at his disposal a quaestor, who made the payments necessary for the administration of the province out of the senatorial treasury, and three legates who supported or deputized for him at assizes or days of legal jurisdiction in Ephesus and other cities of the province. The imperial procurators, appointed from among the knights (*ordo equester*) or second class of society in the empire, effectively functioned as governors in certain "procuratorial" provinces. They also looked after the affairs of the emperor in special areas, especially the imperial treasury (*fiscus*), and served at the same time as the eyes and ears of their master whose paid civil servants they were. This system of indirect spying gradually put an end to the collaboration between tax farmers (publicani) and governor which had operated to the advantage of both and to the detriment of the provincials. The practice, widespread in the time of the Roman republic, was no longer possible in Imperial times and this led to the eventual disappearance of an increasingly less lucrative tax-farming industry that was replaced by direct imperial control. The honesty and clarity of the princeps' well-founded new regulation is one of the reasons - and not the least important - why the provinces flourished.

The metropolis of Roman Imperial times

The imposing public buildings, even in their ruined state, still bear witness that the city reached the zenith of its urban development in the middle of the 2nd century AD in the epoch of peace, the *pax Augusta*, first introduced by Augustus. Ephesus could describe itself with complete justification as the fourth largest city in the east of the Roman empire, after Alexandria in Egypt, Antioch on the Orontes and Athens.

This urban upswing resulted in large part from the activities of a rich upper class driven by personal ambition to use its wealth for the public welfare. Its members held public office and were bound by family honor to make extravagant expenditures out of their own pockets for the good of the city. The most respected position was that of prytanis, chairman of the Prytaneum, where the eternal flame burned on the communal hearth of Hestia symbolizing the life of the city, and where all cults to which the city felt officially obligated were represented. After the prytanis came the agoranomos (supervisor over the market and above all the provision of grain and bread) followed by the men of letters (grammateis) in public or local governmental notarial and secretarial offices (the general secretariats of the people's assembly and the city council which shared the communal administration). Hundreds of inscriptions on the plinths of statues of outstanding citizens along the main streets and squares of the city bear witness both to the wide variety of public offices concerned with communal self-administration, and with the people who held those offices. They provide insight into the supporting corporate class of the city whose families can often be traced through several generations. The inscriptions present us with an exclusive view of a glittering world.

The prosperity of the city depended primarily on its harbour as the centre of trade for all that was exported from further east through Ephesus, or which the rich province produced itself or imported from the west. A powerful economic body was the Temple of Artemis which, as one of the seven wonders of the world, was visited by tourists from all over and widely known as the credit bank of Asia, *the place of refuge of the debenture* as the famous rhetor Aelius Aristides called it in the 2nd century AD, and at the same time an important employer of labour.

Fig. 1: map of Ephesus according to E. Falkener (1845)

Fig. 2: reconstruction of a view over the city in Imperial times according to E. Falkener (1859)

The city's reputation was based, to a not inconsiderable extent, on its having two Imperial temples. The older of the two was erected around the year 90 AD for the rulers of the Flavian dynasty. After the fall of Emperor Domitian the dedication was transferred to his father, the divine Vespasian. The second Imperial temple was called Olympieion because it served the cult of Hadrian who had become Zeus Olympios. Ephesus, in continuous rivalry with the other cities of the province, especially Pergamum and Smyrna, proudly called itself *the first and greatest metropolis of Asia*, and warden (*neokoros*) *of two Imperial temples*. In addition, there was the guardianship of the Temple of Artemis, but that played no role in this struggle for status and was therefore not part of the city title. What counted were only the Imperial wardenships. In the short period of the joint reign of Aurelius Antoninus (better known as Caracalla) with his brother Geta, Ephesus was awarded

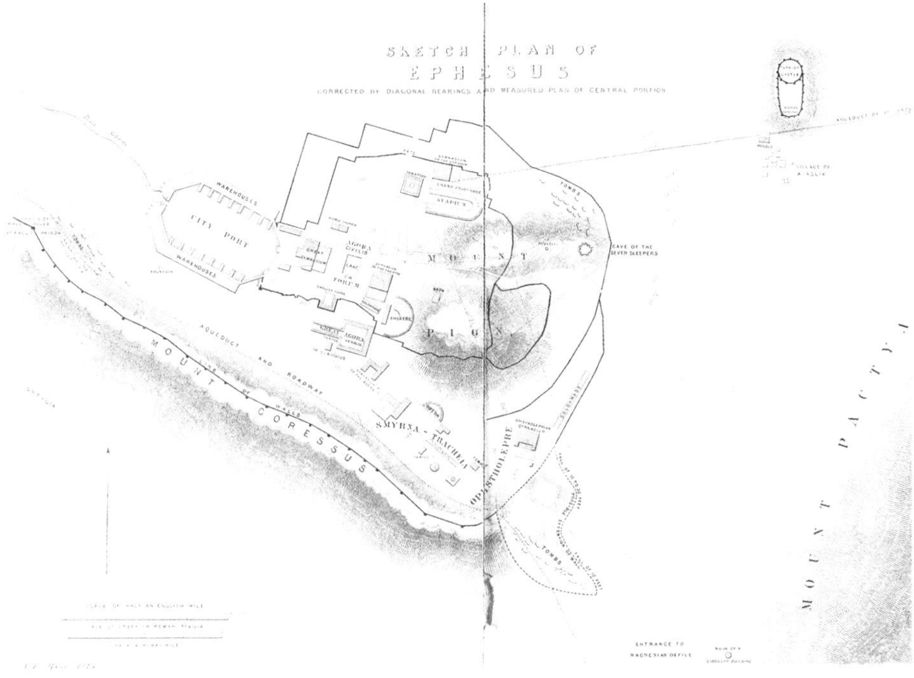

Day & Son Lith^rs to the Queen

THE CITY OF EPHESUS
(From Mount Coressus)

neocoros a third time. Caracalla, however, declined it after the murder of his younger brother, much to the chagrin of the ambitious city which had, with a heavy heart, to have several inscriptions referring to three wardenships altered back to two.

Public life was sparkling and complex. Elementary education under the supervision of *paidonomoi* included the subjects grammar, geometry, drawing and music. The library, which had been built in about 125 AD over the heroon for the former governor Tiberius Julius Celsus Polemaeanus, was available to those desiring higher education, in addition to the Museion, the "University" of Ephesus, where the "faculty of medicine", under the direction of *archiatroi*, held competitions at regular intervals in four medical disciplines (manufacture of instruments, surgery, dietetics and diagnosis).

Nevertheless, Ephesus was not a city in the intellectual class of Athens or Alexandria. Nor could the Ephesian school of medicine match the medical academies of Pergamum or Kos. Sons of the urban elite, who wanted more than Ephesus could offer, went elsewhere to find a teacher to instruct them in philosophy or rhetoric. The city's many gymnasia, organized according to rank or age with their adjacent baths, served for physical training and were, apart from the culture of the bath offered there, important centres of social communication and entertainment. **A series of important representatives of the so-called Second Sophistic worked for shorter or longer periods in Ephesus. Referring to the great Attic speakers of the 4th century BC, they set their own great past and Greek identity against the Roman egalitarianism with rhetorical perfection. Here, the rich Ephesian Titus Flavius Damianus should be mentioned for his sophistic activities as well as his munificence towards the** city.

The requirements of religion were provided for by a great variety of cults which, at the same time, offered social support and kept a hold on their believers with occasional gifts of money, wine or oil, and free meals. This was particularly so in the case of the Artemision (Temple of Artemis) which, following the great sacrificial feasts which took place from time to time, was a sort of free meat market for the man in the street. The rich looked after their clients, who at the same time formed their political lobby, and donated or repaired public buildings and had streets and squares paved at their own expence. In return, they were honored with commemorative statues whose inscriptions conspicuously praised their works and achievements for the well-being of the general public. They also provided public entertainment in the form of gladiatorial contests and the baiting of animals which, for want of a separate amphitheatre, took place in the elliptical arena at the eastern end of the stadium.

Very rich families, such as the Vedius clan, even had their own gladiator families. Some idea of the scope of such games is given by an inscription which reports that, during the days of a provincial festival, 31 pairs of gladiators competed with sharp weapons (i.e. fought a life or death contest with each other), and an unnamed number of *Libyan beasts* (lions) *were brought to the slaughter.* Numerous competitions (*agones*), including both sporting and musical events, were very popular in which Ephesian competitors were joined by foreign professional athletes who journeyed from *agon* to *agon* to display their prowess and walk off with money and honours. The theatre which, as a multi-purpose building, was also the venue of the people' assembly, served for artistic performances, tragedies and comedies, and the mime, who appealed more to the taste of the ordinary people.

Skilled craftsmen and shopkeepers were organized in trade guilds, the Italic businessmen in the society of the *Roman citizens doing business in Asia* (*cives romani, qui in asia negotiantur*). The multinational and multicultural population was complex and varied as appropriate to a cosmopolitan city. The palette extended from the old-established, more or less romanized locals, Italic nationals, new arrivals more or less Hellenized with time, an impressive Jewish community, Egyptians (from Alexandria), Rhodians and others who maintained commercial trading posts in Ephesus. With eight divisions (*phyle*), each consisting of 6-8 groups of a thousand (*chiliastys*) free adult citizens together with a not inconsiderable number of family dependants and many slaves, the population of the city in the middle of the 2nd century AD was about 350,000. This did not include the civil servants and soldiers of the Roman administration or the many "tourists" and merchants from all parts of the empire who stayed for shorter or longer periods in Ephesus to visit the city and in particular the Temple of Artemis (Artemision), or to further their business interests.

Nevertheless, the appearance at first sight of a beautiful and ideal world upon which the sun would never set, was deceptive. While the empire reached its greatest size under Emperor Trajan (98 - 117 AD), the influence of Artemis declined along with the other long-established gods of the pantheon. Unlike the new salvationist or mystery gods of oriental - mainly Egyptian - origin, they were no longer able to give satisfactory answers to the anxious question concerning the fate of the soul after death, and they tried to compensate for their increasing inner emptiness with ever greater displays of pomp and material splendour.

Somewhere, at first on the lower levels and outer fringes of society, Christianity was already appealing to a people beset by an increasing existential uncertainty. Co-founded by none other than the apostle Paul, the Christian congregation at Ephesus was, after the one in Antiocheia on the Orontes, the oldest of all Christian communities. An equally powerful (if obscure) personality belongs to the turn of the first to the second century AD.: The prophet John, over whose grave on the Ayasoluk hill, centuries later, Emperor Justinian I had an immense domed basilica built, which vied in magnificence and size with the Hagia Sophia in Constantinople, and the ruins of which still bear impressive witness to its former splendour. The Ephesian John is, despite later tradition, in all probability not the writer of the forth gospel and certainly not the favourite disciple of Jesus, but the author of the Book of Revelation, the only prophetical book in the New Testament. The liberality and fairness of the Roman emperors from Trajan onwards gave early Christianity time to gradually establish itself. Apart from incidents caused by their own fanaticism, as in the case of bishop Timotheus who was martyred in the reign of Emperor Nerva (96 - 98 AD) because of his public criticism of a dionysian feast of the Catagogues, nothing worth mentioning seems to have happened to the Ephesian Christians until the middle of the 3rd century when the systematic persecution of the Christians began under Emperor Decius (249 - 251 AD).

The first signs of the gathering storm appeared as Ephesus became, in the years 162 - 166, the staging base on the Roman east front in the great war against the Parthians, the old enemy beyond the frontiers of the empire on the Euphrates.

Although Roman arms were in the end victorious, the legions, which were shipped back to the west of the empire over a period of thirteen months through the harbour of Ephesus, brought with them from Mesopotamia the plague which, for nearly twenty years, afflicted and decimated the population up to the furthest provinces of the empire. These times were difficult, but they were merely an intermezzo after which life went on as before. Even the long Severan reign of somewhat more than 40 years, beginning with the fratricidal conflict between the legions when the army of the Danube fought the Army of the Orient in the war which Septimus Severus waged for the sole absolute dictatorship against his adversary Pescennius Niger, did not directly affect Ephesus, which had apparently backed the right horse, although the conflict took place nearby in Anatolia.

Again, Asia and Ephesus were in no great danger when, in the year 226 AD, under the last representative of the Afro-Syrian dynasty, Severus Alexander, power in the Parthian empire of the Arsacids on the far side of the Euphrates passed to the noticeably more aggressive dynasty of the Sassanians whose new Persian empire was less willing to compromise.

The radical change to late Roman times

Things first began to go noticeably downwards, as in the empire in general, in the era of the soldier-emperors (235 - 284). The army, comprised more and more of Barbarian soldiers, would chose an emperor as their leader –none of which survived for more than eight years– and kill him at their slightest displeasure. The debasement of the coinage, which had already begun under Emperor Caracalla, now reached its greatest extent as a result of natural economic conditions. The periphery of the empire, attacked in the east by the Sassanian Persians and in the north by the Teutons, and able to defend itself now only with the greatest effort, disintegrated into minor states under more or less short-lived usurpers. Now came retribution. Asia was unarmed. It was no longer a province with a standing garrison of legionaries. Ephesus had neglected its city walls which, in the days of the Pax Augusta, had become little more than stage scenery. The sudden advance of a horde of seafaring Goths, who had set out from the Black Sea area to attack the coast of western Asia Minor, weakened in its ability to defend itself by a major earthquake, also struck Ephesus in 262 AD, attracted by the wealthy Artemision (Temple of Artemis) and its immense riches collected in the course of many long centuries. The temple was plundered and set on fire. Although the damage was repaired as well as possible after the barbarians had left, the old glory was over. How could an Artemis who was unable to defend her own house, remain the protector of the city?

The middle of this turbulent century saw the start of the persecution of the Christians to an extent not previously experienced. In the year 250, the Emperor Decius, who had grown up in the provincial military tradition of Pannonia and was committed to the gods of his forefathers, declared that their neglect in favour of the Christian god was responsible for the decline of the empire. He decreed an empire-wide round-up of Christians by special commissions which went from place to place requiring every individual to prove his loyalty by making sacrifice at an Imperial altar.

We do not know how this persecution affected Ephesus, but the legend of the Seven Sleepers, which was also known to the Koran and very probably originated in Cappadocia, shows, in its Ephesian form that there were, in all probability, Ephesian martyrs. It tells of seven devout young men who fell asleep in the caves near the Meter-Cybele shrine on the north-east side of the Panayırdağ at the time of the persecution by the Emperor Decius, and awoke again, unscathed, under the Christian Emperor Theodosius (II). The caves, built up in the 5th and 6th centuries into an impressive Christian necropolis with two funeral churches, seem, in any case, to have been an old crypto-Christian burial place even before the Decian persecution.

The ever greater downhill trend in the empire came to an end in the year 284 AD with the seizure of power by Diocletian, who initiated the late Roman tetrarchic system of government. This emperor, who came from Dalmatia, again started an empire-wide persecution of Christians for similar reasons as Decius, but called it off in the year 303 apparently for political reasons. After the restoration of the integrity of the empire (*restitutio orbis*) Diocletian, no longer as sovereign ruler but as one who wanted to be seen as master and god (*dominus et deus*), introduced a rigorous system for the collection of taxes (*jugatio-capitatio*) which bound the country folk to the soil. It exacted a compulsory levy based precisely on the quality of land the, number of people (*capita*), and the number of yokes of ground (*jugera* = ancient acres of "the amount of land that one yoke of oxen can plough in a day") they worked on. He also set fixed maximum prices for all goods and services to fight inflation and restore confidence in the imperial currency. The former provinces were diminished in size, and historic regions of the old large provinces were made independent under their own names. So it was with Asia, now limited to a narrow band of territory on the Aegean west coast. As before, the proconsuls were governors who were called in other provinces (with the exception of Africa) praesides or correctores. The new regulations of Diocletian, in taking account of the fundamental changes in social and economic relationships, and of military requirements, made the governors into mere civil servants and placed the military command in the hands of duces. In doing so, the new regulations broke with the centuries-old Roman tradition of the unity of the highest civic and military command. This remained the basic principal of the late Roman/early Byzantine Imperial administration - developed but not essentially changed by Diocletian's followers - which was only abandoned by Heraclius at the beginning of the 7th century.

Fig. 1: Fantastic reconstruction of the Temple of Artemis by J.B. Fischer von Erlach (1721)

Fig. 2: The excavations of J.T. Wood in the Temple of Artemis (1871)

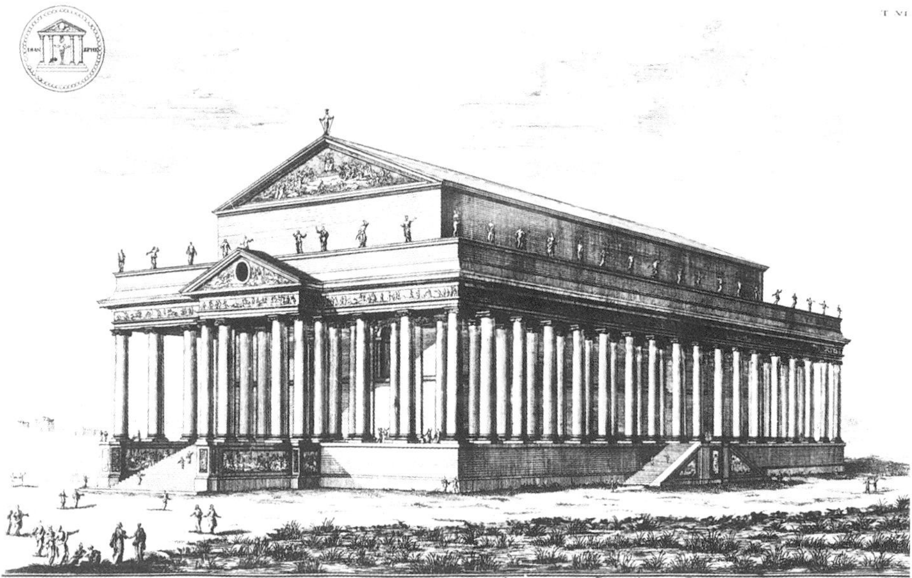

Der Tempel Dianæ zu Ephesus, | woran gantz Asien 220. Jahr gebauet; | hatte in der Länge 425 Schuh; In der Breite 220 Sch; In allen aus und inwendig 127 Säulen von 60 Sch. Kôhe und Ionischer Ordnung. Wie das Vestibulum auf angeführter medaille und die rudera ausweisen

Le Temple de Diane d'Ephese, L'ouvrage de toute l'Asie pendant 220 ans. Il avoit 425 pieds de longueur, et 220 pieds de largeur. Cn y comtoit dedans et dehors en tout 127 Colones de 60 pieds de haut. La medaille ci jointe, qui represente son vestibule, fait voir aussi bien que les ruines, que l'ordre en a été Ionique.

VIEW OF EXCAVATION ON SITE OF TEMPLE LOOKING EAST_ DECEMBER 1871

The tetrarchic system of government invented by Diocletian foresaw that the two *augusti* (Diocletian had shared power with Maximian as *"subordinate augustus"* since 285 AD) would each abdicate at the same time and be succeeded by their assistants and designated heirs - their caesars - which in turn as *augusti*, would again choose *caesars*. This system very shortly became absurd because it tried to bypass the natural bonds of human beings to their offspring. After much turmoil and turbulence, dynastic stability and imperial integrity was again restored when Constantine I became sole *augustus* in the year 324 AD.

The victory of Christianity

Under Constantine, Christianity, formerly outlawed, became an accepted religion (*religio licita*), a formula which he had agreed upon with Galerius, the bitter persecutor of Christians, shortly before the latter died. This was a decision that would change the world.

Ephesus became a Christian city from 350 AD under the absolute rule of Constantius II, the Christian bigot, and the sole remaining of the three sons of Constantine. Nevertheless, the old beliefs continued as they did everywhere, mainly limited to the circle of the educated who sought refuge in philosophy and, in particular, in neoplatonism as founded by Plotinus, in which philosophy met with religious transcendental metaphysics. The edict of Emperor Theodosius I of the year 380 imposed the catholic faith on all who lived in the empire, and paganism was now "officially" dead. A Christian by the name of Demeas was able to boast in an inscription that he *had torn down the demon Artemis and replaced her with the cross of Jesus*. After the victory of Christianity, the Temple of Artemis was soon used as a stone quarry which explains why the remains of the temple are relatively small compared to its former size. An unknown Christian commentator referred to an epigram in which the temple was extolled as the most magnificent of all the wonders of the world: *..... but now it is the most desolate and the most wretched through the grace of Christ and John the Theologian.*

In the year 406, bishop Chrysostomos had the cult image of Artemis, carved out of wood and black from centuries long anointing with oil, burnt, believing that he was performing work pleasing to the sight of god. In the year 431 Ephesus moved to the forefront of church history as the scene of the Third Ecumenical Council when Emperor Theodosius II submitted the dispute, which had broken out between the Patriarch of Constantinople, Nestorius, and his opposite number in Alexandria, Cyril, about the divine and human nature of Christ, to a general assembly of the fathers of the church for decision. The victory of the Alexandrines, who spoke out for a single and divine nature of Christ (monophysitism), was complete when the Council rejected the two-natures teaching of Nestorius who wanted to see the godly in Christ separated from his human nature (diophysitism).

The decision at Ephesus, whereby Mary was seen as *having given birth to Christ* rather than *having given birth to God*, resulted not only in the founding of the cult of Mary but also in the first great schism in the church. This could not be rectified at the Fourth Council of Chalcedon in the year 450 by a formula which tried to square the circle, namely that Christ is truly God and truly man *unseparated* and *unmixed*, a doctrine which persists to this day.

The untroubled time of peace and security in an empire which was Byzantine from the time of Justinian (527 - 565 AD) and in which there were no longer provinces since Emperor Heraclius, but only *themata* (military districts), with Ephesus as capital of the *thema Thracesion*, came to an end in the 7th century.

From the Arabian threat to the establishment of the Ottoman Empire

On the Arabian peninsula, far away from the centres of Hellenistic and Roman civilization, Islam came into being as a new religion-of-the-book after Judaism and Christianity. Islam, which combined representative elements of both beliefs, did not limit itself to uniting the Arabic tribes under its banner, but claimed from the very beginning to be a world religion and thus took upon itself the task of bringing together all the peoples of the world under the teachings of its founder Mohammed, which regulated all aspects of human life without separation of religion and state. The Umayyad Caliph Muawija plundered Ephesus with an Arab fleet on his return from an unsuccessful expedition against Constantinople. The Arab admiral Maslama did the same in 716/17 AD after an equally futile attempt to capture the strongly fortified capital of the empire.

Since the entire area of Ephesus, as originally laid-out by Lysimachus, was now less densely populated than in former times and no longer defendable, the northern slopes of the Bülbüldağ and a portion of the city plain were abandoned, reducing the city to the area enclosed by the so-called Byzantine city wall [77]. The fate of Hellenistic-Roman Ephesus, which still existed after a fashion (though reduced in size) up into about the 10th century, was finally sealed when the harbour, already a constant problem in Roman Imperial times and now only connected by a winding canal to the sea which had retreated to the west, finally silted up. The harbour city of Ephesus became a landlocked town on the Ayasoluk hill. Here, a settlement had already grown up from the 6th century onwards around the Basilica of St. John, which enjoyed air more healthy than that of Ephesus on an increasingly marshy, fever-ridden plain. The acts of the Council of 431 AD already reported that many fathers-of-the-church had become ill with malaria. In addition, a strong ring wall, erected out of stones and parts of buildings dragged here from the ruins of the Hellenistic-Roman city and the Temple of Artemis, offered protection against sea-pirates and enemy fleets. This final Ephesus was later to be called Ayasoluk by the Turks in a misunderstanding of *Hagios Theologos* (Holy Theologian) and is referred to in Venetian and Genoese sources from the Middle Ages as *Alto Luogo*, phonetically understandable and factually not incorrect because it really lay "high up" in comparison to the great city of Artemis. Scalanuova, the ancient Pygela and present day Kuşadası, took over the role of harbour city from Ephesus and henceforth continued the brisk Levantine trade with Genoa and Venice.

Heraclitus once taught that *everything flows*. Only one further episode, albeit long-lasting, remained to Christian Ephesus. Around 1300 AD, Ayasoluk-Altoluogo fell into the hands of the Aydınoğlu, a princely dynasty of the Turkish tribe of the Selçuks. Under İsa bey, one of the sons of Aydın, Ayasoluk-Altoluogo-Ephesus experienced one last golden age to which, in addition to the beautiful mosque (İsa bey-camii) built by the famous architect Ali of Damascus, completed in the year 1375 and named after its patron, the baths (*Hamam*) and mausoleums (*Türbe*) in the municipal area of the present day Selçuk bear witness.

The rule of the Aydınoğlu came to and end at the beginning of the 15th century with the seizure of power by the house of Osman, whose political interests - in view of the claims of the dynasty to a world empire - could not be satisfied with a provincial residence in Ayasoluk but must aim at taking over the capital of the Byzantine empire, the imperial city on the Bosporus to which this empire was in the end reduced; Constantinople would fall into the hands of the sultan Fatih Mehmet in 1453 AD.

The desolate ruins of Ephesus had long become a cemetery of history whose magnificent marble buildings, destroyed by numerous earthquakes, now lay bleached like bones in the sun. So now Ayasoluk, where the splendid buildings of the Selçuk

Fig. 1: The first provisional exhibition of finds from the Austrian excavations in the museum building erected in 1929 in Selçuk

Fig. 2: The Austrian excavations began in 1896 in the Harbour Baths: reconstruction of the so-called marble hall (NIEMANN 1902)

princes, abandoned overnight, stood in sharp contrast to the wretched houses subsequently erected on the slopes of the hill, became a miserable provincial backwater, a nameless and unimportant *kaza* of the great Ottoman Empire, occupied by a military unit which was garrisoned in the former Byzantine fortress at the summit.

Ephesus in the modern era: from history to research history

Nevertheless, the Ephesian region remained in contact with Europe through Venetian businessmen who had commercial interests in the valleys of the Meander and Caystrus; the source material available in the Italian language is surprisingly rewarding. The famous merchant and traveller in the Levant, CYRIACUS OF ANCONA, who interested himself in ancient economics in addition to his own business commitments, came to Ephesus in the year 1448 and made copies of several inscriptions (some of them now lost), which he saw there. The scribbled graffiti of European pilgrims who visited the Seven Sleepers Cemetery, to which pious legend had transferred the graves of famous saints, reach up into the 15th century.

After CYRIACUS, English and French travellers arrived between the 17th and the first part of the 19th century. Their reports on Ephesus and Ayasoluk are so valuable because they represent the only sources for this otherwise completely obscure period of time.

The history of research in Ephesus is also part of Ephesian history which continues up to the present day. The prince who not only visited this Sleeping Beauty but resurrected her to new life was the architect and engineer J.T. WOOD, brought to Ayasoluk in 1863 to build the English railway line from Izmir through the valley of the Meander to Denizli.

WOOD dug in Ephesus up to 1874 on behalf of the British Museum mainly with the aim of finding the Temple of Artemis. No one had been able to locate, even approximately, the place where this Wonder of the World had been built. Wood consulted all available references in the ancient literature. But his main clue was the lucky find of an informative, topographic inscription in the theatre. His dogged perseverance was rewarded in 1869 after long years of searching in vain. WOOD found the sad remains of the once giant building below the water table several metres under the present day surface of the earth. This was all that remained after centuries-long cannibalization, mainly to the advantage of the Basilica of St. John (the ruins of which in turn provided stones for the building of the İsa bey mosque) and its foundation walls. In 1904/5 the English archaeologist D.G. HOGARTH again dug on behalf of the British Museum in the ruins of the Temple of Artemis.

OTTO BENNDORF, Professor of Classical Archaeology in Vienna University, had, however, already obtained a licence to dig in Ephesus in 1895. BENNDORF was the first director of the Austrian Archaeological Institute, which was founded in 1898 and has excavated in Ephesus, with the aim of topographic, historical and architectural research in the city, from that year to the present day. There were breaks in the years 1909 -1910, however, when Turkey, protesting to the annexation of Bosnia and Herzegovina by Austria-Hungary, refused to grant the necessary permite, while in 1914 - 1925 and 1936 - 1954, the dismal conditions during and after the two World Wars made continuation of work unthinkable. Greece, on the other hand, used the opportunity offered by its occupation of western Asia Minor to demonstrate the legality of its claims to the ownership of "Christian-Greek Ionia" to begin immediately with the excavation of the Basilica of St. John in 1921/22, which was continued and completed by the Austrian Archaeological Institute in the years between the wars.

In the century ending with 1995, generations of Austrian archaeologists, architectural historians and scholars of ancient History have endeavoured to carry on with the aims once defined by BENNDORF in friendly cooperation with their colleagues at the Ephesus Museum in Selçuk enjoying the hospitable reception accorded to them by the city of Selçuk. Here must be mentioned, above all, RUDOLF HEBERDEY, GEORGE NIEMANN, WILHELM WILBERG, JOSEF KEIL, KARL HÖRMANN, FRANZ MILTNER, FRITZ EICHLER and HERMANN VETTERS - renowned scholars who devoted their lives to research in Ephesus, often under the most difficult external conditions.

Ephesus is a challenge without end, on account of its size and long history which stretches from the first traces of settlement in the middle bronze age up to the end of the Selçuk era, a period of time spanning more than 5000 years. DK

Overall accounts: BÜRCHNER, RE V, 2773 – 2822; KNIBBE, RE Suppl. XII, 284 – 297; Führer, 12 – 30.

Roman times: KNIBBE, ANRW II 7/2, 248 – 810.

Late Roman times to the Middle Ages: FOSS, Ephesus after Antiquity (1979).

Inscriptions: IvE I — IX.

Numismatical sources: KARWIESE, RE Suppl. XII, 297 – 364.

Archaeology: ALZINGER, RE Suppl. XII, 1588 – 1704; ANRW II 7/2, 811 – 830.

Anastyloses in Ephesus

Abbreviated architectural reconstructions using a few building elements have been attempted from the very beginning of Austrian operations in Ephesus. The first comprehensive rebuilding operations, however, began in the 1950's. The façade of the Celsus Library, completed in 1978, set new international standards and became one of the greatest attractions for tourists in Turkey.

The tradition, begun by O. BENNDORF and R. HEBERDEY at the end of the 19th century, whereby a newly excavated building was marked with a provisional reconstruction consisting of two capitals, an architrave and cornice, was continued until the onset of broader rebuilding projects. The most prominent example from this oldest period of excavation was the setting up of a pediment of the Celsus Library. An installation of this type was erected in 1955 at the Hall of Nero, using concrete pillars (O. SCHOTTENHAMML). The partial-anastylosis of a nave wall of the Basilica of St. John, and, more important the portico of the Temple of Hadrian was done under the direction of F. MILTNER at the end of the 1950's. According to MILTNER, *care was taken to consider each phase in the development of the original building. The supplementary elements, required to replace missing parts, were chosen to fit in harmoniously but nevertheless to be distinguishable from the original.* Important guidelines of the Charter of Venice, first drawn up in 1964, were thus already anticipated. The further re-erection of columns on Curetes Street, in the Prytaneum and in the Basilica Stoa continued the practice of making the results of the excavations intelligible to visitors to the site.

Operations in Ephesus under the direction of F. EICHLER concentrated primarilly on academic research so that only a limited amount of work was done on the preservation of monuments. In the anastylosis of the so-called Nymphaeum of Trajan (H. PELLIONIS), lack of some parts of the columns prevented an estimate of the original height of the façade so that bases were simply separated from their capitals by short stumps of concrete. A. BAMMER worked from 1963 - 1976 on a whole series of monuments (Memmius Monument, Pollio Monument, Fountain of Domitian, columns at the Temple of Artemis and Domitian's Terrace) in which his own very personal style is evident. He reconstructed veritable sculptures out of original parts, blocks of concrete and iron bars. Here the destruction was called to mind rather than the ancient building itself. His installations are of a provisional nature, their aesthetic portrayal must be seen as an improvisation.

Fig. 1: Erection of an architectural - piece in the Imperial Hall of the Vedius Gymnasium (KEIL 1930)

H. VETTERS again followed MILTNER's endeavours and his great projects set new standards in the field of the preservation of monuments. The anastylosis of the facade of the Celsus Library was completed after nine years of building operations under the direction of V.M. STROCKA and F. HUEBER. New methods of anastylosis were developed using modern technical devices, which resulted in a better understanding of ancient building practice - for example, the use of a slight curvature towards the center of horizontal building elements in a facade to increase the effects of perspective. With the re-erection of the South Gate of the Tetragonos Agora in 1989, the layout of the Library Place ensemble was continued and attracted ever more visitors.

In the course of this project, the apartments with their valuable frescoes and mosaics were protected and, with the re-building of the courtyards, the impression of the ancient rooms was restored without resorting to merely hypothetical reconstruction.

The partial anastylosis of the north entrance to the Hall of Nero (HUEBER) was completed in the last period of excavation but the re-erection of the lower storey of Hadrian's Gate (THÜR) is not yet finished. The Turkish Department of Antiquities is carrying out the restoration of the Basilica of St. John and the Church of Mary. GW

The Preservation of Monuments

Traces of the past remain intact for a very long time in the earth - hidden but protected. When they are excavated by archaeologists, these witnesses to civilizations long past become documents of history, but once the protecting earth has been removed, there is also a need to further preserve these monuments.

For this reason scientists began, in the last century, to develope and utilize techniques for the *in situ* preservation of ancient monuments. Today, value is placed on authenticity and faithfulness to the original; the imaginative reconstruction of past glories has become a minor matter considered of little historical value.

The techniques of conservation are variously complicated and expensive according to the durability of the materials used. Metals, ceramics, glass and organic substances such as leather or wood are, in general, easier to conserve because they can usually be taken from the place where they were found to the protective environment of a museum. In the case of ruins, protection becomes considerably more difficult because it is not easy to eliminate the deterioration caused to monumental buildings by the natural environment.

Man himself, indeed each individual visitor to the site, must be included among these environmental hazards, so that the mere presentation of a standing monument to all interested persons as a document of a particular period of history, increases the risk of destruction, and is itself a challange to the conservator.

The visitor to museums and ruined cities must realize that his carelessness may cause serious damage, and is therefore requested to deal gently and responsibly with these irreplaceable monuments to the past so that we can pass on this historical inheritance to those who come after us, unchanged, to the greatest possible extent, for scientific investigation, admiration, and reflection. KH

Figs. 1 + 2: Terrace House 2, so-called theatre room; wall pictures of a wrestling match (Hercules against Acheloos?) before and after restoration.

Figs. 3 + 4: Terrace House 2, burnt wooden beam of wall panelling as it was found and after conservation

Figs. 5 + 6: Terrace House 1, terracotta statue of *Aphrodite taking off her sandals*, rescued as a heap of fragments in debris from early Imperial times

1

2

3

4

5

6

Excavation and Restoration Works of the Ephesus Museum in Selçuk

The excavations undertaken by the Ephesus Museum on behalf of the Ministry of Culture of the Republic of Turkey began in 1959 under the guidance of M. BARAN. Up to 1962, extensive excavation work was continued in the lower (Tetragonos) Agora [61], the great theatre [75] and in the surroundings of the Basilica of St. John [152]. In these years BARAN, together with the architect C. SEZER, supervised the first works of restoration in the Bouleuterion (so-called Odeion [22]), undertook clearance work on Curetes Street [36] and in the lower Agora and had columns re-erected. In one section of the great theatre the seating was repaired with different material whereas in another section it was restored true to its original appearance. Also at this time, the brick walls of the Church of Mary [95] and Basilica of St. John were restored and shored up to prevent collapse. In 1961 the now famous Mycenaean tomb [153] was discovered by accident under the parking place in front of the Basilica of St. John and its excavation was carried out with the assistance of H. GÜLTEKİN.

During the years 1963 - 1979, the cryptoporticus of the Temple of Domitian [30] was excavated under the guidance of the director of the museum S. TÜRKOĞLU, and partially restored. In addition, the repair work to the orchestra floor, the south analemma wall and the Hellenistic well house in the great theatre was continued with temporary interruptions. In the years 1979 - 1995, an important part of Theatre Street was uncovered and restored under the leadership of the director of the museum S. ERDEMGİL. In this period, thorough cleaning and restoration work was also undertaken in the Church of Mary, which was, to a great extent, rebuilt. At the same time, excavations and restoration work began in the Odeion, in the Prytaneum [24 - 25], in the Latrine [43], at the so-called harbour buildings of Pamucak and in the İsa bey Hamam [171], which will be continued at a future time.

The uncovering and restoration of the Basilica of St. John, together with its surrounding structures, has been carried out since 1973 under the direction of E. AKURGAL. The excavation costs will be met by contributions from the Ministry of Culture of the Republic of Turkey, and from a fund set up in the USA by G. QUATMAN and managed, after his death, by his son J. QUATMAN.

Excavations are being carried out in the atrium, baptistery, treasury house and the defence walls. The surroundings of the basilica are being laid out as a park. SE

Fig. 1: The Basilica of St. John, state of the restoration in 1995 (PESENDORFER)

THE ARTEMISION [1]

The sanctuary of Artemis of Ephesus, one of the Seven Wonders of the ancient world, was discovered and excavated at the end of 1869 on behalf of the British Museum by J.T. WOOD, a British railway engineer, after a search of seven years. His successor, D.G. HOGARTH, also working for the British Museum in 1904/05, excavated not only this monumental building, but also older structures in the so-called "central base area" in the interior of the temple courtyard. Excavations were resumed by the Austrian Archaeological Institute in 1965 and continue to this day. This work has brought to world attention not only the temple, first built by Croesus in the mid-6th century BC and re-erected after destruction by arson in the late fourth century, and the great courtyard altar, but also the central base in the interior of the temple. A re-examination of the latter led to the extraordinary discovery of a peripteros temple of the 8th century BC, the oldest known example of post-Mycenaean Greek monumental architecture. In connection with this building, a significant hoard of objects was discovered which mainly consisted of amber, most probably part of the pectoral ornamentation of a cult figure.

The reputation that the Artemision enjoyed brought it many votive gifts. During the archaic period in the 7th and 6th centuries BC, it had a special relationship to Sardis, capital of the Lydian empire. This is reflected not only in the initiative shown by the Lydian kings in building the archaic temple, which according to Herodotus (I 92) was also called the Croesus temple because of the columns which the Lydian king donated, but also in the existence of certain types of pottery that are only found in Ephesus and Sardis (e.g. the so-called Ephesian ware). Animals such as rams, peacocks and oxen stand out among the votives figurines along with gold and ivory representations of goddesses (Ephesus Museum Selçuk, Room 6).

Fig. 1: Cult base made of slabs of local chalk marl from the 7th century BC built over by the foundations of the northern part of the ring of columns around the giant temple

Fig. 2: Water conduit near the altar: lead pipes with marble sleeves, 5th century BC (PESENDORFER)

Fig. 3: Ivory lions head, votive offering from the Artemision

Fig. 4: Collection of gold finds from the vicinity of a 7th century BC cult base: female statuette (53 mm) and lion-headed fibulas

1

2

3

4

The oldest architectural remains in the vicinity of the Artemision consist of a retaining wall of slate and quartz stones. This has been interpreted as a dam wall, built, perhaps, during the Mycenaean period to prevent flooding.

The 8th century BC

A peripteros temple measuring 13.5 x 6.5 m, with 4 x 8 columns and an open cella in its interior, stood, in the second half of the 8th century, in the area which became the courtyard of the subsequent temple. Inside, resting on six columns, a rectangular baldachin housed the cult figure, the *xoanon*.

Walls and foundations were made of local chalk marl. This peripteros temple appears to have been constantly threatened by flooding. For this reason the entire peristasis had to be raised. A tile roof discovered in 1994, which had been re-used to seal a sacrificial trench, probably belonged to this rebuilding. In a third phase of the construction of the peripteros, the peristasis was abandoned but the cella wall itself was strengthened with a casing.

Very little is known about the construction of the peripteros temple. Neither the appearance of the capitals nor of the entablature has been determined. Only the green slate bases of the wooden columns are preserved. Quite primitive, slightly rounded forms which exhibit a smooth supporting surface, exist together with others which suggest a sort of plinth and torus. The soft green slate material used is conspicuously decorative whereas the wooden columns and masonry of yellowish limestone are more in keeping with the character of the surroundings. This temple with its baldachin already anticipates the later Ionic monumental temple.

This peripteral structure cannot, however, have been the oldest building on the site. The stratigraphy shows that the columns of the peristasis belong to an older building phase than the cella wall which must have been inserted later. The existence of a *pre-peripteros* may therefore be assumed. The ceramic continuum of the site has yielded finds, reaching back into Mycenaean times, which are older than the architecture.

Fig. 1: Early cult buildings in the Artemision, overall plan (AB): *peripteros* with baldachin for the cult statue (8th century, pink); so-called *hecatompedos* to the west of it, together with the associated cult base (7th or early 6th century, yellow); older Artemision partly financed by king Croesus (around the middle of the 6th century, green) and late classical altar enclosure (blue)

Fig. 2: The earliest temple buildings in the centre of the Artemision (8th - 6th centuries BC)

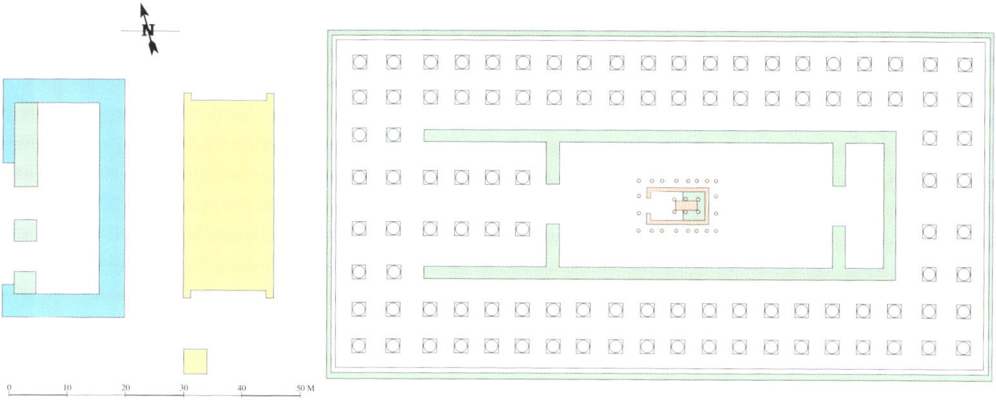
N
0
10
20
30
40
50 M

The 7th century BC

In the 7th century there was a diagonal path towards the later courtyard altar, a water channel and an apsidal building in the south-west of the Artemision precinct. Another contemporaneous apsidal construction lies between Temple C and the archaic marble temple.

This temple C was erected in the late 7th or early 6th century BC. It lies on the site of the peripteros and shows signs of antae on its west side. Its walls and foundations are also made of chalk marl. Building was presumably discontinued when work on the archaic dipteros began.

Construction of a building was begun in the late 7th century on the west side of the Artemision. Its remains were already found by HOGARTH and his architect HENDERSON who, although they did not know how to interpret them, connected them with the so-called Temple C and dated them accordingly.

The foundations of this building are likewise of yellow limestone and the walls built above them were of marble, as was the threshold which lies in situ on the east side of the foundations immediately in front of the west end of the archaic temple. The temple was 34.40 m long, a dimension corresponding approximately to one hundred Ionic feet, and this led to its designation as *hecatompedos* ("hundred footer"). The building lies on the axis of the Croesus temple, exactly at a right angle to its western entrance. Not only the use of chalk marl for the foundations, but also the stratigraphy between them support the conclusion that the *hecatompedos* must be older than the archaic marble temple. Among other things, the fact that the two buildings lie almost fifty metres from one another and have approximately the same dimensions goes counter to a theory according to which the *hecatompedos* was the altar of Temple C. Both were built before 560 BC and both were obviously never finished. This building complex would more likely have been the Apollo temple mentioned in ancient literature. The entire marble structure of the *hecatompedos* was incorporated into the foundations of the Croesus temple. Aligned with the *hecatompedos* on its west lies a base which - like other square or rectangular bases in the later temple courtyard and in the northern temple area - had a cult function, as is indicated by the votive gifts and animal bones found there. The existence of various contemporary cult bases suggests that several deities were venerated at that time.

Fig. 1: Birds-eye view of the foundations of the great altar (left) and the so-called *hecatompedos* with an associated cult base in line with a projection of its west front

The 6th century BC

In the 6th century, three foundations were built in the area of the later courtyard altar. They are oriented north-south and form a parallel line with the west front of the temple. Five stones from the southernmost base are preserved *in situ*, which suggest a square base measuring 3.50 x 3.50 m. These stones bear a numbering system in the form of single Greek letters. A foundation of approximately the same size, adjoining the north side, is entirely preserved and consists of narrow rectangular cut limestone blocks. Just 5.50 m further north there is a third foundation with two steps oriented in a north-south direction which has been called a ramp or stairway-ramp. Pottery finds show that these are early archaic structures. A particularly large number of female goat horns were found here attesting to regular sacrificial activity. Bowls for libations and plates came to light on all sides, in particular, small water vessels (*hydrisks*) and small jugs in which water was brought from a spring for cult purposes (Ephesus Museum Selçuk, Room 6, display case). The spring was supplemented by a water conduit coming from the south-west. This consisted of lead pipes connected by marble sleeves (Ephesus Museum Selçuk, Room 6). Apparently, the spring did not yield much, so that water had to be brought in from the outside.

Around 560 BC, construction began on the first large marble dipteros, the so-called Croesus temple. The building of the archaic dipteros was a milestone for Greek architecture. Up to the beginning of the 6th century all the foundations were laid in a yellow, easily split chalk marl, which came from a quarry at the entrance to the Ephesian bay. Most of the marble used for the construction of the archaic temple was obtained from a quarry near Belevi which lies inland in the direction of Izmir. Such large blocks had never previously been transported and the technological innovations used here were greatly admired. According to tradition, Chersiphron, Metagenes, and Theodoros of Samos were the architects of the archaic dipteros, which was laid out on a east-west axis. The marshy ground presented a special problem when it was erected. Theodoros of Samos recommended laying charcoal under the foundations, and this ash substratum has been archaeologically confirmed. The ash and charcoal of the sacrificial remains were inbedded in a rubble layer to hinder the capillary action of the soil. The foundations of the building consisted of large slate blocks coated with clay. Only the stylobate above was constructed of polygonally cut marble slabs.

The great admiration which the Greeks showed for the technological innovations first used in the building of this giant temple is reflected in the legend that the lintel of the great door was put in place by the goddess Artemis herself (Pliny the Elder, *Historia Naturalis* XXXVI 21, 95). The temple was just under 60 m wide but its length is not known. It probably had 106 columns.

Of particular interest are the temple columns engraved with figures - the *columnae caelatae* -, and the roof cornice, also embellished with figures. Nearly all the roof tiles were made of marble as well, so that each column had to support a weight of over 100 tons. Most of the fragments of architectural sculpture, the *columnae*, and the frieze of the roof entablature were discovered during the English excavations and found their way into the British Museum in London. Many were reused in the pillars of a church built over the temple, which was blown up by J.T. Wood. Fragments of column drums with reliefs, as well as rectangular column bases still survive and portray a procession of people and animals on their way to sacrifice.

Like the temple of Apollo in Didyma, the Artemision was not a temple in the sense of a covered building; the walls enclosed a open court area - the sekos - and only the columned porticos were roofed over. The *sekos* surrounded the old *peripteros* whose cella was now used, in its eastern half, as the foundation for the *naiskos* - a small temple-like building which housed the cult statue - of the Croesus temple.

The 5th century BC

In the early 5th century, a large courtyard altar was erected on the temple axis over a U-shaped limestone foundation which enclosed the three bases mentioned above. Discovered in 1965, this altar (*thrinkos*) lies in the west of the area and encloses a large courtyard, 31.90 x 16.67 m, which opens to the west. It is today protected by a modern wall against flooding of adjacent marshy land. The lower of the two approximately 0.36 m high stone courses supported some sort of structure, probably an undecorated fence-like enclosure.

The 4th century BC

Various ancient sources state that the Croesus temple, also called the older Artemision, was set on fire in the year 356 BC by a certain Herostratus who allegedly wished to immortalize his name through this act. Alexander the Great is said to have been born during the same night on which this occurred. The historical reports of this fire are verifiable because many parts of the archaic temple reveal traces of it.

Paionios, Demetrios, and Cheirokrates are known to have been the architects of the rebuilding. The ground plan can only be reconstructed with the help of the dimensions of the archaic temple lying approximately 2.76 m beneath it. All essential elements of the archaic structure were retained including the columns decorated with reliefs.

The high platform upon which the later temple stands was necessary because of flooding caused by a pronounced rise in the level of the sea in the 4th century BC. In contrast with the older Artemision the ground plan was modified. The high and broad stepped base, as well as the third row of columns on the west front narrowed the space between the altar and the temple. The *sekos* acquired a stepped ramp which led down to the level of the archaic temple. The rear, eastern end of the cella was fitted out with a room accessible from outside, the *opisthodomos*, which probably served as a treasure chamber. No more than 21 columns can be assumed for the long sides of the temple, while eight columns remain on the west front, or entrance side. Three rows of nine columns can be reconstructed on the rear façade. Ancient coins depict doors in the temple pediment; their purpose could have been to allow a portrait of the goddess Artemis to participate as an epiphany in the altar sacrifices, as a direct view from temple to altar was obstructed by the high altar enclosure.

The height of the columns can be reconstructed to approximately 18.40 m using literary sources (Pliny the Elder, *Historia Naturalis* XXXVI 21, 95) and the remaining fragments.

In the 4th century BC, a new altar enclosure was also built. The three structures in the interior of the court, which have been interpreted as a base for the cult figure, an eschara (hearth for sacrificial burning) and a ramp (place for slaughtering the sacrificial animals), were apparently rebuilt on the old foundations. The second building phase of this enclosure, represented by the uppermost preserved limestone course, the construction of which probably began prior to the rebuilding of the large temple, has preserved fragments of sculpture and architectural elements. A hypothetical reconstruction can be made of the altar base as well as the columnar architecture above it, which was decorated with figures in the intercolumniations. Sculpted horses from the decoration of the building's roof have also survived.

Fig. 1: The later Artemision (2nd half of the 4th century). Reconstructed ground plan of the temple and altar (AB) 1:1000

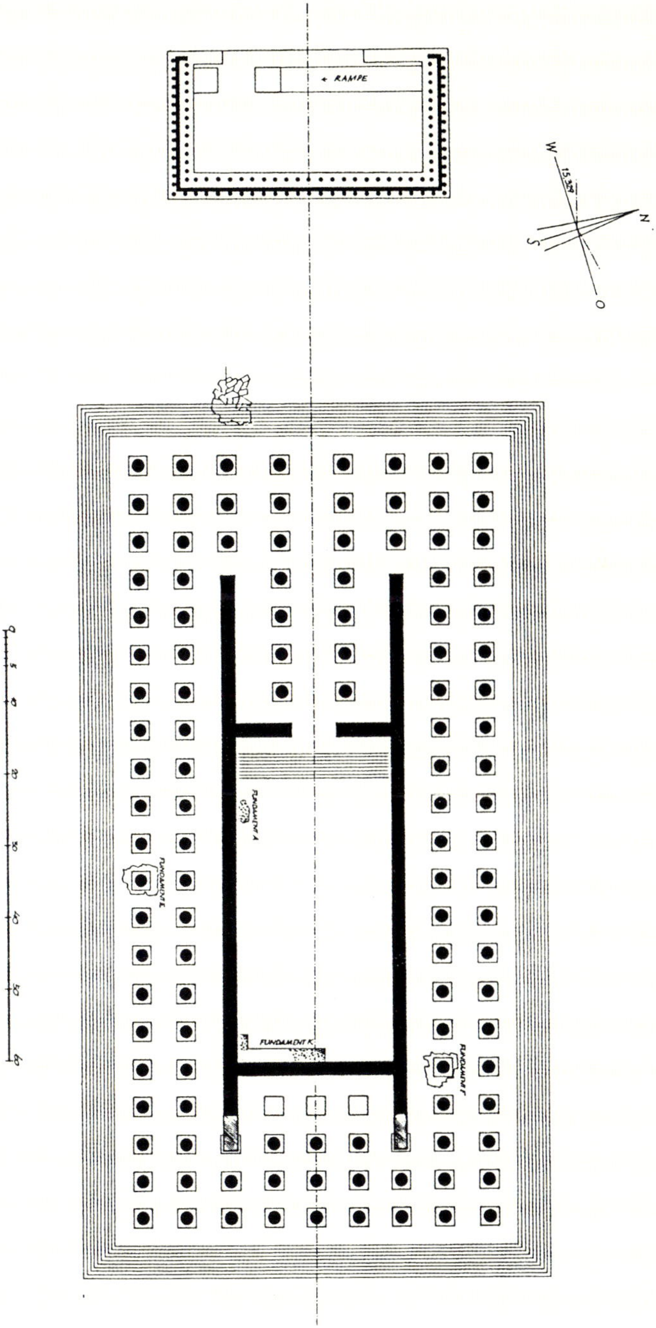
← RAMPE
W
N
S
O
0
5
10
20
30
40
50
60
FUNDAMENT A
FUNDAMENT E
FUNDAMENT K
FUNDAMENT F

Roman Times

The Hellenistic centuries have left behind hardly any traces in that area of the sanctuary that has, up to now, been excavated. The turmoil of the Roman civil wars at the end of the Republic and the associated economic decline, as well as the progressive silting up of the rivers, put Artemis' possessions into disarray. Thus extensive organizational measures, promulgated by the *proconsul* of the years 6/5 BC, came into effect under the Emperor Augustus. All the boundaries, paths and drains in the *temenos* - the cult area enclosed by a wall - were newly surveyed and restored. The *temenos* wall itself, the ashlar stones of which, covered all over with inscriptions of civil decrees, were used in Late Antiquity as spoils, primarily for the Church of Mary and its associated bishop's palace. According to Strabo, the *temenos* wall lay one stad (about 180 m) from the temple and marked the boundary of the age-old asylum precinct. A cult structure known as a *sebasteion* was perhaps set up for Augustus - as for a series of emperors thereafter - in the temenos of Artemis. However, some fifty years later, a provincial governor once again complained that . . . *the sanctuary of Artemis itself, which is the jewel of the entire province both on account of the size of the building as well as the age-old veneration of the goddess, and because of the amount of revenue secured again for the goddess by Augustus, is being robbed of its own possessions, which could have sufficed to provide for the votive gifts and its embellishment.* Under the Emperor Titus (79 - 81 AD), large-scale repairs and construction were again carried out in the sanctuary.

Three Roman buildings have been partially uncovered in the north-west of the Artemision. The oldest building has beautifully carved steps on its western edge. A podium temple, into which the steps of the older building were partially integrated, was later built on to it. An altar stood in a small courtyard in the south of this podium temple. The large marble head of a goddess was found near this building. East of it, a rectangular temple-like building was erected which stood on an orthostat base and perhaps had an apse to the south. North of this, either an altar or a statue base was constructed out of spoils. The buildings, which were erected in late Hellenistic-early Roman times, can be associated with various Imperial cult installations mentioned in inscriptions.

The late Roman and early Byzantine period

The Artemision was plundered by the Goths in the year 263 AD but its actual destruction did not occur until after 400 AD when the ancient cult was discontinued. The altar and its surrounding colonnade, together with its pediment were apparently demolished, sold or reused in the area of the basilica of St. John. The basilica itself, as well as its outer walls, is full of spolia from the Artemision (Ephesus Museum Selçuk, Room 6). A church was erected in the Artemision in the 5th century AD. During the early Byzantine period, pillars were also built into the longitudinal walls of the sekos which were apparently intended to support the church roof spanning the courtyard. J.T. WOOD had already identified these pillars and searched inside for the spoils of the two marble temples.

Many fragments of sculpture from the archaic temple were found which had "survived" the new building phase because a great number of them were used for the foundation of the late classical building and integrated into the pillars when the church was built.

BAMMER, Die Architektur des Jüngeren Artemision von Ephesus (1972); Das Heiligtum der Artemis von Ephesos (1984); Ephesos, Stadt an Fluß und Meer (1988); regular reports in ÖJh, AnatSt and RA; BAMMER – MUSS, Das Artemision von Ephesos (Zaberns Bildbände zur Archäologie 20, 1995); RÜGLER, Die Bauplastik des spätklassischen Artemisions von Ephesus, IstMitt Beih. 34 (1988); MUSS, Jahrbuch der Kunsthistorischen Sammlungen in Wien 80, 1984, 7ff; Die Bauplastik des archaischen Artemisions von Ephesos (1994); WESENBERG, Zur Rekonstruktion griechischer Architektur nach literarischen Quellen, AM Beih. 9 (1983) 32ff.

An apse in the east has not yet been found. The pillars measured some 3 x 4.40 m; the eastern corner-pillars were larger. Eight pillars, with spanning distances of about 15 m, stood before each longitudinal wall so that this building can be considered one of the largest Ephesian churches. Until now, only one impost capital for a column 0.53m in diameter has been found. Whether the associated arch-supporting columns were set up in the upper storey or as an interior colonnade cannot yet be determined. Up to now there are no clues as to the dedication of the building but since the temple itself had been dedicated to a goddess for 1000 years, it can be assumed that this church was consecrated to Mary. The cult of Mary in Ephesus, whether in the Church of Mary or in the so-called House of Mary in Meryemana, has enjoyed a lively tradition to this day, a tradition which can hardly be imagined without the cult of Artemis.

Visiting the Artemision

The Artemision has a large potential for research. But although it is one of the most important excavations in Ephesus and of great symbolic significance, it is for the most part an invisible monument. The excavations have been, in part, re-buried and the whole area is often under water. Excavations take place during the summer when the ground is dried by means of a suction pump.

The towering column in the north-east was set up in 1973 using drums from various columns. It is 14 m high, approximately 4 m short of the original height. This column stands on the remains of the foundations of the 4th century BC temple platform in which numerous spoils of the archaic building were incorporated, some of which can still be seen. In contrast, the archaic column base, insofar as it is preserved, lies *in situ* directly under the late classical, and is also visible. On the south side of the temple are some remains of the foundation of the late classical temple, upon which Wood found what was left of another classical base (today in the British Museum) centered on an archaic plinth, which is still preserved. The courtyard walls of the archaic temple can be seen, especially the point of attachment for the doorframe and the remains of the archaic marble stylobate in the west.

In the west, the remains of the foundation for the stairway which led from the courtyard to the platform of the late classical temple still exist. Also remaining in the western area, the southern anta of the archaic temple with its late classical casing as well as the west and north edges of the archaic and late classical temples, the foundations of the *hecatompedos*, the buildings lying south of it (*naiskos*, channel, path, and apsidal building) together with the archaic and late classical altar foundations and their subsidiary buildings. The pillars of the church can also be seen in the temple courtyard. The impost capital (mentioned above) lies in the north-west corner.

Depending on the level of the ground water some of the older structures in the courtyard can be seen: the remains of Temple C, the walls of the *cella* of the *peripteros* as well as the *naiskos* of the Croesus temple.

A view from the south shows the sequence of the sanctuaries of three world religions: the pagan Artemision, the Christian Basilica of St. John and the Islamic İsa bey mosque.

AB, UM

The so-called Tribune [2]

A vaulted foundation, all that remains of a Roman building, lies in the garden approximately at the assumed west edge of the *temenos* of the Artemision. On top of this, a tribune may have been erected in connection with a festival ground where processions formed up.

HT

Fig. 1: View over the excavations in the vicinity of the temple with the column, partly re-erected in 1973. In the background, the Basilica of St. John and the İsa bey mosque. Above, the Byzantine-Turkish fortress

MONUMENTS ON THE EAST SLOPE OF THE PANAYIRDAĞ

Following the main road from the Artemision, and just before the first standing ruins of the Roman city, the visitor can take a turn to the left off the asphalt road leading to the Lower Entrance (116). This side road, marked with a signpost to Yedi Uyuyanlar (Seven Sleepers), leads more or less along the ancient route (Damianus Stoa), past the old Greek rock shrine sacred to Zeus and the Mother of the Gods (Meter-Cybele shrine [4]) and the legendary Seven Sleepers Cemetery [8], around the east flank of the Panayırdağ to the Magnesian Gate [10], and on to the Upper Entrance [115] to the ruins of Ephesus.

The road first runs along the Late Antique city wall [77], constructed out of older building materials, behind which the massive ruins of the Vedius Gymnasium [106] and the Stadium [104] are visible. The wall bends to the south-west immediately to the east of the Stadium and climbs to the crest of Panayırdağ, going around a small bay in the slope, and follows this to its southern peak at a height of some 150 m. This inlet could have been the site of the settlement established by Androclus, the mythical founder of the city, around the Harbour called Coressus [3] in early Greek times. According to the results of geological drilling, the plain to the east of the road was still marine marshland up into the 2nd century AD.

Burial Sites

Desirable burial sites lay alongside this road. Highly visible tombs, some of them empty barrel vaults, cover the slope of the Panayırdağ up to the Magnesian Gate [10]. In addition to simple burial places hewn out of the rock and originally closed by a large stone slab, there are sarcophagi, some modest, others elaborately decorated with garlands or other reliefs. Next to these were more or less extravagant tomb structures which served as burial places for individuals of high-rank, families, or individuals of lower social status who were buried together as members of burial societies. Today, numerous foundations of such structures are visible on the ground. Tomb inscriptions, ashlar blocks, and ornamental elements of these mausoleums can be seen scattered throughout the area or re-used in other buildings.

A monument set up behind the so-called Upper Entrance [115] was found in 1987 in front of three vaulted burial chambers containing ostotheques which have been studied by the Ephesus Museum Selçuk.

Cİ, PS, HT

Fig. 1: Grave relief of a gladiator on the Damianus Stoa

Fig. 2: Sarcophagus from Roman Imperial times with garland decoration which now stands at the entrance to the Ephesus Museum in Selçuk

Rock shrine sacred to the Mother Goddess, Zeus and Apollo [4]

The eastern promontory of the Panayırdağ - in Greek times, a steep slope on the coast, but today rising directly from the road connecting the Vedius Gymnasium to the Seven Sleepers cemetery - is the site of an important sanctuary. Numerous inscriptions to Meter (the Mother of the Gods, often called Cybele), Zeus and Apollo, were chiselled into the vertical surfaces of the rocks. Mainly upright, rectangular flat niches, now empty, once housed ready-made votive reliefs (presently in the Ephesus Museum in Selçuk or in the Museum of Izmir) which depicted the Mother of the Gods flanked by lions, alone or accompanied by a bearded older god (Zeus?) and a younger god (Hermes?). Of the few niches which exhibit true rock reliefs, only one is easily found directly on the road. The oldest votive reliefs date back into the 5th century BC. The sanctuary was at the peak of its renown in the late classical - early Hellenistic period but also enjoyed a certain popularity in Roman Imperial times. Rock niches and step-thrones bear witness to similar private cult activity in many other places on the mountain slope. PS

Fig. 1: Rock shrine: niches for votive reliefs in the terrace-like subdivisions of the rock

Fig. 2: Meter relief from Hellenistic times (SCHIFFLEITNER)

Fig. 3: Zeus inscription (5th century BC)

Byzantine Aqueduct [5]

The course of a low aqueduct, dating, to judge from the masonry and construction technique, to the Late Antique period, can easily be followed along the southern and eastern slopes of the Panayırdağ where it cuts jaggedly through the rock sanctuary. The aqueduct carried water from the Marnas valley into the area of the Stadium and the remains of the early Byzantine city between the Church of Mary [95] and the Tetragonos Agora [61]. HT

Archaic settlement in Koressos [6]

The shoulder of the slope from contour lines 40 m to 50 m, between the narrow gorge immediately south of the rock sanctuary and the small peak directly east of the presumed harbour inlet of Coressus, is fortified along approximately 300 m of its length by wall, 2.40 m thick. This has often been incorrectly identified as part of the Lysimachian city wall [11] on the basis of superficial similarities in construction technique. Differences in detail are many, however, the most important being the lack of reinforcing towers. The only known passageway through it is situated directly above the Zeus/Meter shrine. The wall, in fact, defended the archaic settlement of Koressos, founded by Androclus and later besieged by king Croesus, who forced the inhabitants to move to a new city near the Artemision. PS

Rock shrine: ÖJh 1915, 66 - 78.
Aqueduct: FiE III, 236 - 238.
Defensive wall: ÖJh 1926, B261.
Graves: ZPE 11, 1992, 283 - 296; ÖJh 1930, B7 -17.

STOA OF DAMIANUS [7]

At the turn of the 2nd to the 3rd century AD, the well-known Ephesian sophist T. Flavius Damianus had the Processional Way, rich in tradition, extending from the Temple of Artemis to the Hellenistic-Roman city, extravagantly roofed over with a covered colonnade so that, as his pupil Philostratus wrote, *Artemis will not miss her admirers when it rains.*

Traces of the Stoa of Damianus still remain in several places on the northern foot and especially on the eastern foot of the Panayırdağ. Massive limestone pillar blocks jut out of the ground here and there on both sides of the path leading from the Magnesian Gate or the East Gymnasium to the area of the Seven Sleepers.

New excavations to the east of the Stadium [104] and north of the East Gymnasium [12] have investigated the more than 2.5 km long and 3.70 m wide colonnade in three places. Bases made out of the local bluish limestone supported brick pillars which carried brick barrel or groin vaults. These rest on extremely deep foundations appropriate to the hydrologically unstable ground and are interconnected at foundation level by sturdy walls. Surprisingly enough, the walking surface in the colonnade was not paved. The excavations also came across sarcophagi, burial chambers and individual graves of various types and quality dating from late Hellenistic times into the late Roman-Byzantine period.

The discovery of a gladiator cemetery on the north side of Panayırdağ quite close to the Stadium was a special surprise. Two grave reliefs show heavily armed men (*secutores*) bearing sword, helmet and shin-guards, posing in the glory of their victories. Another depicts a net-fighter (*retiarus*) with trident and dagger running to the attack. Many of the skeletons found here show evidence of skull and shin-bone injuries.

Roads for vehicular traffic ran along the stoa and these were paved in the $2^{nd}/3^{rd}$ centuries AD with large limestone flagstones on top of several earlier surfaces. In its final building phase it was a simple road of broken brick. The remains of the stoa can best be seen on both sides of the path which bends to the north at a point slightly east of the East Gymnasium. Several pillars lie on its western embankment and a pair of contiguous pillars has been excavated on its eastern embankment.

DK

Via Sacra Ephesiaca I - III (BerMatÖAI 3, 1993; 6, 1995; 7, 2000) ÖJh 1930, B7 -17.
On the graves, see page 58 with illustrations

Fig. 1: Reconstruction of the stoa (HT)

Fig. 2: Road section K IV

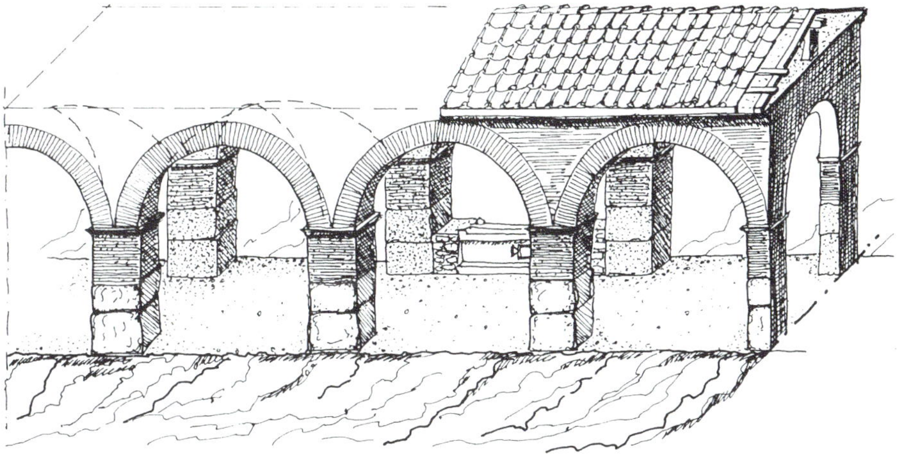

THE SO-CALLED SEVEN SLEEPERS CEMETERY [8]

The Seven Sleepers Cemetery lies outside the city wall on the rugged eastern slope of the Panayırdağ. According to literary tradition, it is this place to which seven young men fled and hid in a cave during the persecution of the Christians by Emperor Decius, in the years 249 to 251 AD. The men were entombed in the cave until the reign of Emperor Theodosius when they are said to have come to life again as witnesses to the bodily resurrection of the dead.

The oldest textual evidence about the clearly legendary martyrdom was probably written (in Greek?) by a Syrian around the middle of the 5th century AD. This was later translated into Latin by Gregory of Tours (*de gloria martyrum* 1, 95), and also became the starting point for the later Islamic tradition (i.e. the 18th sura of the Koran) which, taking note of the many places where the Seven Sleepers were venerated, sees the events as having occurred not only in Ionian Ephesus, but in the Cappadocian Arabissus as well. The results of investigations in the building remains of the so-called Seven Sleepers Cemetery do not, however, allow any identification of the site with the legend. Variations on this tale of suffering are also known in the Coptic and Armenian languages.

Legend: AASS Iul. 6 (= 27), 375 - 397; BHG 2, 1593 - 1599d inc. Auct. and Nov. Auct.; BHL 2313 -2319; BHO 1012 - 1022; ABoll 41, 1923, 369 - 385; Anz 1957, 87 - 95.

Cemetery: FiE IV/2; ÖJh 1972 - 75, B171 - 180; LECHNER – SQUARR, Lex christl. Ikonographie 8 (1976) 344 - 348.

The oldest part of the place of pilgrimage which developed in Ephesus, consists of a cemetery built, probably at the end of the 4th century, around a crevice extending deep into the hill with a two-storey tomb and ten underground chambers in which the graves of the martyrs were to be seen. Shortly afterwards, a church was erected above the underground installation and connected to it by a stairway on the north wall of the anteroom. The church had a domed main room with a mosaic floor together with a raised square presbytery with an apse, built-in bench (for the priests) and an altar. A burial hall, in all likelihood originally barrel vaulted, was built on to west of the church. In time, however, this became too small for the ever increasing number of graves which were dug into the floor, constructed of brick, and built into the walls. In the end, it contained more than 700 multiple burials.

Fig. 1: Seven Sleepers Cemetery, overall view

Fig. 2: Ground plan (after RBK 2 [1971] 193, Fig. 13)

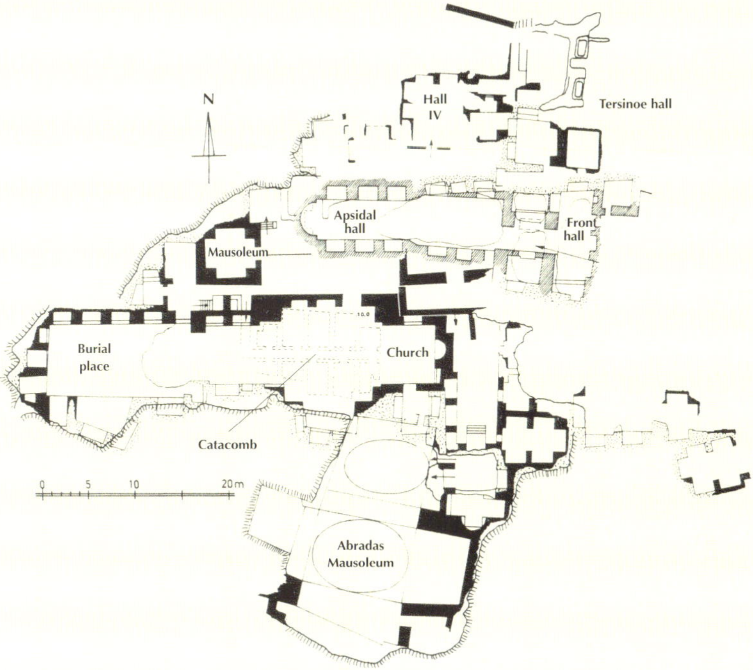
N
Hall
IV
Tersinoe hall
Apsidal
hall
Front
hall
Mausoleum
Burial
place
Church
Catacomb
0 5 10 20m
Abradas
Mausoleum

Unfortunately, the only reference points for dating are over 2,000 oil lamps, most of them from the end of the 4th century and in need of more detailed study, as well as a relatively small number of approximately contemporaneous grave inscriptions, three of which were for deacons. According to the legend, the church was built during the reign of Emperor Theodosius in about the middle of the 5th century. This date agrees entirely with the archaeological finds; as with the burial complex, a prolonged period of building activity - perhaps extending over the entire 5th century - must be postulated, which does not contradict the current dating of the preserved paintings and mosaic decoration. Further investigations, already planned, will hopefully shed more light. RP

The so-called Armenian Place of Worship [9]

Between the two peaks of the Panayırdağ are to be seen the remains of a modern wall in the form of a church apse. This marks the place where, until the beginning of this century, Christians from Smyrna and the surrounding area celebrated the festival of St. John, which gave the hill its present-day modern Greek colloquial name (panayiri, after the ancient Greek *panegyris*). RP

MAGNESIAN GATE [10] — HELLENISTIC CITY WALL [11]

The Panayırdağ was fortified with two not necessarily contemporaneous sections of the Hellenistic city wall [11] of Lysimachus. In the gently climbing terrain between the Panayırdağ and the Bülbüldağ lies the only excavated city gate, the departure point of the road to Magnesia on the Meander, as well as the land connection to the valley of the Caystros and the covered way to the Temple of Artemis as remodelled by Damianus.

J.T. WOOD had already discovered the Magnesian Gate in 1869 during his search for the Temple of Artemis. G. SEITERLE recently continued research on the building. Landslides and post-antique earth dumps have greatly altered the landscape so that the visitor must go a few metres southwards from the asphalt road facing the East Gymnasium [12] before the excavated gate complex first comes into view. The original building was possibly erected in the Doric order with a passageway 3.70 m wide and an almost square courtyard (22.80 x 25 m) on the city side.

Fig. 1: Seven Sleepers Cemetery, view into the apse room

Fig. 2: Seven Sleepers Cemetery: paintings on the triumphal arch, hand coloured drawing (THEUER 1927)

Fig. 3: Magnesian Gate: exterior facade and road with grooves made by wagon wheels

1

2

3

Up to now, however, no evidence has been presented for a Lysimachian date. Parts of a weapons-frieze and three marble lions found in the gate area could have belonged, in a later, secondary context, to the original gate furnishings. In the 2nd half of the 1st century BC, at the earliest, lateral portals and flanking towers (11 m square with walls 2 m thick) were erected on both sides of the main entrance which was embellished with ornamental mouldings. The adjoining curtain walls were thickened from their original 3.40 m to 5 m. Probably in the 3rd century AD, the partially collapsed towers were hastily renovated. A Late Antique cemetery near the gate was apparently associated with a basilica [13] erected in the immediate vicinity in the East Gymnasium at the end of the 4th century.

The city wall extends from the Magnesian Gate in a straight line to the north, where it joins the eastern side of the Roman East Gymnasium [12]. It then climbs the slope of the Panayırdağ, approximately to the 70 m contour which it then follows (still standing in parts to a height of 2.5 m), for some 500 meters. The wall curves to the west along the geological fault-line running between the two peaks of the Panayırdağ and ascends along the broken edge to the 120 m contour.

Seiterle, AntK 25, 1982, 145 - 149; Anz 1982, 69; 1983, 117; 1984, 215; 1986, 83; ÖJh 1915, B280.

Judging from the sparse remains, the Hellenistic wall crossed the so-called Byzantine city wall [77] not far north of the southern peak of the Panayırdağ and finally reached the coastal plain in the immediate vicinity of the theatre [75]. A second ring crossed the ravine between the two halves of the hill at their highest point, and continued around the northern peak. It seems that the section of the wall on the Panayırdağ was already partially dismantled in Roman Imperial times. In any case, ashlar blocks from the Hellenistic wall of Lysimachus were used for the construction of the Byzantine city wall, particularly in the area of the crest of the hill. The remains which still exist, match precisely the well-preserved sections on the Bülbüldağ in respect both to the overall course of the wall and the building technique. The double-faced curtain wall was 2.40 m to 3 m thick, the portion encirceling the northern peak increasing to more than 4 m as it descends into the deep ravine. Towers, almost square in plan (i.e. 8.20 x 9.80 m, or 9.40 x 10.6 m), were erected and loosely incorporated into the wall at strategic points and where the wall changes direction.

PS

Fig. 1: The eastern promontory of the Panayırdağ was secured by two relatively well preserved towers

Fig. 2: View over the double-faced curtain of the city wall by the East Gymnasium

THE EAST GYMNASIUM [12] AND EARLY CHRISTIAN BASILICA [13]

A bath/gymnasium complex, erected in about the 2nd half of the 2nd century AD and covering an area of almost 130 x 107 m, lies immediately north of the Magnesian Gate. Only superficially studied, the enormous ruins of this so-called East Gymnasium still clearly mark the beginning of the Ephesian city area for tourists approaching the Upper Entrance. A three-aisled basilica on the main street originated, in late Roman times, as a cemetery church.

A stoa with market stands occupied the south front of the gymnasium complex with its main entrance on the street leading to the Magnesian Gate. The visitor first enters the *palaestra*, with a lecture hall with rising rows of seats adjoining on the east, and a so-called Imperial hall on the west. During the excavations, which began in 1930, F. MILTNER found the remains of a statue of the healing god Asclepius in the central apse of this Imperial hall. On the two narrow sides, a statue of an Imperial priest faced that of a distinguished lady, probably the donors of the complex. Additional statues, including Aphrodite, Dionysus, Hygeia, Pan and captured barbarians, bear witness to the once rich furnishings. With the exception of the so-called Vedia Phaedrina, which can be seen in the Ephesus Museum Selçuk, these statues are in the Izmir Museum. The enormous bathing halls are located (as was normal in Roman Imperial times) in the centre of the structure, surrounded on three sides by vaulted halls for physical exercise, games, and for strolling after the bath.

East Gymnasium: ÖJh 1927, B25ff.; 1928, B5ff.
Church: Anz 1982, 71; 1983, 116; 1984, 215

A church was built over the Hellenistic city wall to the east of the lecture hall in the late 4th or 5th century. Around the time of Justinian, this was converted into a three-aisled basilica (35 x 17 m) with a narthex (excavated after MILTNER's plan was drawn), and arcades. Most of the floor surface was covered with well-preserved, highly decorative mosaics, which have been removed for reasons of preservation and security. The *solea* in front of the presbytery is decorated with Numidian marble. The church must have been abandoned after destruction by fire in the first third of the 7th century AD. Most of the presbytery, fitted out with a bench for the priest but lacking an apse, fell victim to the construction of the asphalt road. PS

Fig. 1: East Gymnasium, early Christian basilica and Magnesian Gate. Ground plan (1:2000; MILTNER)

Fig. 2: Donor statue from the East Gymnasium; Imperial priest with crowned head (wrongly identified as Flavius Damianus; Izmir Museum)

Fig. 3: East Gymnasium, reconstruction (MILTNER)

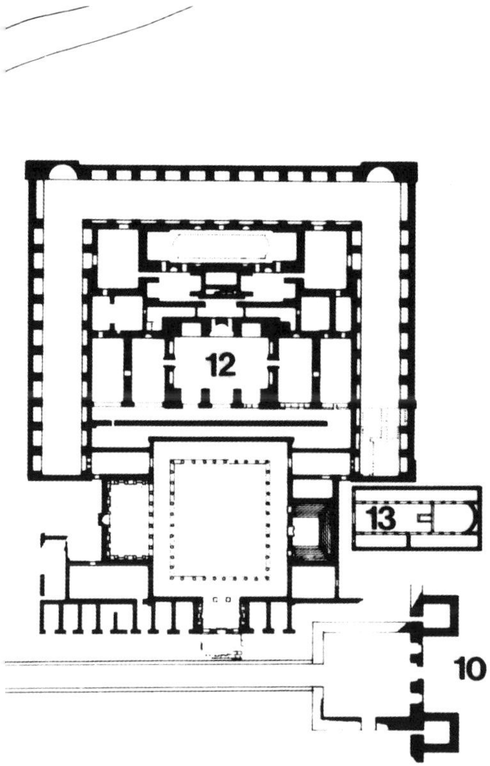

1

2

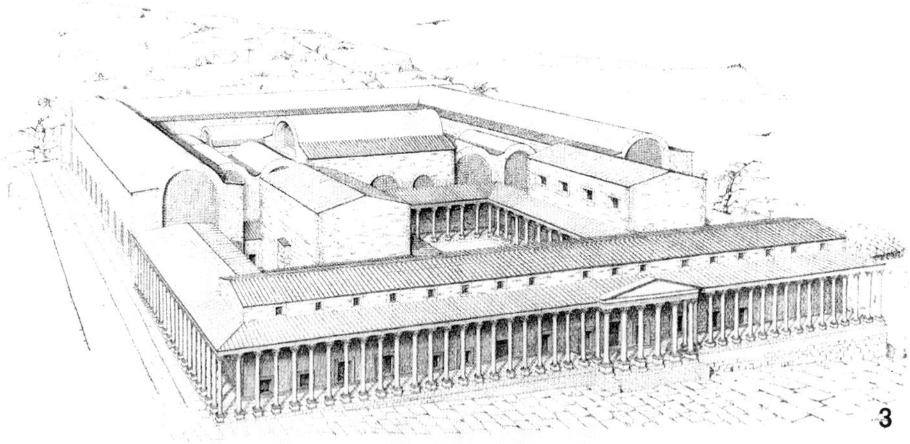

3

MONUMENTS ON THE SOUTH SLOPE OF THE PANAYIRDAĞ

The south slope of the Panayırdağ was densely populated, at least in Roman Imperial times. Most of the ruins visible on the surface in this area are in poor condition and have never been closely studied. The plain near the Magnesian Gate accommodated the potters' quarters of the city.

The so-called St. Luke's Grave [14]

In the 2nd century AD, a rotunda of unknown function (with diameter of nearly 16 meters) was erected above earlier architectural remains. The substructure contained several chambers surrounding a massive central pillar, while the floor above was surrounded by columns. In early Byzantine times (5th or 6th century AD) the building was converted into a church and an apse was added in the east. Only a few additional traces of this early Christian building have been identified during recent excavation work. The church rested on the Roman podium, now without columns, and could be reached from outside by stair cases in the north, west and south. A narrow inner stairway connected this upper, central building with a lower church. Numerous fragments of wall paintings attest to the building's rich decoration. The south entrance to the crypt is flanked by two re-used pilasters. In the western pilaster is carved a cross, while the eastern one shows, in addition, a humpbacked ox, which J. T. WOOD, the first excavator of the complex, interpreted as the symbol of the evangelist Luke and thus called the building "Luke's grave". AP

"St. Luke's Grave": WOOD, Discoveries at Ephesus (1877) 56 - 59; WEBER, RA 17, 1891, 36 - 48; ÖJh 1912, B177ff.; ÖJh 1998, G11f.
Street Fountain: ÖJh 1926, B271 - 277; ÖJh 1978-80, 86, fig. 18.
Cult (?) Building: Anz 1981, 142 Table IX.

The Street Fountain [15]

A fountain installation east of the so-called St. Luke's grave was excavated in 1925 but was buried and built over when the road connecting the Upper Entrance with the ruins and Meryemana was constructed.

According to M. THEUER's reconstruction, the building bore a great resemblance to the Nymphaeum Traiani, with which it shares not only the same building period (102 - 117 AD) but also the same donor and commissioner, Tiberius Claudius Aristion. The two-storey aediculated façade, which framed the fountain basin on three sides, was also richly decorated with statues. HT

Roman Cult (?) Building [108]

A small building on the slope above the East Gymnasium had a mosaic floor (removed for restoration) which shows cupids fishing and birds in 21 picture fields. The single-roomed building, with a water reservoir, might have been used for cult purposes. PS

Fig. 1: View of "St. Luke's Grave"

Fig. 2: Pillar with humpbacked ox relief, and a cross which was chiselled in later

Fig. 3: "Luke's Grave": fresk with female head

1

2

3

THE SO-CALLED ADMINISTRATIVE DISTRICT

The flat saddle between the two city hills, Panayırdağ and Bülbüldağ, directly behind the Upper Entrance to the ruins, contained the administrative centre of the city, at least from the time of Emperor Augustus. In the centre stands the so-called State Agora [18] with a *peripteros* temple dismantled down to its foundations. The north side of the square includes the triple-aisled Basilica Stoa [21] and behind it the Odeion/Bouleuterion or town hall [22]. Adjoining to the west is a *temenos* with a Rhodian *peristyle* [23]. From here a lane [*kathodos* 26] runs westwards forming a connection to the Plateia. On the north side of this lane is the central city cult building, the Prytaneum [24], with a banquet hall to the west [25]. To the east of the State Agora, and to the right of the modern entrance lie the imposing ruins of a bath installation [16]. On the south side of the State Agora the main south road [110] runs from the Magnesian Gate [10] towards the Bülbüldağ with two well- houses of the Flavian period - the so-called Fountain [17] and the Hydrecdocheion of Laecanius Bassus [29] - on either side of it. On the slopes above the administrative district were richly-furnished private houses.

The Baths (Upper Gymnasium) [16]

For a long time, the bath complex adjoining the State Agora was incorrectly identified as the *Baths of Varius* (= Baths of Scholasticia [41]). In contrast to the other great Ephesian baths, this incompletely excavated bath complex is of the asymmetrical ring type and resembles the Faustina Baths in Miletus (erected before 176 AD). Four large bathing rooms are partially hewn out of the rock on their northern side. The room to the west, the *caldarium*, has seven niches with bathing basins and large windows to the west. South of this is a latrine as well as smaller adjoining rooms, some for commercial activity. Halls with mosaic floors adjoin the baths to the west and south. The southern hall can perhaps be called a triple-aisled *Basilica Thermarum*, a type of building that served as a place for relaxing, strolling and physical exercise.

The existence of a palaestra is presumed in the un-excavated area to the south in the direction of the modern entrance. Inscriptions suggest the existence of a (late Hellenistic?) gymnasium - perhaps the *Upper Gymnasium* described above - in this area.

Plateia with Necropolis and the so-called South Road [110]

The straight road, lined with colonnades, which leads towards the Bülbüldağ from

Fig. 1: So-called administrative district and the area around Domitian Square, plan (1:2000)

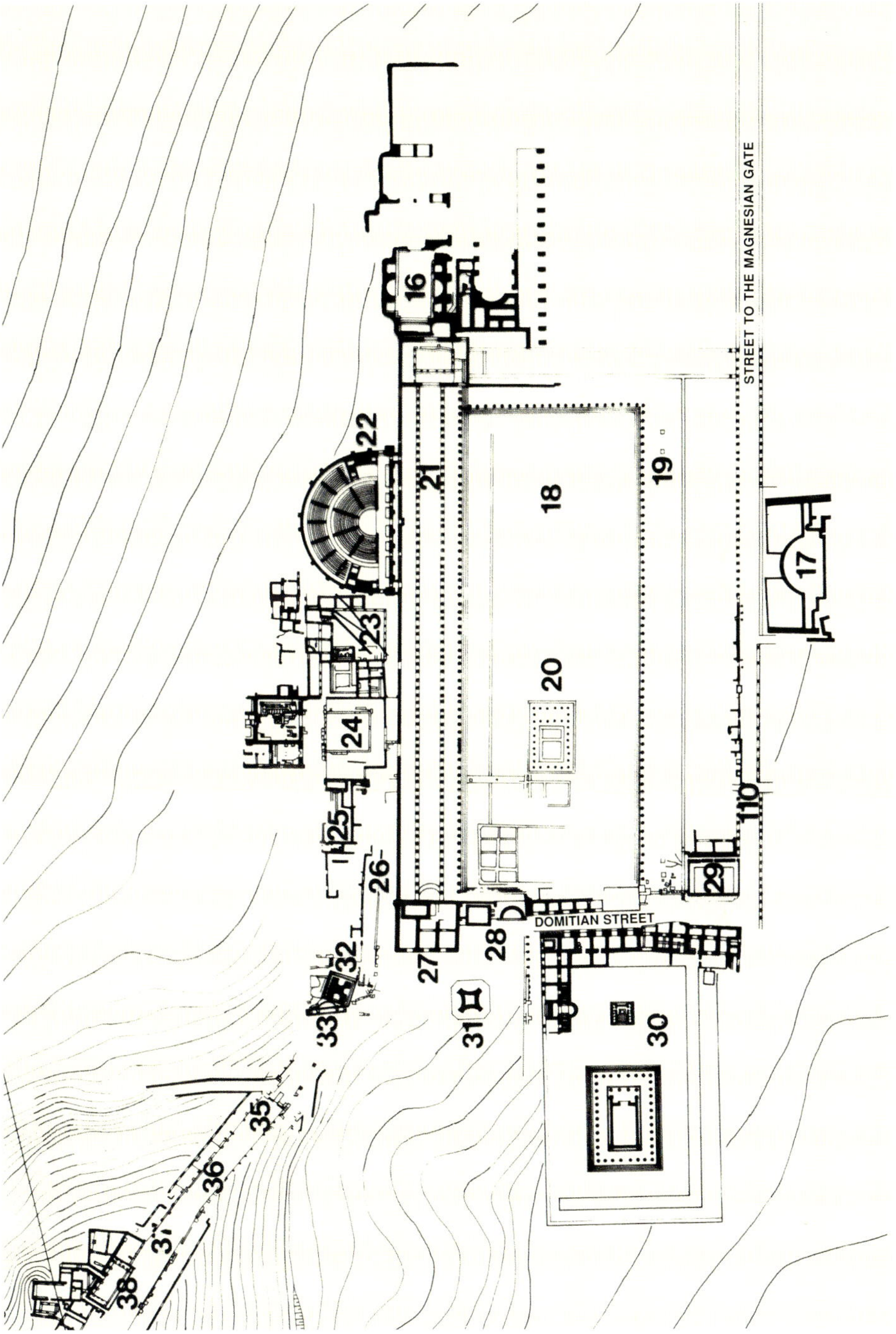
STREET TO THE MAGNESIAN GATE
16
22
21
19
18
17
23
20
24
110
25
26
29
DOMITIAN STREET
32
27
28
30
31
33
35
36
37
38

the Magnesian Gate [1] and known as the South Road, has only been excavated along the State Agora as far as the so-called Domitian Lane, but it continued along the southern side of the terrace of the so-called Temple of Domitian [30]. Its course was determined already in the urban planning of the early 3rd century BC, but the actual construction must have taken place (at the latest) when the State Agora was erected in late Hellenistic to Augustan times, since it took over the function of the Processional Way which had previously cut diagonally across the saddle. Sections of the diagonal road, which dates back into archaic times, were investigated in the eastern edge of the State Agora as well as under the west Chalcidicum [27] of the Basilica Stoa. Clay sarcophagi from the necropolis, which was used from the late 6th century BC and abandoned when the city was re-located under Lysimachus, still lie in the investigative trench left uncovered on the State Agora. The latest burial so far found is the grave of a young girl in the late 4th century BC hidden under the Chalcidicum.

The so-called Fountain [17]

On the south side of the colonnaded road lies the "fountain", which an inscription designates as a *Nymphaeum*. In its first building phase, the high, semicircular middle portion was the terminus, reservoir and distributor of the water conduit by which, in 92/93 AD under the *proconsul* P. Calvisius Ruso Julius Frontinus, brought water to the city from the rivers Marnas and Claseas. In the 2nd century AD, the installation was enlarged and given a more lavish architectonic layout when the two side wings and the fountain basin in front were built. The *Nymphaeum* was restored by the well-known *proconsul* L. Caelius Montius before the middle of the 4th century.

The Water Reservoir (hydrekdocheion) of Laecanius Bassus [29]

In 80 - 82 AD, the governor, C. Laecanius Bassus, erected, on the southwest corner of the State Agora, a magnificent two-storied façade called in an inscription, the *hydrekdocheion*. The fountain installation, aligned with "Domitian Lane" and the terrace of the Temple of Domitian [30], incorporated the western end of a row of houses and taberna which lay between the Doric colonnade of the State Agora and the South Road leading to the Magnesian Gate. The large main basin measuring 12.35 by 8.30 m, which served as a water reservoir, is set in an U-shaped aediculated façade in two-stories. The pavillions and open spaces do not yet alternate in the first and second stories in this oldest building of the type in Ephesus.

Two columns were each connected to niches and *aediculae* in which elaborate arrangements of statues were set up. The sculptures (in the Ephesus Museum Selçuk, Room 2) included portraits and statues of goddesses in addition to representations of sea-creatures and river-gods, parts of which served as water outlets. The rear façade carried a broad crowning pediment with five bays, the motif of which

Fig. 1: Administrative district and Domitian Square, aerial view from the south-west (PESENDORFER)

Fig. 2: Sculpture which decorated the *hydrekdocheion* (Ephesus Museum Selçuk, Room 2)

was repeated across the open side wings. On the street front of the reservoir there were two fountains with running water or wells, the rims of which show deep rope grooves caused by the drawing of water.

The so-called State Agora [18]

It would seem that the area called the State Agora, which in its final form in late Augustan times measured 160 m long and 58 m wide, already existed in the late Hellenistic period. The levelled terrace necessary for its layout was buttressed by a heavy ashlar wall.

The area was not bordered by a colonnade, which was the more usual arrangement. Instead, individual monuments, erected successively, fronted the terrace wall as in the case of the upper part of the Fountain of Domitian [28], built in 92/93 AD. The situation in the east has not yet been clarified, but a colonnade similar to the South Colonnade must have stood here.

The two-aisled **South Colonnade**, built in the Doric order with two gate structures [19], appears to belong to the original building concept. At the eastern end of the South Colonnade there is a 6.75 m wide passageway into the square which was enhanced on the South Street by a **Doric gatehouse**. In front of this, column drums and pillars still stand *in situ* which, along with additional pieces found nearby, allow a theoretical reconstruction. Four Doric columns formed a prostyle gatehouse, 8.40 m wide and approximately 8 m high, surmounted by a pediment decorated with a round shield. Only two pillars remain of the gate itself. The gatehouse can only be dated by the style of its architectural ornamentation which suggests the $2^{nd}/1^{st}$ centuries BC.

The gatehouse gives access to the two-aisled South Colonnade of the State Agora, which was also built in the Doric order. Little remains of this aside from the round cuttings in the stylobate for the middle columns. Well preserved, however, is the rear wall of the colonnade with carefully constructed marble panelling with a row of marble benches in front. The South Colonnade has only been excavated in the eastern part of the State Agora and at its west end adjacent to the *hydrecdocheion* or water reservoir of Laecanius Bassus [29], where it is bordered in the north by another, poorly preserved, Doric gatehouse leading to Domitian Lane.

Along the north side of the State Agora there was, initially, only a single-aisled hall (or a terrace wall). Its west end extended parallel to the Processional Way which

Baths: Aug. Architektur, 55; ÖJh 1976/77, 57; ZPE 97, 1993, 288.
Necropolis: FS F. EICHLER (1967) 103 - 123; ÖJh 1972 - 75; 252 - 265; ÖZYİĞİT, IstMitt 38, 1988, 83-96; BerMatÖAI 3 (1993) 9ff. and 51f.
Fountain and South Road: Anz 1963, 46ff.; ÖJh 1912, B173ff.
Hydrecdocheion: ÖJh 1972 - 75, B301-310; AW 14/3 (1983) 53ff.
South Hall and Gate House of State Agora: THÜR, in: Fremde Zeiten, Festschrift J. BORCHHARDT I (1996) 345 - 361.

Fig. 1: Doric gatehouse in the south-east of the State Agora

Fig. 2: The bull-head capitals of the basilica allude to the sphere of cult activities

crossed the area diagonally. In a second phase (contemporary with the South Colonnade on the opposite side), a one-aisle colonnaded hall with a small room at the west end was built, and above this, the Basilica Stoa [21] and its western Chalcidicum [27].

The Basilica Stoa [21]

Originally one of the most magnificent buildings in Ephesus, the two-storey, triple-aisled Basilica Stoa (royal colonnade) in the Ionic order, donated by C. Sextilius Pollio and his family, was built here in the year 11 AD, according to its building inscription. Access to the building is gained by four steps from the square. The side aisles are 4.72 m and the middle aisle 6.85 m wide. The front side had 67 columns in the ionic order. The double-spaced interior columns carried capitals decorated with widely projecting bull's heads to distribute the static load from the entablature. In spite of this, it appears that the colonnade suffered severe damage some 12 years after its erection by one of the earthquakes which are all too frequently recorded in Ephesus. The rear wall of marble orthostat blocks must have been newly erected afterwards and the number of interior columns was doubled with additional intermediate columns carrying Corinthian capitals.

Under the Emperor Nero, an enormous Chalcidicum ([27], see also below) was built on to the west end, which may have been converted into a church in late Roman times as is suggested by an eastern apse in its middle aisle.

The east Chalcidicum of the Basilica is only preserved in its rebuilt Byzantine form as a peristyle courtyard. The half-column pillars with Corinthian capitals set up here seem to have belonged to the original upper-storey architecture of the colonnade.

The monumental seated statues of the imperial couple Augustus and Livia (Ephesus Museum Selçuk, Room 7) were probably originally set up in the east Chalcidicum. Additional portraits and inscriptions referring to the Julio-Claudian dynasty, gave the Basilica Stoa the appearance of an imperial gallery.

The Temple on the State Agora [20]

In the west part of the otherwise empty square stood a prostyle peripteros temple with 6 by 10 columns, the podium of which measured a mere 28 x 15 m. The dating to approximately the third quarter of the 1st century BC is certain because of the finds from the foundation trenches, but the proprietor of the temple is still disputed among those engaged in research. Its interpretation in the past as an Isis or Dionysus temple with Mark Antony and Cleopatra as patrons was followed by its designation as a temple of Augustus. A more recent suggestion identifies the temple with the sanctuary of the divine Caesar and Dea Roma built by the association of Roman citizens (*conventus civium romanorum*) as recorded by Strabo in the years after 29 BC. In Late Antiquity the temple was completely dismantled and the materials were probably re-used for repair work somewhere in the city. PS, HT

The Bouleuterion (Odeion) [22]

The northern edge of the State Agora is dominated today by the impressive

Fig. 1: Re-erected columns of the front of the basilica (SCHIFFLEITNER)

remains of a theatre-like structure, dated by inscription to the mid-2nd century, and interpreted variously as a city council chamber (Bouleuterion) and a concert hall (Odeion) since its discovery by J.T.Wood in the 19th century. It is likely that the building served both functions. The auditorium (cavea), enclosed by a massive curved wall, was built on the lower slopes of Panayırdağ, probably with the help of vaulted substructures. It consisted of two tiers of seats separated by a walkway (diazoma) and divided into wedge-shaped sections (kerkides) by radial stairways. The seating accommodated about 1500 people. Newly discovered evidence for a colonnade around the top includes faint traces of a single pilaster base carved in the footing of the rear wall, and cuttings in the floor for additional bases, some fronted by euthynteria blocks which originally supported columns. These are probably represented by the red marble fragments first noticed by Wood and still to be seen lying about. At the bottom of the auditorium is a sunken orchestra that was originally paved with stone slabs, and a shallow stage (pulpitum) approached from the east and west by sloping parodos ramps and from the south by five doors in the stage wall. Access to the building was through tall arched entrances at the ends of the parodoi, and through doorways in the north wall of the Basilica Stoa. Five of these are aligned with the stage doors, while two lateral doorways were oriented on vaulted staircases which led to the diazoma at the top of the lower cavea.

Fig. 1: The ensemble of the administrative buildings and the Imperial cult installations: Basilica Stoa, with Bouleuterion behind it. Temenos and Prytaneum with the State Agora and the foundations of the temple in the foreground (SCHIFFLEITNER)

Fig. 2: The Bouleuterion before restoration

Restoration work by the Selçuk Museum in 1970 and 1990 consolidated the remains which had deteriorated badly since the building was thoroughly cleared in 1908. The pavement of the stage and parodos ramps is mostly modern as are portions of the vaulted staircases, while the massive structures in which these terminate are entirely new additions. Moreover, a large portion of the auditorium has been restored in concrete. It should be noted that this measure was aimed at stabilizing the ancient concrete packing underlying the marble seats rather than in restoring the seating itself which has survived more or less intact only in the first few rows.

The attention of the audience focused on the stage, behind which rose the *scaenae frons*, a decorative facade in two stories with columns grouped to form projecting pavillions enclosing statuary. Little remains of this columnar display, but there are some clues for its general appearance of which the most important are the six podia, two narrow and four wide, flanking the stage doorways. Several bear cuttings in their top surfaces for column and statue bases that comprised the lower storey. A small number of architectural elements have survived including an architrave

State Agora, Temple and Basilica: FiE IX/2; Aug. Architektur, 26 - 37 and 49ff.; IstMitt 30, 1980, 241 - 260; ÖJh 1990, 98 - 101. Bouleuterion: FOSSEL, in: FS F. EICHLER (1967) 72 - 81; MEINEL, Das Odeon (1980) 117 - 133; Alzinger, in: Bathron (FS H. DRERUP, 1988) 21 - 29; Bier, in: Steine und Wege, Festschrift D. Knibbe (1999) 7 - 18.

block with an inscription citing as builders Flavia Papiane and another person whose name is missing. This can only have been her husband, P.Vedius Antoninus, a well-known Ephesian benefactor, who was praised in 145 A.D. by Antoninus Pius for his building activities. The surviving statuary, sent by Wood to the British Museum, include a dynastic group of Emperor Lucius Verus and Faustina the Younger, a Silenus torso and the Muse Erato.

Roman theatres offered some protection from the weather in the form of retractable, awnings called *vela*, but smaller theatre-like buildings such as Bouleuteria and Odeia normally had permanent roofs. Little is known about them, but they were probably constructed with large triangular wooden trusses supporting secondary timbers and battens covered with clay roof tiles. At Ephesus, the entire building would have risen no higher than the Basilica Stoa on its south and could not have been seen from the Agora, so it is not surprising that it was not given a monumental facade. The narrow corridor with its deep drain that separates the two structures was nothing more than a catchment for rainwater shed by the roofs of both buildings. LB

Temenos (Rhodian Peristyle) [23]

To the west of the Odeion or Bouleuterion there is an open courtyard (33 x 28 m) bordered by colonnades on three sides; the raised columns on the east side are characteristic of buildings of the so-called Rhodian peristyle type. The Ionic columns with Ephesian bases (a torus with horizontal annular grooves) clearly point to the Temple of Artemis. There is a raised podium, some 15 m wide, with precisely worked orthostat panelling and broad steps on the west side of the temenos.

The badly damaged foundations in the interior of the podium, which were destroyed by demolition work and built over in Late Antiquity, suggest that it once supported either an altar (F. MILTNER) or a small double temple structure (W. ALZINGER and A. BAMMER).

The centre pieces of a front and rear pediment, found nearby, which could also have been part of the temple in the central square, now lie on the rear wall of the podium. ALZINGER saw an unmistakable Roman influence in the building concept, and interpreted the structure as a double shrine for Divus Caesar and Dea Roma. P. SCHERRER, following MILTNER, has recently re-interpreted the precinct as the altar serving the worship of Artemis and Augustus; a portrait head of this ruler (see page 19, fig. 4) and statues of Artemis were found nearby along with an inscription mentioning the erection of a cult precinct for Augustus. PS

Prytaneum [24]

The Prytaneum also belongs to the Augustan building program in the administrative quarter; its Hellenistic predecessor remains unknown. The visitor first enters a large peristyle courtyard (approximately 26 x 22 m and totally devastated in

Fig. 1: Columnar architecture of the temenos (Rhodian Peristyle) with Bouleuterion behind

Fig. 2: Re-erected Doric columns of entrance hall of the Prytaneum almost entirely covered with lists of the cult personnel (SCHIFFLEITNER)

Fig. 3: Administrative Quarter and Temple of Domitian: model in the Ephesus Museum in Vienna

1

2

3

Late Antiquity) the excessively wide north colonnade of which also serves as the entrance hall of the actual building. The six Doric columns, partially re-erected in the course of restoration work, with long lists of the "curetes" or cult personnel and other religious texts, had, like many other building elements, been reused in the late fourth century AD, in the construction of the so-named Curetes Street and the Baths of Scholasticia [41]. The main room with heart-shaped interior corner columns, was apparently used for public feasts for privileged persons so honoured, or for banquets connected with religious events. The ashlar foundation in the centre of the room has been variously interpreted as the sacred hearth, or merely as a sort of buffet sideboard.

Smaller rooms adjoin this hall to the north and the west, but their individual functions have not been clarified. Additional gods, such as Demeter Karpophoros and the oracle god Apollo Manteios, joined the cult of Hestia, particularly in the 2nd century AD. In addition to the inscriptions, which are extremely important for the history of religion, the most outstanding finds from the Prytaneum are three Roman copies of the cult statue of Artemis Ephesia (Ephesus Museum Selçuk, Room 6), which were ritually buried after a catastrophic earthquake in the fourth century AD.

Banqueting House [25]

Excavations resumed in 1990 by the Ephesus Museum Selçuk, uncovered a well-furnished banqueting house or residence in the west of the Prytaneum; the base measures 14 x 11 m and the walls are still preserved to a height of 3.5 m.

The large southern room, with wall paintings and a sumptuous floor consisting of cut marble slabs (*opus sectile*), may have served as an assembly room with four smaller rooms adjoining in the east and north.

A rectangular pit was found in the easternmost of the north rooms, which contained the stored inventory from the first century AD phase of construction (terra-sigillata tableware, kitchen pottery ware, little terracotta figures and bone needles: Ephesus Museum Selçuk, Room 3). Alterations can be dated to the third century AD. It may be assumed that the building was functionally connected with the Prytaneum. MB, ÜY

Kathodos with Embasis [26]

A small street, known as *Kathodos* in antiquity (which simply meant the way downwards), leads to the west from the Prytaneum. Its south side forms the bolstered ashlar wall of the Basilika-Chalcidicum. At the point where it opens onto the Plateia (Domitian Square, see page 90) there is a threshold-like installation, mentioned in inscriptions as *Embasis* [26]. On both sides of it are bases, each bearing a pair of reliefs. One, showing Hermes with his ram, was oriented towards the Processional Way with its graves and shops. The other, depicting Apollo's tripod, faced the *Embasis*. The reliefs possibly indicate the separation of the fundamentally different realms of cult (purity, symbolized by the tripod), and human life and death. PS

Temenos: Aug. Architektur, 55ff..; ÖJh 1972 - 75, 57; 1990, 98 - 101.
Prytaneum: FiE IX/1; Aug. Architektur, 51ff.
Kathodos/Embasis: IvE 1248; 3071.

Fig. 1: Statue of Artemis Ephesia as found

Fig. 2: Embasis between the Plateia and the area of the Prytaneum (SCHIFFLEITNER)

DOMITIAN SQUARE

The so-called Domitian Square, a section of the Plateia, lies one terrace lower than the State Agora and adjoins it on the west. Only the eastern part has been excavated; the western side still lies buried under the ground. The square is bounded on the north side by the Memmius Monument [32]. The so-called Chalcidicum [27] of the Basilica Stoa [21] lies on the east side of the square in front of a Hellenistic retaining wall with a projection and plinth. South of this is the Pollio Monument over which the so-called Fountain of Domitian [28] was later built. The so-called Domitian Street continues southwards and the rest of the south side is bounded by the terrace for the so-called Temple of Domitian [30]. At its northwest corner, Domitian Square merges with the westward sloping, so-called Curetes Street (Embolos). Domitian Square lies within the Hippodamian grid of the Hellenistic city but the extension wall of Curetes Street runs at an angle to the Hellenistic plinth at its eastern boundary, mentioned above. Its shape is thus closely related to the building of the State Agora which necessitated a diversion of the Plateia. The abrupt transition from the Memmius Monument to Curetes Street was ameliorated by the construction of the Hydreion [33] in Roman times, and the Hercules Gate [35] later in the Roman era.

Chalcidicum of the Basilica Stoa [27]

South of the junction with the path leading from the Prytaneum to Domitian Square, a massive construction made out of rusticated ashlar blocks projects 15.90 m from the western terrace wall of the State Agora. It supported an extension of the Basilica, the upper-storey architecture of which consisted of Ionic half-columns and pillars, opening through an arch into the centre aisle of the Basilica. The form of the building corresponds to the extension built on to basilicas which Vitruvius (V 1,4) describes as a *chalcidicum*.

Chalcidicum: Anz 1963, 48f.; ÖJh 1972 - 75, 22; Aug. Architektur, 30.

The three chambers of the plinth were accessible through doorways from Domitian Square. Above this is an architrave with an erased inscription, which was replaced by another inscription in

Fig. 1: Altar of the temple of the Flavian Imperial dynasty (so-called Temple of Domitian) as found (now set up in the Ephesus Museum Selçuk, Room 7)

Fig. 2: The massive west Chalcidicum of the Basilica Stoa with its walls of bolstered ashlar dominates the east side of Domitian Square (SCHIFFLEITNER)

letters of bronze (set up in Domitian Square) that still requires interpretation. The erased inscription probably referred to Emperor Nero (43 - 68 AD). AB

Garland Frieze

West of the Chalcidicum stands a frieze of garlands suspended from bucrania. The remains of a conical roof topped by a pine cone belong to the circular frieze which formed part of one of the honorific monuments described below.

Niche Monument [31]

Of the Niche Monument, a memorial edifice with four niches located in the southern part of Domitian Square, only the foundation is preserved. The original structure probably resembled the niched constructions of the Lion Harbour at Miletus. AB

Pollio Monument and Fountain of Domitian [28]

In front of the western terrace wall of the State Agora [18], and south of the Chalcidicum, stands the base of a memorial monument, measuring 8 x 6.5 m and 6.4 m high, the mortared rubble core of which was clad in pseudo-isodomic marble slabs (now partly re-erected). A small central niche framed by flat pilasters is the only architectonic embellishment on its western façade. According to building inscriptions in Latin and Greek, the monument was erected - presumably as a memorial tomb - for C. Sextilius Pollio by his step-son on a site made available by the city. In this way, the city honoured the donor of both the Basilica Stoa [21] and an aqueduct. Adjoining to the south, and dated by inscriptions to 92/93 AD, the Fountain of Domitian was built with its large apsidal room opening onto Domitian Square. The arch, supported by pillars decorated with acanthus, has been partially reconstructed in concrete using original marble. A group statue depicting the adventures of Odysseus and his companions with Polyphemus (Ephesus Museum Selçuk, Room 2) stood, re-used, in the niche as decoration for the fountain.

Together with the so-called Fountain of Domitian, an architectural background of Corinthian pillars and columns with a projecting and receding entablature was erected above the socle of the Pollio monument on a level with, and oriented towards the State Agora. Water and drainage pipes suggest that this structure also served as a fountain. Statues of the river gods Marnas and Claseas stood in the aediculae, framed by columns on the north and south sides, whereas the central aedicula of the west side accommodated a statue of Zeus (Ephesus Museum Selçuk, Room 2). HT

Pollio Monument: ÖJh 1960, B51; 1976/77, B77ff.

Fountain of Domitian: ÖJh 1978 - 80, 67 - 81; STROCKA, in: Festschrift J. İNAN (1991), 77ff.

Niche Monument and Garland Frieze: FiE VII, 81; Aug. Architektur, 43ff.; ÖJh 1968 - 71, 23ff., 36ff.; ÖJh 1990, 76.

Fig. 1: Fountain of Domitian, reconstructed arch of the main apsis opening on Domitian Square (SCHIFFLEITNER)

DOMITIAN'S TERRACE WITH IMPERIAL TEMPLE AND ALTAR [30]

To the west of the State Agora a large terrace was built over a substructure - two-storied, in places - as a level building site for an Imperial Cult Temple and altar. A multi-storey façade, richly decorated, in part, with supporting figures, masked the vaults to the lower-lying area in the north.

Parts of the façade were re-erected in 1975. Above a lower storey with Doric-like half-columns and a flat-vaulted, coffered ceiling, lies an upper storey with male and female supporting figures. When compared to similar façades in Corinth and Rome, these can be interpreted as barbarian caryatids - a theme in the victory propaganda of the Roman emperors. A double staircase leads from the portico to the temple terrace.

Pieces of the façade architecture were re-used in late Roman times in the Commercial Agora, Curetes Street, and in the Theatre. With the victory of Christianity, even the temple itself was dismantled down to its foundations. From the cuttings in the upper surface of the six-stepped substructure (24 x 34 m), it may be inferred that the temple was a pseudo-dipteros with a cella, pronaos and a peristasis with 8 x 13 columns. The elevation is largely unknown.

ÖJh 1932, B51ff.; 1972 - 75, B399; 1978 - 80, 81ff.; SCHNEIDER, Bunte Barbaren (1986) 125ff.
The head, lower arm and left big toe of the statue of Titus can be seen, together with the reliefs of the altar, in the Ephesus Museum Selçuk, Room 7.

Building remains were uncovered east of the temple, from which a U-shaped altar on a raised podium can be reconstructed. The podium, the exterior of which was decorated with a relief frieze portraying sacrificial scenes and weapons, was the substructure for a small-scale colonnade.

Pieces of colossal statues of emperors were found in the substructure. The only portrait head uncovered was originally thought to belong to Domitian (82 - 96 AD), but has now been identified as his elder brother Titus (79 - 81 AD). The structure is generally associated which inscriptions referring to a *common temple of the emperors of Asia in Ephesus* and was originally erected in honour of Domitian and his deified predecessors. After the murder and *damnatio memoriae* of Domitian, the long sought and arduously acquired Imperial Cult Temple was transferred to his father Vespasian whose name replaced that of Domitian in numerous inscriptions. HT

Fig. 1: Partly re-erected terrace façade of the Imperial Temple built under Domitian

INSCRIPTION MUSEUM, TAVERNS, CRYPTOPORTICUS

The substructure of the Domitian terrace, which served as storerooms in Roman times, is now the inscription depot, and a museum of inscriptions has been set up in the long, straight eastern vaulted passage. The entrance is at the south-west corner of the State Agora.

The museum displays a selection, with bilingual explanations, from the entire spectrum of Ephesian inscriptions, from the seventh century BC up into the Byzantine era, which afford a variety of insights into private and public life in ancient Ephesus. The subjects covered are mainly law, religion, public buildings, honours, victory documents and tombstone inscriptions.

The excavation of the substructure of the Temple of Domitian has been carried out by the Ephesus Museum in Selçuk since 1970. The cryptoporticus is 154 m long and has an angular, U-shaped ground plan. Up to now, the Ephesian cryptoporticus is the only known example of this architectural type in the eastern part of the Roman Empire. The doors at each end face north. An additional smaller door - only used temporarily - in the south-east corner of the cryptoporticus opens onto Domitian Street. The north end of the eastern part, which extends under the caryatid façade, is completely destroyed.

Adjoining this façade of the temple podium stood a hall, oriented east-west, with central columns and a flat roof. A door in the south wall leads into the cryptoporticus.

The interior of the substructure has a total of 102 built-in niches, spaced at intervals of 1.25 m to 1.35 m, which served partly for lighting and ventilation. During the excavations of the substructure of the Temple of Domitian, important finds from Roman and Byzantine times came to light, including parts of statues of Aphrodite as well as portraits of Trajan and Germanicus, the nephew of Tiberius.

The paved street - a part of the Processional Way - leading down between the State Agora and Domitian's terrace was flanked by taverns.

These vaulted rooms are arranged at right angles to the street and possibly served for business and trade, although a fresco featuring Demeter (Ephesus Museum Selçuk, Room 1) could point to cult usage. Deep excavations under the temple substructure revealed sparse remains of late Hellenistic or early Imperial period houses which cannot be individually reconstructed.

BT, DT

Inscriptions and inscription museum: IvE; Knibbe – İplikçioğlu, Ephesos im Spiegel seiner Inschriften (1984)
Enquire at the entrance for opening times.

Fig. 1: Inscription museum in the eastern cryptoporticus

Fig. 2: View into the hall in the north-west of the temple terrace

THE MEMMIUS MONUMENT [32]

In the third quarter of the first century BC, a honorific monument was erected for C. Memmius, a grandson of the Roman dictator Sulla, at a particularly prominent place on the Plateia as it bends towards the Embolos. The structure, excavated in 1959/60, is one of the few remaining architectural monuments from late Hellenistic times in Ephesus. Its re-erection as an architectural pastiche is more a modern interpretation than an illustration of an ancient edifice.

The nearly square ground plan of the building is developed over a massive foundation of rusticated ashlar blocks. According to investigations by A. BAMMER, the elevation of the main storey had spherical recessed niches fitted with benches in the east, south, and west sides. The arches framing the niches were supported by caryatids supportinging basket capitals. The north side, which faced the slope, probably remained unaccentuated. BAMMER, in his initial reconstruction, envisioned a two-storey facade surmounted by a kind of attic. Recent investigations, however, have turned up additional architectural elements which point to a traditional tower-like structure reminiscent of Hellenistic tombs and honorific monuments. An upper storey with three display sides supported by columns has, therefore, been placed above the ground floor construction. Reliefs would have been arranged on the walls of the "cella" corresponding with the intercolumniations. The figures have been interpreted as members of Memmius' family and personifications of his characteristic virtures. The inscription in Latin and Greek, which gives the monument its name, was cut in the architrave of the first storey.

FiE VII; ÖJh 1990, 57 - 85; TORELLI, ScAnt 2, 1988, 403ff.

On the basis of corresponding measurements, the fragments of a round structure decorated with garlands and bucrania, as well as fragments of marble roof tiles, all found in the immediate vicinity, have been assigned to the Memmius monument. UO

Hydreion [33]

Probably during the Augustan period, a fountain was added on to the west side of the Memmius Monument. It was remodelled around 200 AD, and, about a century later, statues of

Fig. 1: Memmius Monument, present day condition (PESENDORFER)
Fig. 2: Original suggestion for reconstruction (BAMMER)
Fig. 3: More recent proposal for reconstruction (OUTSCHAR)

1

2

3

Diocletian and his co-regents were set up in front of it.

The structure, 11.70 m long and 1.60 m deep, is divided into three water basins. The middle portion of the rear wall is accentuated by a semicircular niche containing another basin two meters higher. In front of the water basin stand four columns on pedestals between which are stone slabs that served as the basin wall. The midddle columns, which correspond with the semicircular niche were joined with two columns resting on the outer basin walls to form a pavillion.

Hercules Gate [35]

In late Roman times, a monumental gateway spanned the eastern end of Curetes Street. Two now re-erected pillars had framed the middle gate since the fifth century AD, so that vehicular traffic was no longer possible. The pillars, which bore reliefs depicting Heracles, carried an arch with a building inscription with an adjacent spandrel bearing the figure of a flying Nike holding a palm branch in her right hand and a laurel wreath in her left. A. BAMMER related the Hercules pillars to a first building phase of an attic storey.

On the basis of the remains of the building inscription on the archivolt, from which a Flavius Constantinus can be deciphered, the construction could be dated to the third quarter of the fifth century. At least parts of the arch, including the Nike relief, may be from the first half of the fourth century.

Round Monument on the Panayırdağ [34]

High up on the slope, roughly in the direction of a lane leading northwards between the Hydreion and the Hercules Gate, lies the square foundation of a formerly two-storey honorific monument. The lower storey had a Doric half-column architecture with some unusual decorative elements, and the upper storey was in the Ionic order. Parts of the architecture may be seen in the Ephesus Museum in Vienna. The interpretation of the building is disputed. It was either erected as a trophy for the naval victory at Kyme in 133/2 BC, or as a heroon for P. Servilius Isauricus (47/6 BC). HT

Hydreion: Führer, 122.
Hercules Gate: ÖJh 1959, B353; 1972 - 75, B383; 1976 - 77, B93.
Round Monument: FiE I, 143; Aug. Architektur, 37.

Fig. 1: Round Monument on the Panayırdağ, reconstruction (NIEMANN)

TERRACE HOUSE 1 [50]

Terrace House 1, the easternmost of the two uncovered insulae, was excavated between 1960 and 1967 under the direction of H. VETTERS. Further instigation was devoted to the first phase of building in the first century BC. This *insula*, in the modern sense of a city block, has a total surface area of some 3000 m². It once encompassed six residential units which were erected on three terraces at the lower end of the slope of the Bülbüldağ. The oldest building dates back into the first century BC and continued in use as a residence until the seventh century AD.

The individual residential units were laid out according to the conventional Hellenistic ground plan of rooms arranged around a central peristyle courtyard. This type of plan and the luxurious furnishings of the individual apartments clearly justify their position in an important part of the city. One or two of them can be shown to have had their own small bath installations (in SR 5a, XI/2b and XI/2c). Without exception, the rooms are small, each with an apse on the narrow side. Terrace House 1 underwent extensive alterations during its long period of occupation, so that the peristyle house form is now discernible only in the southeast corner of the *insula*. In addition, Terrace House 1 is not nearly so well preserved as Terrace House 2.

Entrance to the apartments was from the narrow stairway alleys. Deep investigatory trenches in the northwestern part of Terrace House 1 revealed a peristyle house which had been erected in the first century BC.

At the beginning of the second century AD it was abandoned in favour of a large building project, which may be interpreted as a meeting-house of an association, serving especially for banquets. This new structure occupied about half of the entire *insula*. The main entrance from Curetes Street through Tavern III was immediately opposite the so-called Temple of Hadrian [40]. The taverns originally served only as supporting structures to enlarge the area available for building on this sloping site.

The axis is oriented towards Curetes Street and thereby diverges from the general Hippodamian plan of the city. No side rooms are evident in this representative building with the exception of a small watchman's room (SR 1'), the only heatable chamber in this large and luxuriously furnished banqueting house. The large peristyle should be restored with 6 x 10 columns.

Fig. 1: View over the Terrace Houses from the northeast, with the new roof protecting House 2 (Gail)

Fig. 2: Hero-relief from the debris of the oldest building phase

2

Most of the rooms had a richly decorated fountain and a well, as was usual also in the middle-class dwellings (SR 14 and G), where they were smaller and more modest. The walls were clad with marble panels of various colours to a height of some three meters. The upper parts were painted, and the apse-arches and niches were emphasized with glass mosaics. The floors were also decorated colorfully with small marble slabs.

Refurbishing, in keeping with a desire for increased ceremonial function, especially in the banqueting house, can be dated to the 2nd half of the 2nd century AD. More modest living standards were necessitated by earthquake destruction and the generally poor economic conditions at the end of the third century AD but at the same time, workshops and small businesses also emerged. The shops along Curetes Street resulted from this situation. Of the rooms on the south frontage, only the cellars, which were used as storage rooms and water depots, are preserved.

In the 5th/6th century, the rooms G/H were rebuilt as a chapel. A fountain, similar to the one in SR 14, stood at the west side of G and was redesigned as a basin, which incorporated a panel set between pillars decorated with crosses. In the south niche of room H, lateral pillars were set up and crowned by simple double capitals with crosses. Another Ionic capital with an abacus decorated with a cross, was found here. The actual cult room H could be closed off with a lattice partition.

Fragments of two refectory slabs were found in the immediate vicinity - yet another indication of sacral usage. At the beginning of the fifth century, when the mosaic floor of the Alytarchus Stoa was laid, a revival in domestic culture can be discerned not only in the apartments but also, to some extent, in the shops. However, this did not nearly approach the standards of the 2nd and 3rd centuries. In the area of SR 1, 2, 6 and B, a three metre high heap of rubble was levelled, and new dwellings were built on top, which could be reached over stairways. The cross-shaped ground plan of the rooms on the east side of the *insula* (XII/2b, J and K) can be counted among the most notable alterations of this time. CL

FiE VIII/1 - 3; ÖJh 1972 - 75, B331 - 358; Anz 1961 to 1968, passim.
Outstanding finds are displayed in the Terrace House room of the Ephesus Museum Selçuk, Room 1.

Fig. 1: View into the taverns behind the Alytarchus Stoa as they were in the spring of 1995

Fig. 2: Large peristyle court overlooking Curetes Street with Varius Bath and the so-called Temple of Hadrian

The next two pages: Plan of the Terrace Houses 1 and 2 (1:500)

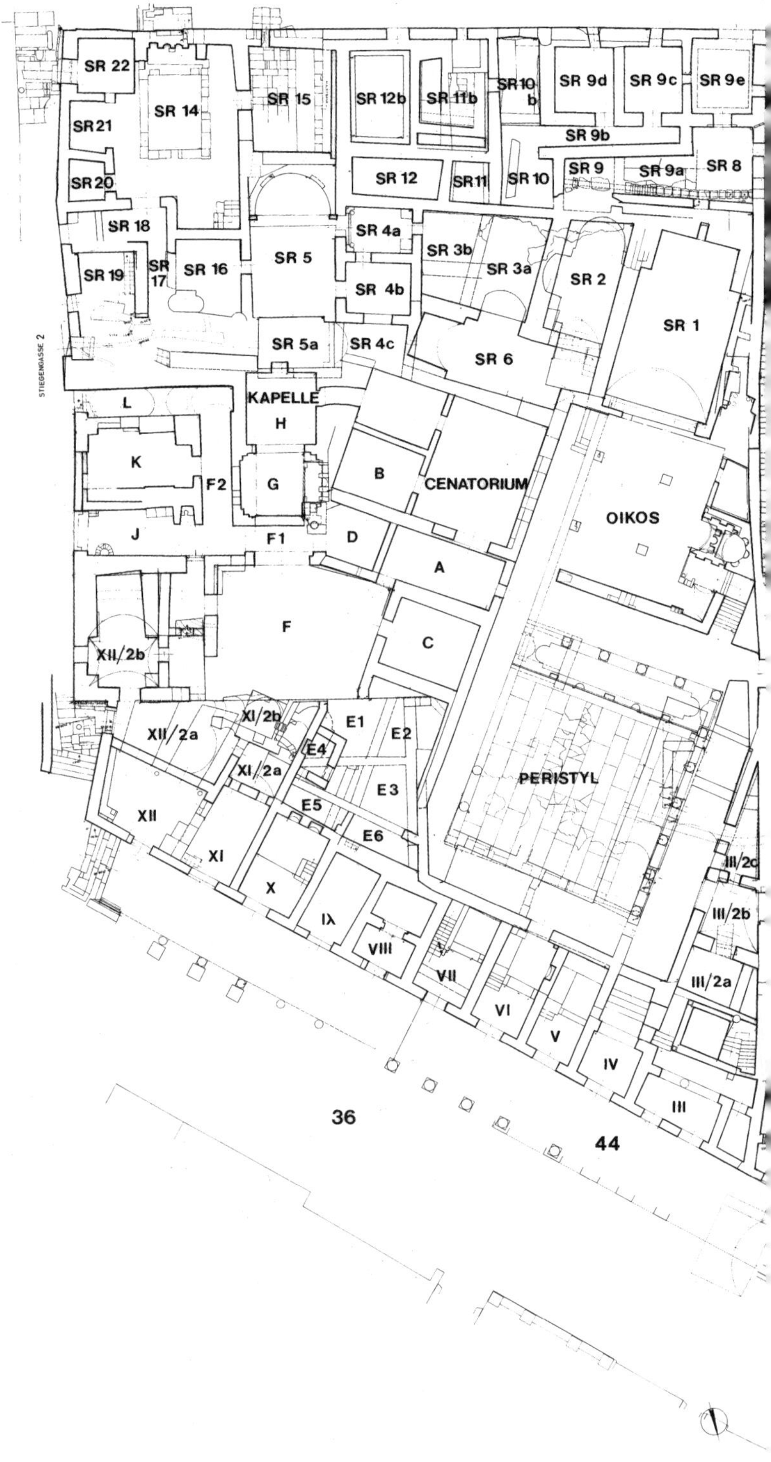
SR 22
SR 14
SR 15
SR 12b
SR 11b
SR 10 b
SR 9d
SR 9c
SR 9e
SR 21
SR 9b
SR 20
SR 12
SR 11
SR 10
SR 9
SR 9a
SR 8
SR 18
SR 4a
SR 3b
SR 3a
SR 2
SR 19
SR 17
SR 16
SR 5
SR 4b
SR 1
SR 5a
SR 4c
SR 6
STIEGENGASSE 2
L
KAPELLE
H
K
F2
G
B
CENATORIUM
OIKOS
J
F1
D
A
F
C
XII/2b
XI/2b
E1
E2
XII/2a
E4
XI/2a
PERISTYL
E3
XII
E5
E6
XI
III/2c
X
IX
III/2b
VIII
VII
III/2a
VI
V
IV
III
36
44
0
5
10
15
20
25
30 M

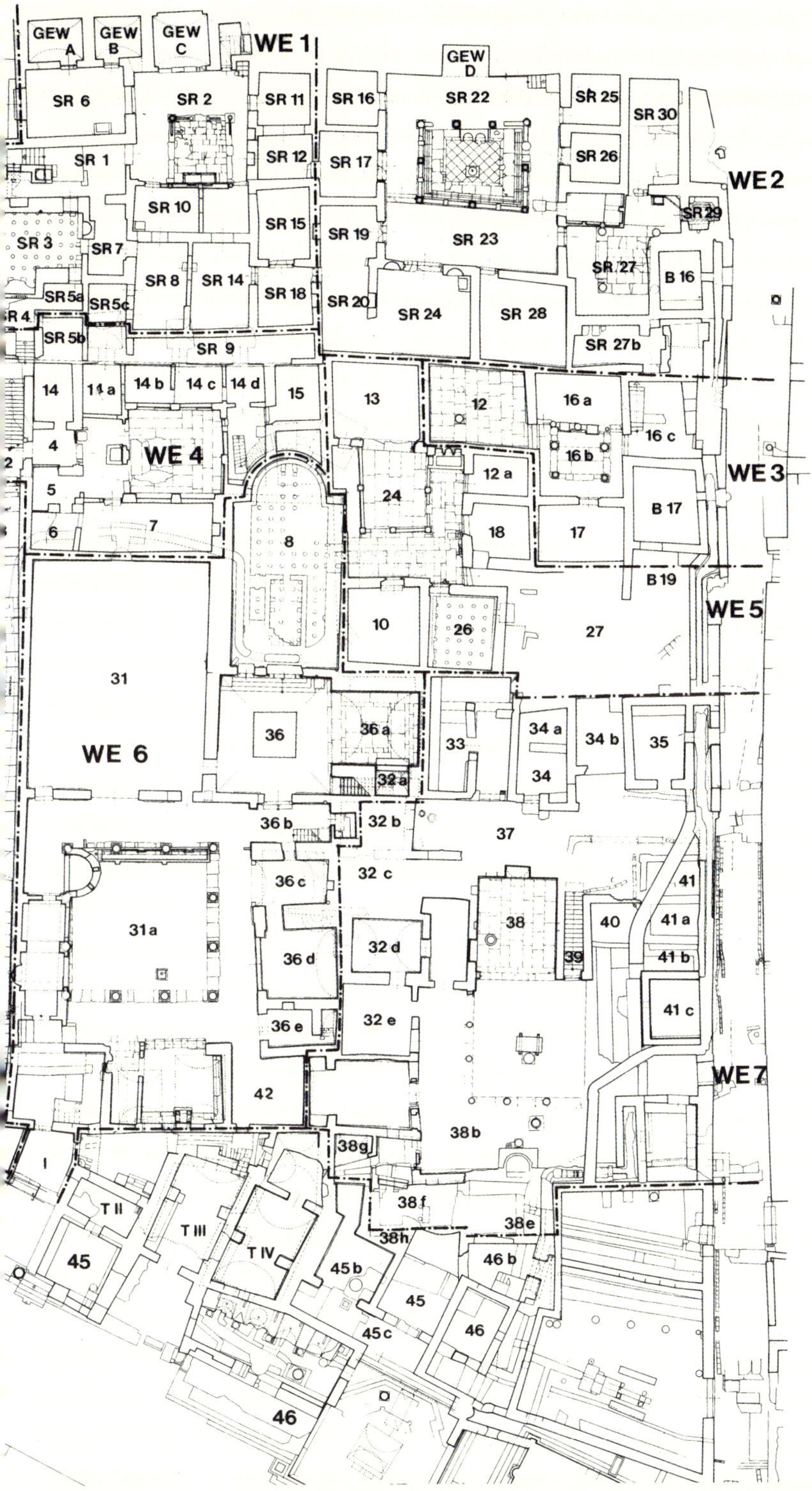

GEW A
GEW B
GEW C
WE 1
GEW D
SR 6
SR 2
SR 11
SR 16
SR 22
SR 25
SR 30
SR 1
SR 12
SR 17
SR 26
WE 2
SR 10
SR 15
SR 19
SR 23
SR 29
SR 3
SR 7
SR 27
B 16
SR 8
SR 14
SR 18
SR 20
SR 24
SR 28
SR 5a
SR 5c
R 4
SR 5b
SR 9
SR 27b
14
14 a
14 b
14 c
14 d
15
13
12
16 a
4
WE 4
16 c
16 b
12 a
WE 3
5
24
B 17
6
7
8
18
17
B 19
WE 5
10
26
27
31
36
36 a
33
34 a
34 b
35
WE 6
32 a
34
36 b
32 b
37
36 c
32 c
41
31 a
38
40
41 a
32 d
36 d
39
41 b
41 c
36 e
32 e
WE 7
42
38 b
38g
I
T II
38 f
38 e
T III
38h
T IV
46 b
45
45 b
45
46
45 c
46

TERRACE HOUSE 2 [51]

The westernmost of the two excavated *insulae* in the centre of the city on the north slope of the Bülbüldağ, lies behind the honorific monuments at the west end of Curetes Street. The compact built-up area covers some 4000 m^2 and the self-contained residential units are, in each case, arranged in pairs on the terraces. On the lowest terrace, workshops and taverns opened onto Curetes Street. The rich decoration of the apartments, with wall paintings, mosaics, and marble panelling, mirrors the big-city style of living of the sophisticated upper levels of society in Roman Imperial times.

The excavation of this *insula*, directly in the centre of Hellenistic-Roman Ephesus, was carried out by H. VETTERS in the years 1967 - 1983 and brought to an initial conclusion in 1999 with the roofing-over making a museum-like presentation of the building possible. Archaeological research is still going on in the complex together with conservation measures to preserve the building fabric and its decorated surfaces.

The north front of the *insula* is oriented on the line of Curetes Street; the south front, however, follows the orthogonal street system of the Hippodamian plan. Here a road runs along the contour of the slope and joins Curetes Street at the level of the Memmius Monument. Steep alleys, on average 3 metres wide, run at right angles to this road. These are adapted to the slope with flights of steps to overcome a difference in level of up to 26 metres. Curetes street runs diagonally so that the adjoining *insulae* have trapeziform ground plans.

The original building scheme can be traced particularly well in the area of Terrace House 2. It shows two dwellings, approximately equal in size and based on the Greek peristyle house tradition, built adjacent to one another on three terraces. Their original building concept is a self-contained complex, with individual rooms arranged around the central, open inner court: the peristyle which provided adequate lighting for the chambers opening onto the covered ambulatory. Openings onto the street are rare and probably served mainly for the ventilation of the rooms.

Fig. 1: View into residential unit 5 (Gail)

Fig. 2: Peristyle of residential unit 2, south side: niche with the mosaic of Dionysus and Ariadne in the paradise garden

The last two pages: Plan of the Terrace Houses 1 and 2 (1:500)

The space available for construction was optimized by directly joining the apartments to one another. Radical changes in the respective ground plans allow the conclusion that the property situation altered in the course of their existence. This, together with the concept of individual "plots of land" in the *insula* owners-association, led archaeologists to draw comparisons with the modern idea of the "condominium" or block of individually owned apartments. In addition, the archaeological finds shed some light on the wording of one or two laws and case studies of ancient jurisdiction (i.e. disputes about the maintenance of common roofs, drainage pipes etc.). According to the examination of the foundations and evaluation of the finds, the entire site was first built upon during a short span of time at the close of the 1st century BC. In most cases it can be shown that the apartments were in use after numerous phases of rebuilding and renovation, up to at least the end of the 4th century, and some until the beginning of the 7th century. Among the events which led to radical changes in the construction of buildings and their usage, the earthquakes of 262 AD and 369/70 AD, known to us from inscriptions and numismatic evidence, should be particularly emphasized. The changed circumstances of social and urban development in late Roman times led to the installation of various workshops in premises, sometimes only primitively adapted or newly built on levelled rubble. A row of mills, driven by overshot water wheels, was installed along the west front of the *insula*. Channels in the tops of the ruined walls provided an efficient water supply by taking advantage of the changing ground level. A workshop in the north-west of the complex housed a stone-cutting saw which was also driven by hydraulic power.

The apartments in the south of the *insula* extended right up to the street, whereby the building terrace was extended deep into the exposed rock to optimize the steeply rising building site; this is the reason why only the rooms of the upper storey are above street level. On the middle and lower building terraces, the slope usually allowed a ground level entrance from the stairway alleys. In the north-eastern section of the *insula* frontage, some of the taverns which face Curetes Street form an integral part of the built-up area.

As a rule, all apartments had several heatable rooms. In some cases the upper storeys were also equipped

Fig. 1 + 2: Theatre room in residential unit 1: allegorical figure (before and after restoration)

Fig. 3 + 4: Residential unit 3/5, east wall of the internal courtyard, series of philosophers: Socrates of Athens and Chilon of Sparta

1

2

3

4

with hypocaust heating systems. A public utility network provided internal running water and removed the waste of interior latrines. In addition, cisterns and wells dug into the rock ensured a supply of water to individual households. A system of city drains under the stairway alleys disposed of waste water.

The furnishings of the ground floor are of ceremonial character throughout, and of outstanding cultural and art historical interest in variety, quality and unity. It mirrors not only the prevailing tastes and artistic requirements of the occupants, who are mainly unknown to us, but also demonstrates the need of a high standard of culture and art appreciation through the selected themes of figural representation. This include theatre scenes, portrayals of philosophers and muses, illustrations from popular novels, mythological and genre painting.

Residential Unit 1

An entrance from the terrace house alley to the south gave access to the area of the ground floor used for official and private ceremony, while the commercial rooms could be reached over steps from stairway alley 1. From the former, a vestibule SR1 led to the inner court SR2 with four columns, and from there to the so-called theatre room SR6. Representations of scenes from the comedies of Menander and the tragedies of Euripides were augmented by personifications of hospitality and generosity. The decorated area in the upper part of the north wall, painted with architectural motifs, shows as a central picture a mythological scene, possibly Hercules in combat with the river-god Acheloos. The small structure in the north ambulatory in the peristyle court can probably be attributed to a need for more rooms in late Roman times due to the fact that the upper stories had not been rebuilt.

Residential Unit 2

Entrance was from the west into a small atrium (SR27) with four Doric columns which, in later use, became the centre of the commercial area of this apartment. The actual centre of the apartment consisted in late Imperial times of a nine-columned, Rhodian peristyle court, on the south side of which was an exedra with a magnificent glass mosaic showing Dionysus and Ariadne in the vineyard of paradise. The floor mosaic of the ambulatory in front of the exedra shows a mythological maritime scene: Triton pulls a hippocamp with a nereid. The arch placed above the columns, assembled from *spolia* on the south side of the peristyle, was partially reconstructed when the protective building was erected. Room SR24 can be considered a triclinium because of its position and floor decoration. The broad white border zones indicate the position of the *klines*, while the decorated central field had the decorative function of a carpet. Also part of the interior architectural design of the room were two niches with marble panelling, the conches of which were likewise decorated with glass mosaics.

Residential Units 3 and 5

Originally one unit, but separated diagonally when its function was changed, these apartments lie on the western upper section of the middle terrace. The individual rooms are relatively small and arranged around a three-sided interior court. Their furnishings are of special art historical interest because the walls of room H2/12 are decorated with portrayals of the nine muses, as well as of Sappho and Apollo. Portraits of well-known philosophers, certainly parts of a then current series, have been preserved on the east wall of the interior court H2/24.

Residential Unit 4

Originally arranged around an open courtyard, the floor plan underwent numerous modifications. The wall paintings, including the famous portrait of Socrates (now in the Ephesus Museum Selçuk) and the portrayal of the muse Urania embellishing a door in the eastern part of the apartment, can be ascribed to the oldest remaining period of furnishing. Building operations, undertaken when the apse of the basilica on the lower terrace was raised, appreciably disturbed the usability of the apartment. This, as well as the existence of a connecting staircase, suggests a common ownership with residential unit 6 adjoining to the north. Over a certain period of time (2nd/3rd century AD), this unit may have served as a commercial wing for residential unit 6.

Residential Unit 6

This unit has a certain position of prominence because of its size (ground floor surface area 950 m^2), room arrangement, and also the naming in an inscription of the presumed owner at the close of the 2nd century AD., C. Flavius Furius Aptus.

The two-storey peristyle court, still to be reconstructed, marks the beginning of an impressive combination of rooms. It gave access not only to the rooms on the west and north sides, but also to the impressive marble-panelled room (H2/31) to the south and, through a small atrium (H2/36) with a groin vault, to the barrel-vaulted *basilica privata* (H2/8) in the south-west.

Furius Aptus belonged to the circle of leading citizens of Ephesus at the close of the 2nd century AD and had, at least once, organized the Ephesian games as festival leader (alytarch). His function within the framework of the cult of Dionysus was reflected in the decorative layout of his premises, and would certainly have been the reason for the theme chosen for the stucco vault decoration of a small room (H2/8) which adjoins the main room of the basilica. Creatures out of the *thiasos* of Dionysus populate the geometric fields of the vaulted ceiling; the figurative portrayals flanked by cupids in the lunette possibly represent the marriage of the god with Ariadne. The social position and cultic responsibility of a prominent person during the Severan Imperial period are here vividly demonstrated by the archaeological finds.

Residential Unit 7

This apartment adjoins residential unit 6 to the west and was at times connected to it. The built-up ground area, also 900 m^2, is arranged in a traditional manner: rooms grouped around the central interior court (H2/38) can be classified as a "private" living area.

In the exedra aligned with the peristyle in the south of the ensemble, busts of Livia, the wife of Augustus, and her son, the later Emperor Tiberius, were uncovered, both having been in secondary use in this context with a huge bronze serpent between them. The destruction of the complex can be dated to the reign of Emperor Gallienus (262 AD).

The area adjoining to the north, though one terrace lower, was used for residential purposes up into late Roman times. Room H2/45b contains wall paintings from a phase of decoration in the 3rd/4th century AD (?), which are preserved in several layers and probably display, in three fields, illustrations from the famous novel, *The Golden Ass* by Apuleius of Madaurus.

FK, UO, GW

Fig. 1: Residential unit 4: garden paintings in the courtyard, behind which is the rear side of the apse of the basilica in residential unit 6 (Pesendorfer)

Fig. 2: Residential unit 6, R8: stucco vault, Pan and the head of a satyr

Fig. 3: Residential unit 7, mural inscriptions

FiE VIII, 1 - 2; Anz 1970 - 1988 passim; ÖJh 1972 - 75, B358 - 380; ÖJh 1996 to 1999, G passim.

Outstanding finds in the Ephesus Museum Selçuk, Rooms 1 and 3.

Until further notice, terrace House 2 is only accessible in exceptional circumstances, as restoration work is still going on.

1

2

3

CURETES STREET [36]

In ancient times, the Processional Way in the valley between Bülbüldağ and Panayırdağ may have been called Embolos or Plateia. The upper part of the marble-paved street was lined with colonnades whereas more and more public buildings - Nymphaeum Traiani [38], Varius Bath [*41*], Temple of Hadrian [*40*] - were erected on the north side of the lower part, and tombs and honorific monuments on the south side.

Curetes Street runs from the so-called State Agora [18] to the Tetragonos Agora (Commercial Market) [61], cutting diagonally through the regular Hippodamian grid of the Hellenistic-Roman city. Not only does this suggest that the street is very old but also that it was of ritual importance as the route of the Artemis procession. The modern name is derived from the re-used column-drums of the Prytaneum which are inscribed with the lists of *curetes*.

The side streets follow the orthogonal system and thus intersect at an acute angle. Four narrow lanes lead down from the north slope of Panayırdağ but only two are continued in the narrow stairway alleys. Sewers run under the streets, lined with limestone blocks and in some parts with marble spolia, and flow into a large main drain.

The street for vehicular traffic is between 6.80 and 10 m, wide, and flanking halls, which served as shaded walk ways, 3.50 to 4.50 m wide. Behind them are the tabernae, which were rented out as shops, hot food stalls, drinking parlours and small workshops. The street has a gradient of 10% and drops a vertical height of some 20 m along its 210 m course.

ÖJh 1959, B346ff.; BerMatÖAI 6 (1995) 84-95.

In the upper part, only the columned porticos on the north side have been excavated. A statue base, inscribed with a dedication, usually to a victorious athlete, stood in front of each column. One of these honorific marble statues, a headless togatus, is now erected on the base for the physician Alexander.

Trajan's Gatehouse [37]

An only partially excavated side street branches off just before the Nymphaeum Traiani; it was flanked by two pedestals, now partially sunk in the ground. These were probably part of a propylon named in a building inscription, dated to 114/115 AD, on an architrave found here. It is likely that the gate formed an ornamental entrance to the side street.

Fig. 1: The partially re-erected, late Roman Hercules Gate turned the Embolos (Curetes Street) into a pedestrian precinct

Fig. 2: The numerous honorific statues, the plinths of which still stand on the north side of Curetes Street, are an excellent example of the thirst for glory in Imperial times

NYMPHAEUM TRAIANI [38]

The two-storey tabernacle façade **of the monumental fountain installation was erected as the magnificent terminus of an Ephesian water conduit, by the Asiarch Tib. Claudius Aristion before 114 AD. According to a building inscription on the frieze and architrave of the lower storey, it was dedicated to Emperor Trajan.**

The building is one of the three great Ephesian fountain installations whose columnar façades are designed in the tradition of the theatrical *scaenae frons* but enriched by additional projecting side wings. In ground plan, the building consisted of a long, rectangular fountain basin, which was framed on three sides by the 9.50 m high façade. The basin, 11.90 m long and 5.40 m wide, was fed by a water channel, which terminated in an outlet shaped like a shell. The rear wall and side wings were two storied. The columns of the lower storey rested on pedestals and carried composite capitals. An aedicula stood between the columns in each of the lateral projections. The column pedestals in the upper storey were octagonal and their columns carried standard Corinthian capitals. The rear wall of the building was subdivided by pilasters, one behind each column.

ÖJh 1959, B326; 1972 - 75, 386; 1978 - 80, 88f.; IvE II 424; FLEISCHER, in: Pro Arte Antiqua, Festschrift H. KENNER I (1982) 123 - 129; FiE X/1, 53ff., 62f., 70ff., 124ff.
The statues found during excavation in the fountain basin are displayed in the Ephesus Museum Selçuk, Room 2.

In the lower storey, the paired columns framing the centre were combined into pavillions. In the upper storey the columns of the wider middle bay are covered by an entablature with pediment. In this way, a two-storey high centre niche was formed, in which a double life-size statue of Trajan was displayed. Remains of this marble statue - a bare breast and a plinth with a foot and a dedication on its base - have survived.

While the middle intercolumniation is accentuated by a triangular pediment, the corners were surmounted by horizontal volutes and the projecting wings with round pediments.. The façade was richly decorated with statues: Dionysus, Aphrodite, a reclining satyr, Nerva, several female robed and portrait statues and one which can be interpreted as Androclus as a hunting youth. Following severe earthquake damage (probably in 362 AD) the building was partly restored. HT

Fig. 1: Nymphaeum Traiani: the architectural installation was carried out in 1962 with concrete supports instead of columns which are missing (PESENDORFER)

Fig. 2: Reconstruction (PELLIONIS 1963)

THE TEMPLE OF HADRIAN [40]

A building inscription identifies the small temple-like monument on Curetes Street, which was incorporated in the Varius Bath [41] complex, as being "in homage to Emperor Hadrian". Though incomplete, its anastylosis, carried out in the late 1950's, has achieved a "heraldic" character among the Ephesian monuments.

A partial reconstruction of this monument as it was in late Roman times, by the architect F. Göschel after excavations carried out under MILTNER, has attracted special attention for many years. It was endowed and dedicated to Emperor Hadrian (117 - 138 AD) by a renowned representative of the citizens of Ephesus by the name of P. Vedius Antoninus Sabinus. Facing the street, the building is fronted by a porch with a "Syrian pediment" supported by a Corinthian order. The building itself consisted of a cella, 7.50 m wide and some 5 m deep, occupying a space appropriated from the bath complex.

The organisation of the ornament is remarkable. Decorative zones, such as frieze or pilaster ornament architectonically bound together, are dominated by apotropaic elements: laurel on the pilasters, mythical beings in the vines, as well as the sprig of leaves underneath the crowning bust of Tyche are, in general, indicators of a certain relationship to the hereafter.

Statues of the tetrarchs were set up on the street front around 300 AD; the pedestals for Diocletian, Constantius, and Maximianus Galerius are preserved, while the renegade Maximian (senior) was later replaced by the father of Emperor Theodosius I.

A re-erection of the building, possibly after earthquake damage - the date is disputed - mainly used the original building elements. The late Roman aspect of the small building, displaying myths of the city's founding (see the reliefs above the lintel) and presenting images of the tetrarchs, represents a historical phenomenon which saw the integration of "private and public attitudes" in Imperial and late Roman Ephesus. UO

ÖJh 1955, B34ff.; 1956 - 58, B17ff.; 1959, B250ff.; **1955**, **B2ff.**; Anz 1956, 44ff.; 1957, 16ff.; FLEISCHER, Festschrift F. EICHLER (1967), 23ff.; IvE 429.

The descriptions of the frieze blocks with reliefs are based on the originals in the Ephesus Museum Selçuk, Room 7.

Fig. 1: The re-erected Temple of Hadrian. In the foreground, the pedestals for the statues 122 of the tetrarchs (PESENDORFER)

VARIUS BATH [41], LATRINE AND SO-CALLED HOUSE OF PLEASURE [43]

The Varius Bath (also called the Baths of Scholasticia) occupies the north side of Curetes Street between Bath Street [39] and the formerly covered Academy Street [42]. The small temple of Hadrian [40] is interposed in the bath complex. Residential buildings, incorrectly interpreted as a house of pleasure, as well as a large latrine, occupy the corner-*insula*.

A 250 m stretch of **Bath Street** has been uncovered, up to a point beyond the theatre, which climbs 70 m without a street intersection. It is lined with unexcavated buildings, probably residential quarters.

The entrance to the large apsidal room of the **Varius Bath**, the apodyterium (see plan on page 129) which served as a changing room and entrance hall, is located at the beginning of Bath Street. The seated statue of Scholasticia, who had paid for the renovation of the building, was set up in a niche in early Christian times. This statue too is a re-used 2nd century piece. Another entrance by a stairway from Curetes Street lies to the east of the Temple of Hadrian.

The apodyterium gave access to the other bathing rooms, the frigidarium, the tepidarium, the caldarium and the sudatorium. The walls and the floors of the rooms and bathing pools were covered with marble revetment. The efficient heating system of the baths, with hypocaust floor and, in some places, wall heating, was operated from the praefurnium, accessible from the lane called by archaeologists, Academy Street.

This street, in its late phase roofed over with groin vaults, connected the baths with the **latrine** in the corner-*insula* which has been extensively renovated by the Ephesus Museum Selçuk. The seats of these public communal toilets are arranged around three sides of an open peristyle courtyard, and fresh water flowed in the channel in front of the seats. Rain water was conducted over cistern heads on the down pipes into the sewers.

The adjoining residential building, in part richly furnished with figurative mosaic floors, has been interpreted as a **house of pleasure** on the basis of an inscription on an architrave re-used here, which mentions a *paidiskeion*, but this word also means public latrine and the architrave may originate from there.

In late Roman times, the street colonnade in front of the corner-*insula* was roofed over with low groin vaults, which rested on re-used column drums from the prytaneum, inscribed with the lists of curetes. Late Roman Doric and Ionic capitals with monograms belong to this building phase.

MB, HT, BT

ÖJh 1955, B35ff.; 1956 - 58, B17ff.; 1959, B251ff.; 1976 - 77, 61ff.

Fig. 1: Varius Bath, statue of Scholasticia (Pesendorfer)

Fig. 2: Varius Bath with Temple of Hadrian. To the right, Bath Street. In front, Alytarchus Stoa (Pesendorfer)

Fig. 3: Restored latrine (Pesendorfer)

2

1

3

ALYTARCHUS STOA [44], HELLENISTIC WELL [45], SO-CALLED NYMPHAEUM (HEXAGON) [46]

In front of Terrace Houses 1 and 2 on the south side of the street, the so-called Alytarchus Stoa was laid out in late Roman times with a lavish mosaic. It was formerly a Hellenistic well house and an honorific monument which was converted into a workshop.

The **Stoa**, 4.70 to 5.50 m in depth, is divided into two sections, because steps in the eastern section were needed to compensate for a 2.50 m difference in street level. The polychrome mosaic is largely composed of geometric patterns and is enriched by fields of birds and flowers, as well as one field with two bowls (*canthari*) and pairs of doves.

An architrave-frieze block with a building inscription naming a certain Alytarchus as the sponsor, has been ascribed to the colonnade. The hall and mosaic floor were probably restored during the same building phase and must have been finished prior to 440/441 AD because a letter of this year to proconsul Flavius Heliodorus is made public on one of the columns.

Tabernae 2 and 2a, whose use in late Roman times is still uncertain, lie at the end of the stoa on the lower street level. Originally, the south wall and the adjoining portions of the east and west walls, formed part of a **Well House**.

Made from carefully joined marble blocks, they still bear the remains of truncated lion's heads with small, round openings as water spouts. The simple form of this building is reminiscent of the Hellenistic Well House [74] near the theatre.

ÖJh 1959, B282f.; FiE VIII/2, 31ff.

The easternmost of the three monuments has traditionally been called a **Nymphaeum**. Steps to the street were built over an older, hexagonal monument. To the south, the remains of four marble basins from the upper storey are preserved. In the bottom of each is a small drain opening into large pithoi which stand in small vaulted, tiled chambers.

The structures west of the Alytarchus Stoa mark the beginning of the last row of tombs and honorific monuments which line the lower Embolos up to the Tetragonos Agora.

Fig. 1: Alytarchus Stoa: the mosaic, which was removed when it was uncovered, has now been re-laid in its original position

Fig. 2: Reconstruction (THÜR, approx. 1:300) of the honorific monument. Right, Hadrian's Gate

THE OCTAGON, TOMB OF THE PTOLEMAIC ARSINOË IV [47]

A rectangular base, constructed of cast mortar masonry, was erected around a vaulted burial chamber and clad with marble. Over it was built an octagonal structure surrounded by Corinthian columns supporting a pyramid roof with a garland frieze. Murdered in Ephesus in 41 BC, the youngest sister of the famous Cleopatra VII was probably buried here.

The massive socle storey, 9 m long and 3.40 high, rests on a three-stepped base and is clad with concave orthostats between an upper and lower moulding. The upper structure consisted of a closed octagonal cella surrounded by an octagonal peristasis. The upper part of the cella wall was decorated with a bucranium-garland frieze, and a bench ran around its base. The columns of the peristasis carried Corinthian capitals. The frieze is unusual: upright acanthus leaves alternate with palm leaves and griffins. The tops of both the leaves and the heads of the bird griffins supported alternating block-shaped and curved consoles. A roof in the form of an octagonal step pyramid may be assumed from the finds of numerous stone steps cut to match an octagon. On the top of the roof was a stone sphere (see page before, fig. 2).

The skeleton of a young woman, fifteen or sixteen years old, was found in a simple marble sarcophagus in the burial chamber, which was entered from the rear through a lockable passageway. The building decoration (capitals, garland and acanthus frieze, wreathed consoles) is dated almost unanimously into the period 50 - 20 BC. This, together with the age of the young woman, supports the interpretation of the building as the burial monument of Arsinoë IV.

Two letters of the co-emperors Valens, Valentinian and Gratian were made public on the street-side of the base in the fourth century AD. The letter on the left, in Latin, is addressed to the Proconsul Eutropius (371 AD) and regulates the sharing of public funds between the cities of Asia Minor heavily damaged by earthquakes. The letter on the right, written both in Latin and Greek, is addressed to the Proconsul Festus (372 AD) and distributes the financial burden of the provincial festival games over four cities.

Aug. Architektur, 40ff.; ÖJh 1990, 43 - 56; Concerning the death of Arsinoë, see Flavius Josephus, Antiquities of the Jews, 15, 89; Cassius Dio 43, 19, 2.
A pair of columns and the adjacent entablature from the octagonal upper structure is re-erected in the Ephesus Museum Selçuk.

Fig. 1: Orthostats on the north-west corner of the octagon socle with the letter to Festus

Fig. 2: The Octagon as uncovered in 1906; in the background, the so-called Curetes Hall, erected using columns from the Prytaneum

MONUMENT (HEROON) AND FOUNTAIN OF KTISTES ANDROCLUS [48]

The U-shaped monument had, over a massive sockel decorated with a blind Doric order, an open upper storey with Ionic columns and entablature. Although the structure has usually been called a Byzantine Fountain because of its late Roman enclosure panels, it was probably built towards the end of the 2nd century BC as an honorific monument (heroon) for Androclus, the mythical founder of the city.

The long rectangular ground plan of the heroon has a U-shaped recess in the middle of the north front which faces the street. The outline of the lower storey (see p. 125, Fig. 2./3) can be seen in the ruins which stand to a height of almost four meters. The blind Doric architecture, surrounding a core of re-used bolstered ashlar, is articulated by pilasters at the corners and in the recessed middle section, and in the middle of the shorter sides with half-columns. The blind architecture in the middle section was never executed.

The ashlar masonry, covered in its lower portions with marble revetment, served as the rear wall of a fountain which was supplied with water by a channel running from the south through the massive core. The fountain basin was converted to a water reservoir in late Roman times when its wall panels were decorated with lozenges and crosses.

The Ionic upper storey had an open, U-shaped arrangement of columns facing the street and was closed off by a wall in the south. The broad middle bay was accentuated by an arch. The structure, originally 13 m high, was crowned by a broken pediment whose lateral fields displayed figurative reliefs which continued as a frieze in the middle section.

The reliefs portray scenes of combat. In one fragment, a rider with fluttering cloak raises his right hand to throw a spear. On the so-called temple of Hadrian across the street [40], Androclus, similarly clothed, and raising his arm in the same manner, is shown killing a wild boar - possibly a reference to the myth depicted on the Androclus monument. The interpretation of the building as an Androclus monument is supported by the relief scenes, the topographical position on the Processional Way, its location near the Tetragonos Agora, and Pausanius' description of the site (VII 2,8; 4,2). The fountain could have surrounded the spring called *Hypelaia* in the founding legend.

ÖJh 1995, 63 - 103.
The pediment relief and the frieze are displayed in the large courtyard of the Ephesus Museum Selçuk.

Fig. 1: The ruins of the Androclus Monument with the late Roman enclosure panels

Fig. 2: Garland frieze

HADRIAN'S GATE, THE NEW TRIODOS GATE [49]

The construction of the three-storied gate, whose third storey resembles Hadrian's Gate in Athens, was apparently already begun as a decorative southern prospect of the Marble Street in a topographically and culturally significant position during the time of Trajan (prior to 117 AD). After an earthquake in the 3rd or 4th century AD, water basins were added in the side bays during a rebuilding. A partial re-erection of the lower storey was finished in 1997.

The structure has a tri-partite plan in which the broad street gateway is framed by two narrower passages. Only the four rectangular bases survived the earthquake. These formed the plinth of a two-sided blind architecture with densely concentrated elements. The 11.40 m width of the gate building and its original height of 16.60 m, stand in contrast to a depth of only 1.50 m. An early collapse, presumably in the earthquake year 262 AD, and the late Roman rebuilding betray the fragility of the construction.

The bases of the lower storey carried pillars with engaged half-columns in the south and free-standing columns in the north. This system of supporting elements carried composite capitals, decorated with reed leaves, each carved from a single piece of stone. A straight entablature spanned the lateral column bays and bent to form an arch at the center.

Framing the arch in the second storey were pillars which were aligned with the outer columns below, and above this was a zone of capitals supporting the second entablature.

Gate: FiE XI/1.
Demeas inscription: IvE IV, 1351.

The upper storey had six supporting elements combining half-column pillars and free-standing columns. The Corinthian-like capitals are again carved from single blocks of stone. The entablature was recessed, and a pediment, into which a small arch jutted in the middle bay, accentuated the three intercolumniations.

Statues of gods, members of the imperial family, and doners, were set up in the intercolumniations next to the large arch and in the upper storey. Underneath, there was also a statue of the city's patron goddess, Artemis, that was later cast down by a Christian called Demeas as being an *evil demon*, and replaced with a cross . The base with the relevant inscription stands in the altar building adjoining to the west. The topographical situation of the gate structure can be explained by the alterations carried out in this quarter of the city in the 1st century AD (see Library Place). HT

Fig. 1: General plan of the excavations in the centre of the city (1:2250): Library Quarter, Tetragonos Agora [61] with Hall of Nero [62], Marble Street [60], West Road [65] with Medusa Gate [66] and Temple Precinct (so-called Serapeion) [67]

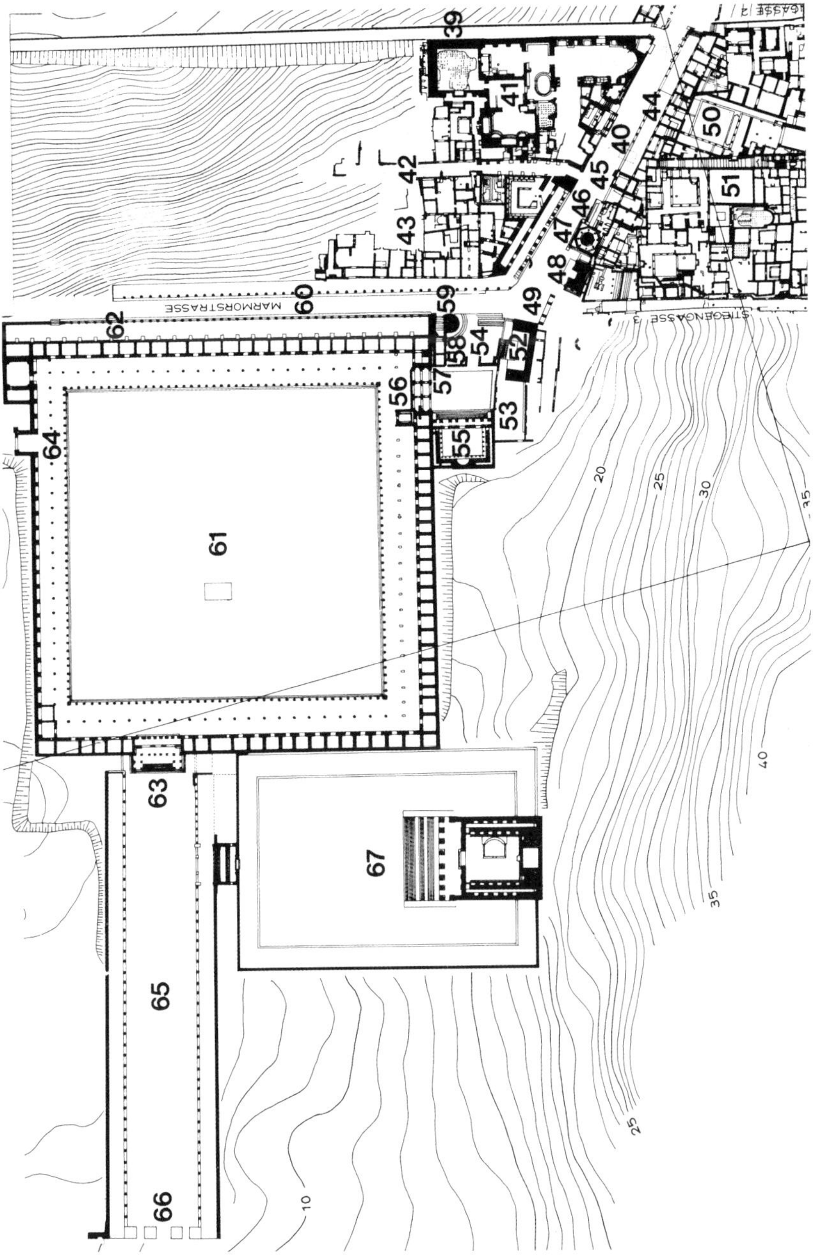
39
41
42
43
44
40
45
46
47
48
49
50
51
52
53
54
55
56
57
58
59
60
61
62
63
64
65
66
67
MARMORSTRASSE
STIEGENGASSE 3
20
25
30
35
40
35
25
10

CELSUS LIBRARY [55]

The library was erected as a heroon over the grave of the Roman senator Ti. Julius Celsus Polemaeanus in the first quarter of the 2nd century AD. Its sumptuous façade marks the western end of the lower Embolos with an impressive architectural configuration.

Directly adjoining the southwestern corner of the south gate of the Tetragonos Agora, the library building stands on a rectangular plot of land obtained by the appropriation of half of a peristyle house [53] in the south of the square. The façade of the building, already excavated in 1905/1906, was re-erected in the course of anastylosis in the years 1970 - 1978 under the direction of F. HUEBER and V.M. STROCKA.

Nine steps flanked by two statue bases lead up to an aediculated façade, which can be entered through three axially symmetrical doorways under corresponding window openings in the upper storey. The most significant compositional elements are the alternately projecting and receding members of the façade which are so arranged that both the lower and upper stories are subdivided into clearly aligned bays or pavillions. The four narrower, and thus apparently elongated, pavillions of the lower storey are complemented by three broader ones in the upper storey which are flanked by single columns, each with a separate entablature. The curvature of the horizontal components (observed in the course of re-building) resulting from the increased height of the vertical elements towards the center gives the illusion of a wider façade, and was deliberately intended by the architects who planned it.

Plaster casts of statues (the originals are in the Ephesus Museum Vienna), allegorically embodying the virtues of Celsus - and typically expected of all high-ranking Roman civil servants - are placed In the four aediculae of the lower storey. From left to right: *Sophia* (wisdom), *Arete* (character), *Ennoia* (power of judgment) and *Episteme* (expertise).

In contrast to the two stories of the façade, the interior of the building was laid out in three stories on a rectangular ground plan which was dominated by an apse on the middle axis of the room. Underneath, and accessible

Fig. 1: The façade of the library as re-erected in 1978. To the right the south gate of the agora. Left, the Hellenistic peristyle house

Fig. 2: Detail of the architectural decoration

Fig. 3: Statue of Sophia

1

2

3

from the north, is the burial chamber with the sarcophagus of the donor who is buried here. The actual contents of the library –the book scrolls– were housed in cupboard-like niches in the two upper stories of the room, which were accessible from the galleries. The interior decoration - the layout of the floor surface and the panelling of the walls - was executed in marble revetments of various colours.

Inscriptions on the bases flanking the steps outside offer information on the social position and official career of Ti. Julius Celsus Polemaeanus, who probably came from Sardis, and was consul of the year 92 AD and *proconsul Asiae* in 106/107. The motifs of the rich architectural decoration refer to his judicial function (the *fasces* in the area of the wall pilasters) and the sepulchral character of the building. Inscriptions, most of which have survived, name C. Julius Aquila, the son of Celsus and *consul* of the year 110 AD, as the builder of the library as a heroon for his father. Legacies in his last will and testament provided for the furnishing of the building as well as for the further purchase of books.

The library burned down as a result of the devastating earthquake in 262 AD and the interior room was destroyed and not refurbished. In late Roman times, the façade formed the decorative backdrop of a fountain structure with water basins built of large, re-used relief slabs erected over the former entrance steps. These reliefs, which became famous under the name "Parthian Panels", were originally component parts of a mid- 2nd century monumental frieze honoring the Imperial dynasty. The main exhibit is now in the Ephesus Museum Vienna, and new finds in the Ephesus Museum Selçuk.

Perhaps the statues of the Virtues were replaced at this time, and the *Ennoia* of a Philippus inserted. A verse inscription in the upper storey refers to a certain Stephanos who was said to have adorned the *Ptelea*, a poetic term for Ephesus.

The final destruction of the façade, probably also the result of an earthquake, occurred in the high Middle Ages. UO

FiE V/1.
For the re-building and new information gained as a result: HUEBER, AW 6/4, 1975, 3ff.; DiscAB 4, 1983, 175ff.; AW 15/4, 1984, 1ff.
Notice boards illustrating the ancient methods of construction and the modern re-erection of the library, are set up in the interior of the building.

Fig. 1: Celsus Library: reconstruction of the three-storey interior room (NIEMANN)

Fig. 2: Condition of the library when uncovered in 1905 with slabs of the so-called Parthian Monument

THE LIBRARY QUARTER

The topography of the library quarter reflects extensive changes from Augustan up into late Roman times. On the one hand, these changes are connected with the shifting of the road junction on the venerable Processional Way and, on the other, are linked to earthquake devastation in the 3rd and 4th centuries AD as well as to the Christian elimination of pagan cult buildings. The ensemble, which excavation and restoration work presents to today's visitor, never existed in this form in antiquity. The south side of the library quarter is occupied by the Foundations of an Altar [52]; the sockle of another monument and a Peristyle House [53], its north side by the South Gate of the Tetragonos Agora [56]; the stairs up to the Hall of Nero [62] with the Grave of Dionysios Rhetor [57] underneath; and the Base of a Circular Monument [59].

What was later to become the South Gate of the Tetragonos Agora was originally erected as a triodos (three-way) gate at the point where the Processional Way branches off to Ortygia (valley of Arvalia), the legendary birthplace of Artemis and Apollo. On the 6th of May, the birthday of the city's patron goddess and her twin brother, there was a procession to that place. The new Celsus Library was built over the old Processional Way to Ortygia and the road junction shifted further up the slope at the south end of Marble Street [60]. The new Ortygia road passed through, and its beginning was marked by Hadrian's Gate [49]. It then ran westwards on the south side of the altar structure [52]. The Plateia probably extended across Marble Street from the time of the enlargement of the Tetragonos Agora [61] and the associated erection of the Hall of Nero in the course of the 1st century AD.

After earthquake destruction and the prohibition of pagan cults in the 2nd half of the 4th century AD, events which resulted in the demolition of the altar structure, a mill was built in the south-east corner of the no longer significant library plaza, to supply water through a channel over the steps of the former altar.

In the 6th/7th century this mill was abandoned, and the plaza rearranged for the last time. A wall built out of spolia, and nicknamed "Tube" or Culvert Gate [54], is thought to have closed off the square

ÖJh 1978 - 80, B53 - 64; 1983, B150 - 250; AW 15/4, 1984, 3 - 30; BerMatÖAI 1 (1991) 5 - 18; 3 (1993) 9 - 15. 54.

Fig. 1: Circular Monument, provisionally reconstruction of the conical roof

Fig. 2: South Gate, Hecate relief

Fig. 3: Marble arch with burial inscription of a Rhodian sophist

1

2

3

against the south-eastern part of the city as part of a Byzantine fortification system. A stairway over the Grave of Dionysios Rhetor [57] in the southern front of the Tetragonos Agora and its eastern colonnade, gave access to Marble Street.

Library Plaza was dominated by the monumental **altar** [52] measuring 22.20 m x 8.40 m, which directly adjoined Hadrian's Gate. The foundations, which contained a sewer reservoir, and the 9.5 m wide stairway to the altar courtyard, are all that remains. What was built above them has not yet been determined. It has been suggested that this was the location of the so-called Parthian monument, the relief slabs of which, along with other marbles, were re-used in late Roman times to construct the water basin in front of the library façade. The altar could have served the association of Artemis worshippers, known from an inscription, in the area around the Embolos. It was built in early Imperial times and the northwest corner of the foundations adjoin another building, of unknown purpose, from the same period.

To the west, excavations have revealed a **peristyle house** from late Hellenistic-early Roman times, which had been partially sacrificed for the construction of the library. In the 4th century, a **hall** was built over the altar and the peristyle house. Its mosaic floor, now removed for restoration, was partly decorated with figurative panels showing, among other things, two lions fighting. The hall could be entered by steps from Marble Street and probably formed a connection with buildings adjoining to the west, which have not yet been excavated.

East of the South Gate and underneath the late Roman ramp [57] to Marble Street, a formerly vaulted **burial chamber** was excavated which contained a sarcophagus decorated with garlands and an inscription naming **T. Claudius Flavianus Dionysius Rhetor**. The sophist, celebrated in the time of Hadrian, is primarily known to us from his biography by Philostratus who states that he was buried *on the agora* in Ephesus. Originally, in Imperial times, a broad staircase led above the burial chamber to the main entrance of the Hall of Nero [62] in its south wall. The staircase incorporated the bossed ashlar plinth of a **Circular Monument** [59]. The associated architectural elements, only partially identified, permit a theoretical reconstruction. The plinth carried a six-columned monopteros with Corinthian capitals and a conical roof. All the components of the building exhibit strongly sintered round holes and slits so that the structure must have functioned as a decorative fountain of a type which was very popular when it was built at the end of the Hellenistic age.

In the 2nd century AD, a climbing brick barrel vault [58], the function of which is still unclear, was placed in front of a small apsidal structure which formed the western boundry of the staircase up to the hall. HT

Fig. 1: Late Roman hall: mosaic floor with picture of lions fighting
Fig. 2: Burial chamber and sarcophagus of Dionysius Rhetor

THE SOUTH GATE OF THE TETRAGONOS AGORA [56]

The north side of Library Plaza is dominated by a monumental gate building called *triodos* in Antiquity. Erected as a kind of triumphal arch by two Imperial freedmen, it formed the south entrance to the enlarged Tetragonos Agora since Augustan times. It was re-erected in this form between 1979 and 1988 under the direction of F. HUEBER.

The gate house has three deep passageways spanned with arches, of which the central one is recessed on the south facade. The passageways are interconnected by richly decorated doorways, and each of the outer walls has two semicircular niches. Above the exquisitely decorated entablature, with its triple fascia architrave, vine frieze and denticulated cornices, there is a high attic zone framed by an elaborate cornice molding at the top, and by a guilloche moulding at its base. This carries the building inscription and served as a base for statues of the imperial family.

The text of the building inscription, given in an abridged Greek version in the middle section and in greater detail in Latin on the sides, states that Mazaeus and Mithridates, freedmen of the imperial house, had the gate erected in the year 3 BC in honour of the Emperor Augustus, his wife Livia, his son-in-law Agrippa (already dead), and his daughter Julia. The entire building is covered with additional inscriptions which refer to the supply of grain to the city, contain public price edicts and other official decrees, or are concerned with building activities in the surrounding area.

Reliefs of Hecate, sacred to crossroads, decorated the outer, narrow walls of the gateway. A curse formula In the south-east conch is addressed to those who answer the call of nature here.

The original appearance of the north façade was lost during re-building in the 1st century AD. According to an inscription, the floor level inside the South Gate was then raised so that rainwater cascading down the Embolos could be collected in sewers leading across the agora to prevent flooding in the market place.

There were originally two-storey wings on each side of the gatehouse which probably housed the graves of the two donors. The eastern one was reduced in size when the agora was rebuilt. The western one, for Mazaeus, was torn down, at the latest, when the library was erected. SK, PS, HT

For bibliography, see Library Quarter and Agora

Fig. 1: Library Plaza, north side: South Gate, slanting brick vault and so-called "Tube" or Culvert Gate

Fig. 2: South Gate: condition before the re-erection

TETRAGONOS AGORA [61]

From the time King Lysimachus relocated the city at the beginning of the 3rd century BC, the commercial market, named in an inscription as the *tetragonos agora,* was located in the flat valley area to the west of the so-called Marble Street [60]. Parts of the Hellenistic storerooms and halls have been excavated, particularly in the western area of the market. The square form, closed on all sides by two-aisled colonnades, each about 112 m long, was the result of a complete rebuilding on a larger area beginning in the late 1st century BC. After heavy destruction by earthquakes, the agora was rebuilt, using spolia and retaining the same ground plan, first in the 1 century AD and again under Emperor Theodosius I (379-395 AD), and continued in use up into the 7th century.

The excavation of the agora in its late Roman form took place mainly between 1901 and 1907. The re-erection of a part of the columnar architecture, in connection with additional excavation work, was carried out some sixty years later by the Turkish Department of Antiquities.

The re-used building components for the enclosure - now called the Forum of *Theodosius* - came partly from Imperial cult buildings; thus the west stoa was erected out of elements of the façade of the Temple of Domitian [30]. Capitals and entablatures were also brought to the agora from the Vedius Gymnasium [106] and the Harbour Gymnasium [93]. The majority of the architraves and cornices come, however, from colonnades of the time of the Emperor Caracalla (211 - 217 AD), which is the reason why it was long assumed that the rebuilding of the Agora took place under his rule. Today we know that these architectural elements only became part of the Agora as spolia in Late Antiquity.

The construction of the late forth century AD used the foundations of an enclosure erected sometime during the decades around the birth of Christ, with two-aisled, 11.20 m wide colonnades, behind which were a total of nearly one hundred rooms. These were mainly used for commercial purposes, but guild associations and political organizations of the city probably also had meeting places here. Of the ashlar walls of the Augustan agora, destroyed by an earthquake in 23 AD, only small areas remain in both corners of the south stoa. Obviously, the colonnades all had upper storeys, as remains of stairways in the south-east corner, near the West Gate and east of the North gate prove. The rebuilding was started on the same foundations and the agora could be used

Fig. 1: The north hall of the agora, partly restored in 1967, had been re-erected in the 4th century AD on its Augustan foundations, and altered again in the 6th century exclusively with re-used marble elements.

again twenty years later, as in 43 AD a statue of Emperor Claudius was erected in the courtyard by the association of Roman merchants. Leaf capitals of the so-called Pergamene type, re-used in late Roman times (now collected in the north stoa), originally were set upon the columns of the mid first century upper storey, while only few fragments of the Ionic capitals of the ground floor have been found.

Along the east side of the Agora (although not actually forming part of it) and facing Marble Street, there is a Doric, two-aisled basilica some 150 m in length. This was called the **Hall of Nero [62]** by the archaeologists because of the inscribed dedication to Artemis Ephesia, Nero, his mother Agrippina and the citizens of Ephesus. The two doors at the south side, facing the so-called Library Plaza, could be reached by a stairway, still partly preserved. The north end of the building, redesigned in late Roman times with a floor raised about one meter for ceremonial purposes, was separated from the two-aisled main room by a transverse wall. The façade facing Marble Street was closed with the exception of an entrance at the north end. The western half of the Hall of Nero, erected above the row of rooms behind the east colonnade of the agora, collapsed along its entire length, so that nothing can be said about its appearance on the agora-side, or about whether it was connected to the actual agora colonnade adjoining on the west.

When the Augustan **west stoa** was built, the originally lower-lying ground was used for a cellar storey with basement windows set at an angle in the front wall. Supplies were probably brought into this storage room through six entrances in the western outer wall so that the traffic did not affect activity in the agora. After the earthquake of 23 AD, this basement was partly filled with debris, especially with the sherds of many thousands of broken vessels.

The agora had gates on three sides. The **South Gate** [56], the only major part of the Augustan building phase to survive the earthquake, and the **North Gate** [64], preserved in its later, very simple form, clearly marked the course of the Plateia before the Augustan widening of the agora. The connecting way from the north gate of the agora to the forecourt of the theatre - a rather odd arrangement from the point of view of urban planning - is only a remnant of the main roadway which was rerouted in early Imperial times to coincide with the Marble Street.

The main entrance of the agora was the **West Gate** [63], which also served as a magnificent eastern termination to the so-called West Road [65], the boulevard leading from the harbour. A stairway with ten steps led up to the gate with its double colonnade and projecting wings, each with an additional pair of columns. The bases, some of them still

Fig. 1: Reconstruction of the west gate as it was originally thought to have appeared, after the excavations of 1904 (NIEMANN)

Fig. 2: View over the harbour plain from the Panayırdağ: in the foreground, the agora, The darker green land, partly under water, marks the basin of the Roman harbour

TAFEL I

P FRANKENSTEIN HELIOGR. DRUCK v F. SCHÖNDLE, WIEN

WESTTOR DER AGORA

in situ, and the Ionic capitals (now stored near the gate) carry rich decoration. Marble benches on both sides of the doorway invited those passing by to linger and look down the West Street. The most recent excavations have proved that, contrary to earlier suggestions for dating, the Gate was built after 23 AD upon a somewhat smaller Augustan foundation.

Soon after the market opened, it became apparent that the gate, though attractive, was unsuitable for goods traffic, and so, during the reign of Domitian (81-96 AD), a businessman of Alexandrian origin set to work on alterations. We see it today as it appeared in late Roman times; three passageways in the actual gate, two large water basins, and lateral approach ramps for heavy vehicles can be attributed to these first alterations.

In the course of centuries, the vast courtyard of the agora was filled with numerous honorific statues and votive monuments, but only their foundations remain *in situ*. Several dozen inscribed bases for statues of high imperial dignitaries and outstanding citizens of Ephesus were found in their late Roman usage as building stones in walls. These contain important information about urban building history, cultural events, and aspects of political administration and religion. The foundations of a building measuring 10.00 by 5.87 m and oriented north-south, excavated slightly west of the agora centre, were thought to be those of the *horologium* (clock) mentioned in a late Hellenistic inscription. The most recent research, however, has shown that the structure was most probably erected in the 6th century AD, as part of a larger building program, when the agora north hall was totally rebuilt as a two- or three-storied arcaded stoa with its rear wall supporting an artificial hill. On the top of this hill today, military barracks and depots of the Ephesus Museum Selçuk are located.

Deep excavations, initiated by G. LANGMANN in 1977 and only temporarily kept open, have revealed that the early **Hellenistic agora** lay as much as 3 m lower than the present ground level. A warehouse of the Lysimachian period in the south-west corner of the agora, had two rows of chambers, each measuring some 4.30 x 4.07 m on the interior. Over these, a stoa developed in three phases of modification in the course of the 3rd and 2nd centuries BC, which extended to the road near the later west gate. Excavations brought to light additional colonnades north of the west gate and at the western edge of the presumed course of the Plateia, mentioned above. It now appears that the Hellenistic agora, with sides 100 to 110 m long, only occupied about half of the area of the Roman agora.

With the founding of the agora, a settlement was demolished which can be identified as the village with the name

Fig. 1: The Italic manufacturer of terra *sigilata*, C. Sentius also had founded a factory in Asia, probably in Tralleis (Aydın); his depot on the agora fell victim to an earthquake (in 23 AD?)

Fig. 2: Hellenistic Warehouse in the south-west of the agora (3rd century BC) below the facade of the Roman west stoa

of **Smyrna**, mentioned by the poets Callinos and Hipponax in archaic times. Since 1987, its remains, comprising five periods of settlement beginning in the 8th century BC, have been uncovered at the west edge of the agora. All the buildings were constructed with clay walls on stone foundations. An early house with oval ground plan measuring 7.30 by 4.50 m and oriented north-south, was replaced in the next building phase by a similarly oriented rectangular building of 10.30 by 5.0 m, which had an anteroom open to the east. In the course of the 7th century BC, this was joined by almost square, single-room buildings along a narrow lane. In the 6th century, large residential houses were erected in the course of substantial changes, which partly made use of the older walls. Probably because of the rising sea level, the houses were abandoned, and, in the 5th and 4th centuries BC, the area was used by potters and other craftsmen.

During deep excavations, burials from the late archaic and classical periods were found along the Plateia, in the east of the Roman agora and under the Library Plaza. The most remarkable single find from the burial ground is a grave-lion from the 6th century BC, found in the Byzantine debris when the street near the north gate of the agora was uncovered.

Roman and Late Antique Agora: FiE III, 1 - 168; FiE XIII/1/1; Aug. Architektur, 45 - 49; HÖRMANN, ÖJh 1929, 22 - 53; 1996, G7 - 10; 1997, B253 - 318; 1998, G7 - 12.

Smyrna and Hellenistic agora buildings: ÖJh 1993, G12 - 14; 1994, G11 - 14; 1996, G10 - 12.

Graves: STROCKA, AA 1977, 507 - 510; BerMatÖAI 3 (1993) 53.

West Road and Medusa Gate: FiE III 32 - 38; ÖJh 1902, B62; 1926, B270f.

West Road [65], Medusa Gate [66]

The west gate of the agora forms the east end of a plaza-like boulevard measuring 160 by 24 m), now called the West Road. The 6 m wide colonnade along its length - excavated only near the West Gate - and the chambers behind are in the Doric order. The southern colonnade contains the doorway to the so-called Serapeion. The crossroads at the west end, with the side street from the four-columned Arcadiane monument, is marked by a gatehouse with three passageways, the plan of which, already uncovered in 1901, goes back to building activities around 400 AD. Assorted spolia may have been used to renovate a building core from early Imperial times. The newly created capitals of the entrance pillars, with frontal reliefs of peculiar Medusa heads, give the gate its modern name. On the sides are palmettes which bear a striking resemblance to those on the so-called Hercules Gate [35] on Curetes Street. Pagan mythology was still a welcome theme in building decoration in Christian times. PS

Fig. 1: Foundation walls (7th - 4th century BC) of the Smyrna settlement. Complex courtyard houses built in the 5th century BC over archaic single-room structures.

Fig. 2: Medusa Gate: pillar crown (capital?)

TEMPLE PRECINCT (SO-CALLED SERAPEION) [67]

The temple traditionally called the Serapeion directly west of the agora, one of the best preserved ruins in the city, was built in the 2nd century AD and converted into a church in late Roman times. At its southern narrow side, a massive podium temple rises from a temenos surrounded by two-storey colonnades. The cult, connected with water, of an unknown divinity was practised in the cella of the temple.

In the early 2nd century AD, a large terrace, approximately 100 x 75 m, was laid out on an outcropping of Bülbüldağ, over the ruins of late Hellenistic buildings, for a temple precinct. The terrace, symmetrically arranged about a north-south axis, was achieved by quarrying into the rock and using the excavated debris for levelling. The main entrance lay on the northern narrow side where a magnificent flight of steps led up from the West Road some four meters below. Another stairway led, at least from late Roman times, from the southwest corner of the agora directly to the temple.

The centre of the northern side of the terrace is occupied by a prostyle-like podium temple measuring 29.20 x 36.70 m, the portico of which rises in an eight-columned facade over an open staircase divided by a landing into two flights. The monolithic columns, approximately 14 to 15 meters tall, were crowned with Corinthian capitals, while a pediment with three doors rose above the richly decorated entablature. Engaged pilasters subdivided the rear of the portico.

Six small niches are set into each of the longitudinal walls of the cella and two more flank the 7 m wide central niche for the cult figure in the middle of the south wall. Vertical slits in all the niches served to let in water which was then drawn off by a peripheral channel in the cella floor. Two extremely narrow side aisles (only 1.23 m wide) also had five niches in their outer walls which, however, were not connected to a water supply. On the south side, narrow flights of steps led to the area above the cult figure, but it is not, at the moment, clear whether these were an exit at the rear of the temple or simply a means of reaching an attic room above the cella. The walls, made of massive blocks of local limestone from the Bülbüldağ covering a mortared rubble core, gave sufficient support for the wedge-shaped stones of conglomerate which comprised the barrel vault.

Fig. 1: Temple precinct west of the agora; overall view from the north-east

Fig. 2: Unfinished frieze block from the temple portico

Two-storeyed colonnades, each some 6 m deep, surrounded the precinct and were the subject of an exemplary investigation in the northeast corner of the temenos in 1991/92. The Corinthian architecture of the porticos rose to a height of 15 m, above which was a shed roof edged with marble tiles, but otherwise covered with clay tiles. On the surface of the stylobate, In front of each of the columns, erected 3.10 m apart, stood a base, perhaps a receptacle for votive offerings. Fragments of at least two bronze statues, found during the excavations, bear witness to the once rich furnishings. The rear wall of the colonnade was panelled, at least on the ground floor, with marble slabs, which were articulated by pilasters with relief bases and Corinthian capitals. The architecture of the colonnade is closely related to that of the palaestra of the Harbour Gymnasium [93] and, judging from the ornamentation of the capitals, was probably designed, like the entire, uniformly planned temple precinct, by the same guild of masons brought to Ephesus from Aphrodisias.

An earthquake, probably the one reported for 262 AD, and resulting fires, left the eastern temenos hall a heap of rubble. During the work of rebuilding under Theodosius I, the area was simply filled in with debris, while the architectural components of the west side, which had survived in better condition, were taken away for re-use to the neighbouring agora and elsewhere.

It was probably at this time that the cella of the temple was converted into a Christian cult room, and a presbytery, measuring 8,40 x 9m, which had been built against the east wall of the cella, was partitioned off. The surviving foundation walls suggest that a half-domed ceiling now rose above the bench for the priest, which was oriented towards the east. Adjoining to the south are the remains of a baptismal (?) font. Invocations in inscriptions to a certain John suggest that the church was consecrated to him.

The temple ruins offer a picturesque view only slightly marred by the excavations of 1913 and 1926. A portion of the facade architecture, displaying unfinished details, lies scattered over and around the open staircase, undisturbed since its destruction by an earthquake in the Middle Ages.

The names of the divinities worshipped here remains uncertain because of a lack of building inscriptions. Early on, the building was interpreted as a nymphaeum, and later as a Claudius temple. In 1926, J. KEIL gave it its current, though still not undisputed, designation of Serapeion. Indeed, the extensive use of water in the cult suggests the worship of a god of healing. PS

ÖJh 1915, B77 - 87; 1926, B265 - 279; Anz 1954, 217 - 228; 1993, G14 - 16. KEIL in: Halil Edhem Hâtıra Kitabı I (1947) 181 - 192; WILD, ANRW II 17.4 (1984) 1829ff.; EPRO 87 (1982) 188f.; Hölbl, EPRO 73 (1978) 33ff.; KOESTER in: IBID. (ed.), Pergamon. Citadel of the Gods (1998) 131f.

HARBOUR PLAIN AND NORTH SLOPE OF THE BÜLBÜLDAĞ

The harbour plain and the adjoining terraced foothills of the Bülbüldağ were among the most densely populated areas of the Hellenistic-Roman city. However, hardly any excavations have taken place here. Many buildings important to the history of the city are known only from inscriptions or, like St. Paul's Grotto, only accessible with difficulty. An inscription seems to suggest that the **West Agora**, founded by King Lysimachus, may lie in the flat, little investigated area between the Medusa gate and the marshy harbour basin. Most of the inscribed blocks found south and west of the harbour basin probably came as spolia and were not necessarily set up there. A grave relief and a sarcophagus with scenes showing sculptors at work were found at the foot of the Bülbüldağ, and may have originated from a little- investigated necropolis along the coastal highway outside the city walls. In the Byzantine period, the graves encroached on the former municipal area on the south edge of the harbour. Some of the inscriptions are, however, assumed to have been discovered *in situ*. A guild of merchants from Rhodes had a meeting house here with a **shrine of Aphrodite** and one member was honoured by a portrait crowned with a wreath. A **fishery customs house** is known from an inscription found near the southeast corner of the harbour marsh in 1929, probably in the site of the building or its vicinity. The consecration to the Emperor Nero, his wife and his mother allows a dating to the years 54 -59 AD. The site was made available by the city. At least 92 fishermen and fishmongers contributed to the costs of building. One of them contributed the building plans and supervised the work. Others donated labour and materials such as plastering, bricks and a total of at least 18 columns. Many donated from five to fifty denarii, altogether a total of over 1,100 denarii. From the contributions in work and materials the building costs can be calculated at more than 2,300 denarii, although they were probably much higher. The inscription also names a **Samothrakion** that must have housed a branch of the mystery cult of this north Aegean island. In the time of Hadrian, Junia Cominia, a member of the fishermen's guild, donated an image and altar of Isis. A **shrine of the Egyptian gods**, known since the time of Ptolemaic rule in the 3rd century BC, could also have been located in the harbour area. A trial excavation on the slope west of the so-called Serapeion [67] revealed evidence of well-furnished late Roman residential buildings. Older layers underneath can be traced back into archaic times.

AE, PS, ÜY, HZ

FiE III, 18; ÖJh 1902, B62; 1930, B48; 1993, 125 No. 17; TürkAD 30 (1992) 71 - 82; IV. Müze Kurtarma Kazıları Semineri (1993) 405 - 423; KARAGÖZ, in: Steine und Wege, Festschrift D. KNIBBE (1999) 55 - 59.

The so-called St. Paul's Grotto [71]

This building complex, normally closed to the public, was discovered by O. Benndorf around 1900 and lies opposite the so-called Serapeion, some 100 m above, on the north slope of Bülbüldağ. The grotto is a partially rock-cut room, approximately 15 x 2 m, which ends in a slightly widened chamber, once lined, perhaps, with stone slabs. It lies some 20 cm higher than the remains of a carefully levelled passageway which is now strewn with fragments of ancient buildings.

In the south part, 0.5 m above floor level, are two smoke-blackened, arched niches of different sizes. The larger one, reaching down to the floor but irregularly hewn to the right of the entrance, is covered with layers of plaster like the walls of the passageway. The upper layer, bearing chalk or charcoal inscriptions, was applied early in the 20th century. More interesting are the ancient layers with numerous scratched inscriptions containing prayers such as *Lord, help your servant, Timotheus,* and other appeals to (Saint) Paul. In 1998, unique frescos illustrating the story of St. Paul and Thekla were discovered.

Immediately adjacent to the east of the grotto was a second unworked cave. A domed anteroom erected in the Byzantine era gave access to both. RP

Circular grave: ÖJh 1956 - 58, B49ff.; Aug. Architektur, 57ff.
Water supply: FiE III, 233f.
St. Paul's Grotto: ÖJh 1956 - 58, B54.

Circular Tomb [70] and Water Pipe on the Bülbüldağ

A circular tomb, located above the agora at the edge of vegetation, may well be an interesting link between the Ionic tumulus graves and Roman tomb structures. The circular building, made out of mortared rubble masonry clad in marble, has an exterior diameter 9.7 m. Its outside wall is preserved to a height of 2.7 m. This consists of a strongly projecting base, two orthostats separated by a string course and a crowning cornice. A block with a spherical surface suggests that the roof was a cupola externally clad in marble. At the time of excavation, only the base slabs of four marble sarcophagi remained in the interior room. Construction technique, molding profiles, and several oil lamps discovered inside, all suggest a date in Augustan times.

A water pipe, the remains of which are also preserved in other places on the slope, runs above the tomb. It probably brought water from Değirmendere, a river near Kuşadası, into the city. HT

Fig. 1: Entrance to St. Paul's Grotto, present day condition

Fig. 2: View into St. Paul's Grotto

Fig. 3: Relief with representation of *homonoia* (city partnership) between Ephesus and Alexandria, found above the harbour area

1

2

3

HELLENISTIC CITY WALL ON THE BÜLBÜLDAĞ [11]

The city wall, erected under King Lysimachus and at least nine kilometres long, was built according to the most modern theories of strategy and fortification of the day, but without much consideration of aesthetic criteria. More than 3 kilometres of it is extremely well preserved on the Bülbüldağ.

A four-roomed watch tower, excavated in 1912, some 400 m west of the harbour bay (and now inaccessible), formed the starting point of the city's fortifications on the coast and guarded the highway which lead to Pygela (Kuşadası).

From here, the wall led in a straight line up the slope of a hill, called astyages in an inscription, to the vicinity of a similarly constructed tower which, in memory of the apostle's imprisonment, has been called **St. Paul's Prison [69]** since the 17th century. Its good state of preservation and convenient position make it an easily visible reference point in the Ephesian landscape.

Following a bend to the west imposed by the terrain over a small hill called *hermaion*, the city wall continued upwards and approximately eastwards rising to more than 300 m above sea level along the crest of the Bülbüldağ. From its eastern end it descended again, on a route which can no longer be traced, to the plain and on to the Magnesian Gate [10].

The defense of the Bülbüldağ area was directed from a three-roomed watch tower on a plateau probably fitted out with arsenals and cisterns. The wall is also subdivided along its length at irregular intervals by 48 single-roomed towers, each originally at least nine metres high, which served as lookout posts and emplacements for heavy weapons. The tower walls are between 1.60 and 2.50 m thick and the curtain-walls, 2.90 to 3.60 m thick and 6.50 m high. All the walls are constructed in *emplekton* technique - wall faces of bonded ashlar masonry with the space between filled with earth and small stones. The walls also had battlements and, in some places, possibly also covered walkways with arrow-slit embrasures facing the enemy. Twenty-three stairways allowed quick access to the walls. So far, nineteen sally-ports have been discovered in the eastern portion of the Bülbüldağ, but not a single one in the west between the *hermaion* and tower 23.

PS

ÖJh 1915, B183 - 196; SEITERLE, The Hellenistic city wall of Ephesus (Ph. D.-Thesis Zürich 1970).

Fig. 1: Course of the city wall on the Bülbüldağ

Fig. 2: So-called St. Paul's Prison

MARBLE STREET [60]

The marble-paved street running tangentially to the east side of library place and the Tetragonos Agora [61] was, in Imperial times, both main street and a part of the Processional Way. It was lined on the east by a colonnade, and on the west by the Hall of Nero [62], which was higher up and therefore inaccessible from the street.

The eastern colonnade ends some 40 m before the corner of the southern analemma wall of the great theatre [75] which projects into the street. Behind, lie single rooms which were used for commercial purposes, and entrances to the partially excavated multi-storied residential buildings. In size and furnishing these are much more modest than the terrace houses [50 - 51] on Curetes Street. The entire slope of the Panayırdağ above was probably covered with residential houses with their entrances on two roads with the modern names of Academy Street [42] and Bath Street [39].

The west side of Marble Street is also occupied by the colonnade of the so-called Hall of Nero (see above, s.v. Tetragonos Agora [62]), whose floor level is 1.70 m above the street. An observation platform at the entrance to the Hall of Nero, close to its north end, allows a nice view over the agora.

The appearance of the street was determined to a large degree by the terrace wall of bolstered ashlar. A marble block, set in plaster near the middle of the hall, has drawings carved into it - a female bust with a polos crown, a foot and a heart with an arrow - which have frequently, but incorrectly, been interpreted as a signboard for the so-called "House of Pleasure" [43].

In a late phase of the city, Marble Street was crossed in front of the

theatre, by the city wall [77] which was built up against the rear wall of the stage building. The immense marble frame of the "city gate" consists of re-used blocks. Behind it, the street widens out into the Arcadiane [82] and the **Theatre Plaza**, measuring 20 by 30 m, with its flight of several wide steps up to the theatre.

An elongated fountain was built along its south side; the structural form of this installation has not yet been closely examined. Stairs led from the north end of the Hall of Nero as well as from Theatre Plaza to the lower lying street which also gave access to the north gate of the agora.

HT

Fig. 1: Marble Street and the Hall of Nero; some of the broken pieces of the great columns and entablature of the hall lie along Marble Street

THE GREAT THEATRE [75]

This giant structure faces west from an appropriate site on the slope of the Panayırdağ, and was an important station on the route of the Artemis procession. Because of its function as urban focal point and place of assembly, the theatre, with its performances and artistic competitions, was especially important to the infrastructure of the city. When it was completed in Roman Imperial times, the theatre seated some 25,000 spectators. The present day appearance is due largely to renovation in late Roman times. According to the Bible (*Acts of the Apostles, XIX. 24 - 34*), the silversmith Demetrius opposed St. Paul in the theatre and provoked the shouted chorus *great is Artemis of the Ephesians.*

There seems to be no evidence of a theatre prior to the 1st century BC so that the old assumption that Lysimachus had it built for his founding of *Arsinoeia* could only apply to selecting its location. Only after about 100 BC, when the small well house [74] at the northwest corner of the stage building was constructed, can the existence of a theatre really be verified. It is probably not by chance that the lists of the *agonotheteis* (contest referees) begin here in 51 BC. Since lively building activity took place in general at the end of the 2nd century, it is likely that the theatre came into being as the centre of the new, Romanised harbour city of Ephesus, probably in connection with the establishment of the Roman province of Asia in 133 BC. Certainly it began as a smaller structure consisting of a simple scene or stage building and an *orchestra* with a drainage channel and a auditorium (koilon) of, perhaps, only one tier of seats. Undoubtedly the ground plan extended beyond a semicircle, with its diagonal side entrances (*parodoi*), already extant.

With the rapid growth of the city under Augustus, an enlargement of the theatre soon became necessary. Thus, from the time of Nero, especially during the great building boom in the reign of Domitian (according to an inscription, between 87 and 92 AD), the upper storey of the stage building was erected with a richly structured aediculated façade. In front of this, a *logeion* was built in the orchestra on a low *proscenium* and the orchestra was enlarged. A second tier of seats was constructed at this time, with the seating built on vaulted substructures adjacent to the lateral retaining walls (analemmata).

The first circular walkway (*diazoma*) is set between the seating circles. High

Fig. 1: Aerial view from south-west (SCHIFFLEITNER)

vaulted staircases **within the *analemmata***, completed shortly after 100 AD according to a building inscription in the south, gave access to the upper part of the theatre. It is still unclear when the theatre attained its final form with the building of the third seating circle, which rests partly on even higher vaulted chambers, and the blind top storey of the stage building, although this must have occurred before 262 AD.

Narrow stairways divided the lowest tier of seats into eleven wedge-shaped *kerkides* or *selides* and, by doubling the number of stairways, the two upper tiers of seats each had 21 sectors, whereby the number of rows of seats in each sector rose from 19 to 20 and 23. On the wide second *diazoma* stood stone benches called *prohedria*, in which sat the directors of the performances and the referees of the contests.

Originally, these officials had seats at the edge of the smaller *orchestra*. We learn this from inscriptions, which also tell us in which sectors the various *corporate* civic groups had their reserved seats: the *boule* (city council), the *gerousia*, (council of elders), the *ephebes* (youth association), the *phyles* (tribes), the *theologians* (main speakers), etc.

The text of a long inscription put up in the theatre states that in 104 AD a C. Vibius Salutaris gave an extremely generous donation for the Artemis procession and had silver statues of the goddess and of the Emperor Trajan set up here during the public gatherings. Around the middle of the 2nd century an awning was put up, which was repaired in the year 205 and again around 240 AD.

The uppermost zone of the theatre was partly occupied by a sort of tribune, in front of which stood a colonnade. This could possibly be the *Nemeseion* named in an inscription, the sanctuary of Nemesis, the goddess of contests, which was given a portico prior to the middle of the 3rd century AD.

Parts of the building collapsed during the great earthquake of 262 AD. This led to fundamental alterations to the staircases in the north analemma. Further destruction as a result of a later earthquake (between 359 and 366 AD at the earliest) resulted in the complete abandonment of the uppermost area of the north analemma. In the meantime the classical purpose of the theatre gave way to more plebeian usage, including vulgar games and gladiatorial contests, as is shown by several graffiti on the front wall of the stage. In the 8th century AD, the theatre was incorporated into the defense system of the city, by then much reduced in size. SK

FiE II; HÖRMANN, JdI 38/39, 1923/24, 275 - 345; JdI 41, 1926, 67 - 73; ATALAY, EfesHMY 1, 1972, 46 - 48; KAYAN, EfesHMY 1, 1972, 56 - 64; ÖJh 1994, G29 - 31; ÖJh 1998, G 24 - 29. 41 - 43.

Fig. 1: Reconstruction of the stage façade (WILBERG – NIEMANN)

Fig. 2: Scratched drawings of coarse theatre scenes on the base of the stage wall

HELLENISTIC WELL HOUSE [74]

North of the stage building of the great theatre [75] is a simple, well-preserved well house from Hellenistic times.

The well house, initially 3.82 m long and 1.45 m deep, is of marble with high stretcher and low header courses. The orthostats of the rear wall are set off with a cornice molding and have three lion-head gargoyles which spouted water into a water basin, now missing. The side walls end in antae with capitals which, together with two Ionic columns, supported a triple-fascia architrave and a denticulated cornice as well as the marble coffered ceiling of the well house.

With the exception of the Ionic capitals, none of the moldings show relief ornamentation; perhaps the decoration was painted. In Roman times, the modest Hellenistic structure was extended about two metres in depth, and the front of the new anteroom was separated from the street by two un-fluted columns (see fig. 2. on page 171). An inscription on one of these columns states that the water was conducted here from the Marnas. MB, DT

THEATRE GYMNASIUM [79]

The building at the eastern end of the Arcadiane [82] is of the Ephesian bath-gymnasium type. The form of its palaestra with a tribune shows that it had a specific function.

The large courtyard of the palaestra, measuring 70 x 30 m, is surrounded on three sides by colonnades with mosaic floors. In front of the baths are four rows of seat-steps and an inclined area for standing-room, so that a larger number of people could observe and perhaps judge or referee the activities in the palaestra courtyard.

The bathing portion of the complex, only partially excavated and thus inaccessible, has a series of large halls on its north and south sides, oriented respectively on a transverse and longitudinal axis.

The large middle room (IV) housed warm bathing pools and the narrow outer rooms can be interpreted as apodyteria. Between these are two elongated U-shaped rooms which served as recreation rooms and lobbies. The middle part of the inner room is thought to be a frigidarium (III) because of its *natatio*. The large middle room (V) in the north of the structure was probably used as a hall for the Imperial cult. Training for sports may have taken place in the adjacent Xystoi (so-called Halls of Verulanus [94]). HT

Hellenistic Well House: FiE III, 266ff.
Theatre Gymnasium: ÖJh 25, 1929, B42ff.; 1930, B 18.

Fig. 1: Plan (1:4000) of the ancient district of the city, called *Coressus*, between the theatre and the harbour and north of the Arcadiane

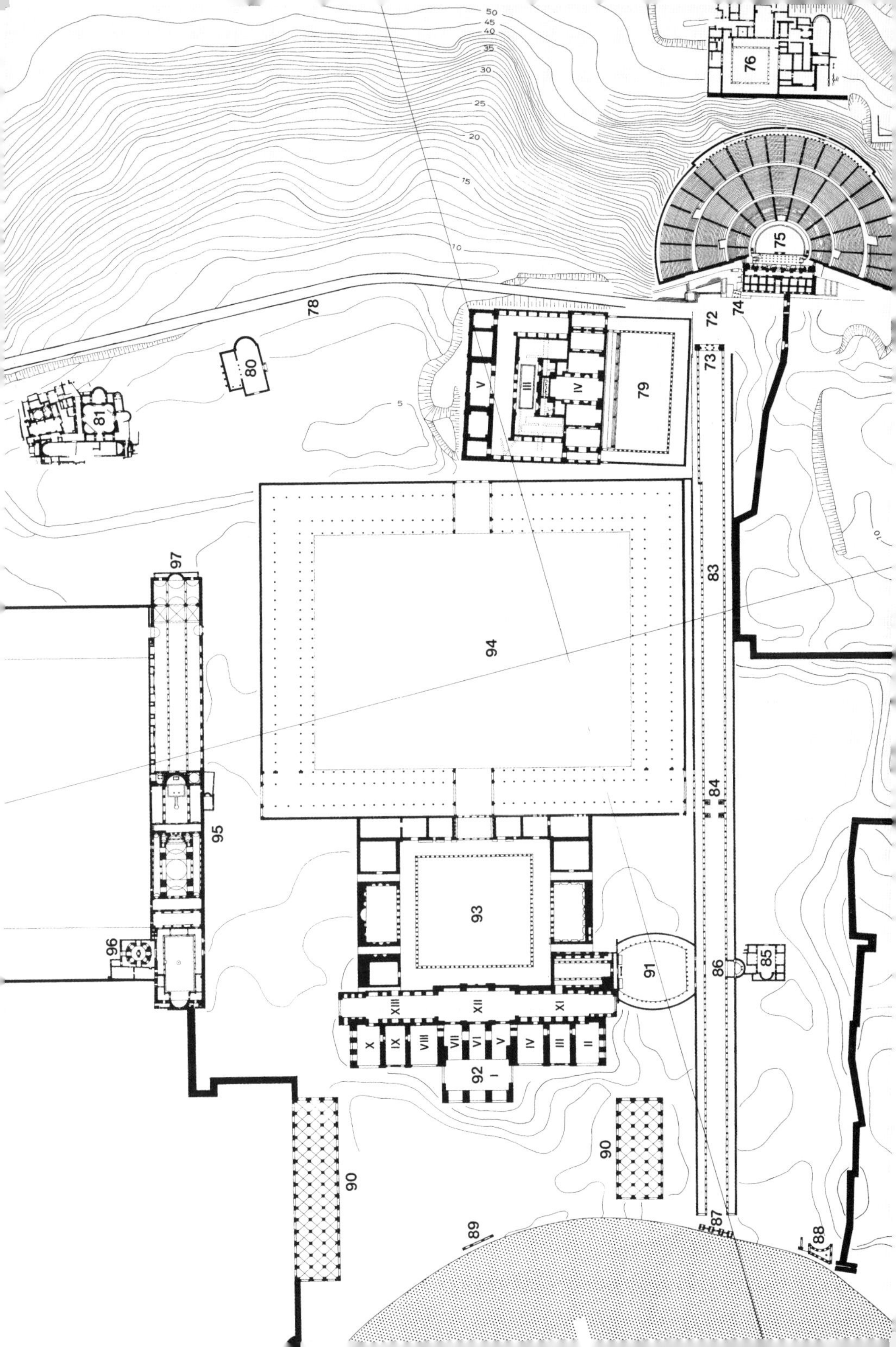

50
45
40
35
30
25
20
15
10
5
10
72
73
74
75
76
78
79
80
81
83
84
85
86
87
88
89
90
90
91
92
93
94
95
96
97
III
IV
V
I
II
III
IV
V
VI
VII
VIII
IX
X
XI
XII
XIII

THEATRE STREET *(PLATEIA IN CORESSUS)* [78]

The continuation of the Plateia, already slightly displaced towards Marble Street [60] by the theatre [75], starts to diverge from the rectangular city grid at the north-east corner of the Theatre Gymnasium and again follows, as at the Embolos [36], the route of the old Processional Way, which was at this point apparently called *plateia in coressus* in ancient times. It first bends slightly to the north-west, then turns again to the north-east in the direction of the Byzantine well house [101] and the Byzantine Palace [81].

The street owes its appearance, as revealed by excavations conducted by the Ephesus Museum Selçuk since 1974, to late Roman renovation following earthquakes. Column bases and monolithic columns of the porticos were found *in situ* on both sides of the marble - paved street, with shops arranged behind them. The street was 7.7 m wide and the porticoes 4.1 m (east side) and 3.7 m (west side) deep. One of them was perhaps called the *Stoa of Servilius*. Inscriptions on columns describing an endowment by Dionysius Nicephorus in the 1st half of the 3rd century AD states that the halls, which he had restored, were made over bay by bay by various craftsmen's guilds. The beginning of another street was discovered on the west side of the street 15 m south of the apsidal building [80], which ran in an east-west direction at a right angle to the Plateia.

A Byzantine well, the relief blocks of which come from the Temple of Domitian [30], is located on the west side of this road. Today, the Plateia provides the only access to the Stadium [104] and the Vedius Gymnasium [106]. There is a plan to extend the tourist path to this part of the site after completion of excavation and restoration work by the Ephesus Museum Selçuk. PB, DT

Plateia: ÖJh 1985, 71 - 77.
Absidal building: ÖJh 1926, B261 - 265.

Apsidal Building [80]

North of the road junction mentioned above, lies an almost 40 m long building of the 5th or 6th century AD with its surviving high eastern apse. Apparently the structure consisted of only two rooms and is oriented similarly to the older part of the Byzantine Palace [81] further to the north. The ground plan and orientation, as well as a giant marble basin lying next to it (the so-called baptismal font of St. John), suggest an early Byzantine church, but it was more likely a secular building. The marble basin comes from one of the baths, like the one in the baptistery [96] of the Church of Mary. SK

Fig. 1: The *plateia in Coressus*, view to the south. It is intended that the tourist path shall, in future, be laid out on its ancient course in the direction of the stadium (SCHIFFLEITNER)

STADIUM [104]

At the base of a spur of the northwest flank of the Panayırdağ is a largely unexcavated depression covering an area of 3.3 hectares. The site has always been recognized as a stadium from the shape of the depression, and the immense ruins on its west side, but research to determine the precise nature of the structure, its ground plan, as well as its architectural development, only began in 1993.

It is presumed that, originally, there was seating only on the southern slope of the spur, and that in front of this was the running track and, in the western end, a starting-gate (*aphesis*) from Hellenistic times.

The monumental expansion of the stadium, which probably took place in the time of Nero, was made possible by the donations of individuals such as the freedman C. Stertinius Orpex. Thus, the ground plan was completed with the construction of an enormous chamber and a vaulted substructure in the north, which supported seats as in the south. The north front, through which stairways led to the seating zones, must have been an impressive sight with its towering ashlar wall. Arched gates in the monumental west façade gave access to tunnels which supported the seating and permitted circulation around the stadium. The running track of well-tamped earth was lined with orthostat slabs bearing reliefs and was some 180 m long. The elliptical area (*sphendone* = hollow), set into the curve in the east, measured about 50 x 40 m. Its original purpose is uncertain. It seems to have been sealed off from the running track in late Roman times, and the general opinion is that gladiatorial contests were held here. An unusual feature is a water channel under the southern seating, the continuation of an **aqueduct [5]** leading to the city.

ÖJh 1912, B 180ff.; 1994, G21ff.; 1995, G22f.; 1996, G18 - 20; 1997, G19 - 22; 1998, G20 - 23.

The earthquake of 262 AD destroyed whole sections of the stadium. The north façade was not rebuilt, but the south gate and the western portions were re-erected using the old building elements. The *sphendone* seems to have attained its characteristic form at this time.

The later series of earthquakes between 359 and 366 AD presumably also caused damage in the stadium. In the 5th century, a **church [105]** was built into the west end of the northern tunnel, of which only the entrance-atrium has been uncovered. As a result, the running track was filled in and apparently used as a field. A cemetery with brick masonry tombs developed around the church. This late phase lasted at least into the 12th century. SK

Fig. 1: South gate of the stadium. View from the so-called Ionic acropolis

Fig. 2: Stadium and Vedius Gymnasium (SCHIFFLEITNER)

VEDIUS GYMNASIUM [106]

The Vedius Gymnasium lies in the far north directly against the city wall, and covers an area of 135 x 75 metres. Like most Ephesian gymnasia, it is a bath-gymnasium complex with the baths and palaestra symmetrically arranged along an east-west longitudinal axis. In Roman times the building was known as the *Gymnasium in Coressus.*

The colonnaded street between the gymnasium and the stadium leads to an opening in the Byzantine city wall at the east end of the stadium, the so-called Coressian Gate. This triple-gated *propylon*, the side walls of which are richly articulated, gave access to the 40 x 50 m courtyard of the palaestra. The architrave of the five metre wide columned hall which surrounded the courtyard on all four sides, bore an inscription dedicating the building to Antoninus Pius and the entire imperial family. Another inscription names M. Claudius P. Vedius Antoninus Phaedrus, a well-known Ephesian patron of public buildings, and his wife Flavia Papiana.

Next to the propylon lies the latrine, a structure 17 m long, that is open in the middle and surrounded by columns. The latrine was accessible from the colonnaded street through an anteroom, and a doorway connected it to the baths. Inscriptions on its columns bear witness to the fact that latrines were leased out to nearby business associations and craftsmen's guilds.

Öjh 24, 1929, B20 - 45; Öjh 25, 1929, B21 -38; 1930, B17 - 20; 1959, B23ff.

A large exedra lies on the western side of the palaestra and is delimited by an additional row of columns. Magnificently fitted out with a two-storey columnar display, incrusted with marble, and containing relief panels, its centre portion is accentuated by a semicircular niche. Statues, among them one of Androclus, the founder of the city, portrayed as a hunting youth, and one of the donor, were placed between the columns. The exedra has been interpreted as an Imperial hall for Antoninus Pius who did not have his own temple in Ephesus. A statue of Emperor Antoninus Pius was certainly set up in the centre niche, in front of which an altar was found *in situ*. The Imperial hall was flanked by two small rooms which were also accessible from the palaestra and had doors to the adjoining large hall. This double T-shaped hall was framed at its eastern end by the Imperial hall and two small rooms (I and II) and to the west by the frigidarium (IV) with the large natatio (cold plunge). This large room (III), subdivided by pillars which supported the vaulted ceiling, can be considered as a spacious lounge and ambulatory.

Fig. 1: Plan (1:2000) of northern Coressus

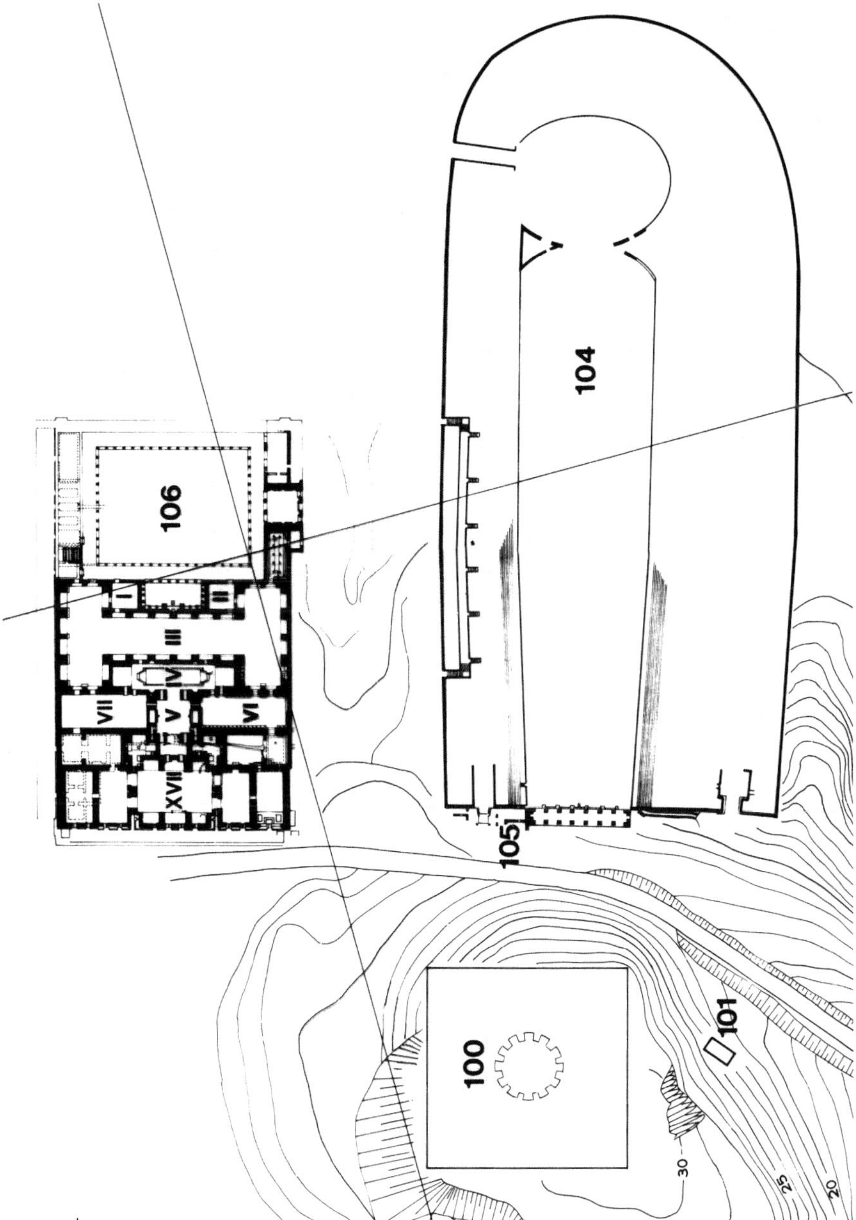
104
105
106
I
II
III
IV
V
VI
VII
XVII
100
101
99
102
30
25
20
N

The three main bathing rooms are arranged along the longitudinal axis of the bath building: the frigidarium with the natatio, the tepidarium (V) which served as a sluice and, at the western end, the large caldarium (XVII) on both sides of which are two additional bathing halls, all fitted out with wall and floor heating. Two elongated rooms (VI and VII) lie on the north-south axis of the bath building. The southernmost room, which originally had direct access from the colonnaded street, was provided with a bench and small securable box, which identify it as an *apodyterium* (dressing-room). Outdoor clothing was probably hung on wall hooks.

SK, HT

THE SO-CALLED BYZANTINE BANQUETING HOUSE ON PANAYIRDAĞ [76]

On a building terrace above the theatre, a spacious residential complex was erected with its accommodations grouped around three sides of a peristyle court oriented towards the west.

The ground plan of this splendid residential home, which was discovered at the beginning of the century in the course of survey and excavation work, can hardly be seen today because of the heavy overgrowth of vegetation which covers the area - only a few stray architectural building elements point to the existence of a building. The complex, designed in Hellenistic times, and altered through renovations and extensions into a residence which must have satisfied the expectations of the highest levels of society, was occupied into Late Antiquity.

Fig. 1: Statue of a river god (now in the Archaeological Museum İzmir), found in the cold water basin of the Vedius Gymnasium

Fig. 2: Hellenistic well house near the theatre (SCHIFFLEITNER)

The usual designation as banqueting house is incorrect. Exedrae with mosaic floors were arranged about the north-south axis of the spacious peristyle court which was probably open to the west. The surrounding rooms adjoin a private bath complex in the north-east and an apsidal banqueting room in the south-east, also with richly decorated mosaic floors.

South of the villa stands a single-room building. KEIL designated it as a gathering place for devotees of Dionysus mentioned in inscriptions on the wall revetments. The room measures 40.5 m by 11.5 m, and was divided longitudinally into five units by columns and walls.

Directly above the theatre lie several heavy, limestone foundations which are thought to have been substructures for honorary tombs or victory monuments.

UO

Living accommodation: ÖJh 1932, B8ff.; Anz 1981, 142; MILTNER, Ephesos, Stadt der Artemis und des Johannes (1958) 79f.

Club house: ÖJh 1932, B12ff.

ARCADIANE [82]

Between the harbour and the theatre runs a magnificent boulevard, 528 m long (1,800 Roman feet, or 3 stadia), which must have been in existence at least since early Roman times. It received its final form under Emperor Arcadius (395 - 408 AD), probably during restoration work after the earthquake of 359 - 366 AD. The colonnades on both sides were re-erected using older building materials, and the roadway between was 11 m wide. In the fifth century, the Arcadiane was equipped with street lights.

Originally, the Arcadiane could be closed at each end by a gate (see the middle Harbour Gate [87]). In the sixth century AD, a **four-column monument [84]**, a structure consisting of highly decorative, free-standing columns on individual stepped bases, was erected approximately in the middle. The round pedestal bases, two meters high, have niches bearing Christian symbols. It is assumed that the capitals carried statues of the four evangelists. The monument was no doubt intended to make new arrivals aware of the Christian character of the city.

A construction known as the **church south of the Arcadiane [85]**, stands directly opposite the *atrium thermarum* of the Harbour Gymnasium [91] behind an exedra with water basins [86] on the south side of the Arcadiane. The building, 22 m long, might appear, at first glance, to be a church, but the existence of an apse at the west end weakens this interpretation.

LATE ANTIQUE CITY WALL [77]

A new city wall surrounding the Coressian quarter was certainly built in the sixth or early seventh century BC as protection against the Arabs. This wall ran from the South Harbour Gate [88] at a distance of 70 m from the Arcadiane, opening out south of the four-column monument, apparently to include a large building, before continuing directly alongside the street to the middle of the theatre, whose towering south analemma was incorporated as a bastion.

To the north, this late city wall can be identified at the western end of the Church of Mary [95], the western edge of the Olympieion [98], at the so-called Crevice Temple [103] and in front of the Vedius Gymnasium [106]. From there, the eastern ring wall follows the western semicircle of the Stadium [104], running over the ridge and around the two peaks of the Panayırdağ before returning in the direction of the Theatre. The Hellenistic-early Roman centre remained outside the new fortification. SK

Arcadiane: RE Suppl. XII, 1597.
Four-column monument: FiE I, 132 - 142.
Byzantine city wall: MÜLLER-WIENER, IstMitt 11, 1961, 86ff.
So-called church: ÖJh 1902, B60f.

Fig. 1: Four-column monument, perhaps a memorial for the evangelists

HARBOUR BATHS AND HALLS OF VERULANUS [91-94]

The large bath-gymnasium complex north of the Arcadiane [82] is planned symmetrically about an east-west axis. It consists of three parts: baths, gymnasium and athletic grounds (see the plan on page 165). The building may have been begun at the time of Domitian and it was rebuilt before the middle of the 4th century AD - probably after a destruction. A round forecourt and an atrium then formed the main entrance.

Three gateways lead from the Arcadiane, 90 m west of the four-column monument [84], onto a square monumentally laid out in Late Antiquity. Directly opposite the south side of the colonnaded street is a semicircular **exedra [86]** which, in Late Antiquity, was given a columnar display that certainly contained statues, to form the decorative rear wall of a water basin.

The forecourt of the baths [91], approximately 45 m long, is noteworthy for the curved east and west boundaries. Three sides are surrounded by colonnades with mosaics. The courtyard, on the other hand, had a marble pavement in which many spolia were found, among them, numerous relief fragments of the so-called Parthian altar. In the middle of its north side, a stairway flanked by two spirally fluted columns led into a room which an inscription calls *atrium thermarum Constantianarum* (337-350 AD).

On either side of the stairway stand fountain basins, each made of five reused relief slabs from a bull's head garland frieze, and possibly parts of the Parthian Monument whose structure has yet to be identified. The atrium, 33 m long and 15 m wide, is subdivided by two rows of columns into a wide centre aisle and two side aisles. The outer walls are articulated by brick pillars and the niches between them were spanned by vaults which, together with the columns, carried the barrel vaults of the ceiling. The columns and capitals are also reused. It is believed, on the basis of finds, that the atrium also functioned as a shop.

FiE I, 182ff.; ÖJh 1898, B63ff., 71ff.; ÖJh 1912, B161ff.; FRIESEN, Twice Neokoros (EPRO 116, 1993).

A visit to the imposing ruins, whose piers have seemed to be on the verge of collapse for some 100 years, is rewarding even though only the forecourt, the atrium and the marble hall have been excavated. All the rest is piled high with debris and therefore somewhat confusing.

Fig. 1: The fountain on the forecourt of the Harbour Baths

Fig. 2: Buildings on the harbour (model in the Ephesus Museum Vienna)

The atrium served as the entrance to the baths complex adjoining to the north-west, and to the gymnasium in the north-east. The purely investigatory excavation of the **baths complex [92]** revealed a ground plan which was extended by a second suite of rooms.

The atrium gave access to the apodyterium, a changing room and lounge (XI), with a symmetrically arranged counterpart (XIII) lying opposite. Between these rooms is the frigidarium (XII) with its large cold plunge (*natatio*). Three intermediate rooms (V - VII) adjoining directly to the west, were probably tepidaria (lukewarm bathing rooms), which formed the transition to the large caldarium (I) projecting from the west front, with its six warm bathing pools arranged in the niches between the pillars. This spacious room, with vaults 18 m high, had large west windows and a heating system for floor and walls. The remaining rooms (II - IV, VIII - X) were used for ball games, boxing, physical training, massage, personal hygiene, and cosmetics. Both floors and walls of the rooms were panelled with marble, as can be seen from the numerous holes in the pillars and walls for metal mounting hooks.

The middle part of the complex, the so-called **Harbour Gymnasium [93]** - its ancient designation was probably *Gymnasium of the Emperors* - consists of a square peristyle court, 90 m on each side which corresponds to the palaestra of a Greek gymnasium. It is surrounded on three sides by rooms of varying size and furnishings and served, in Roman times, for cultural and spiritual edification. Two large rooms in the middle of the north and south sides are conspicuous by their lavish furnishings. The so-called marble room, already uncovered in 1898, was luxuriously fitted out on the three wall sides with a three-storey display of columns and niches containing numerous statues carved from thirteen kinds of coloured marble. This can be interpreted as the Imperial hall and was, according to inscriptions by the well-known Ephesian, Tib. Claudius Aristion, erected in honour of the Emperor Domitian. The bronze statue of a victorious athlete cleaning his bronze scraper - now displayed in the Ephesus Museum Vienna - was found in the Imperial hall.

On the middle axis of the gymnasium, a gate with two rows of four columns led onto a large sports field, which measured 20 x 240 m, called ***Xystoi*** [94] in antiquity. It was surrounded by a three-aisled colonnade, whose broad middle aisle, perhaps uncovered, served as a running track. The square, open court was used for different kinds of sports, and, planted with tree, had a park-like atmosphere. In the Hadrianic period, the Imperial priest Claudius Verulanus donated the marble panelling of the colonnade walls, but the structure itself is older. HT

Fig. 1: The Harbour Gymnasium in the morning mist

Fig. 2: The Harbour Gymnasium (Reconstruction NIEMANN, 1902)

a
b

HARBOUR GATES AND QUAY STRUCTURES [87 - 89]

The harbour, vitally important as a place of transfer from land to sea transport, was also a deciding factor in the development of the city. With the progressive silting up of the Caystros, the harbour area steadily moved westward from the archaic period to Roman times. In its present form, the harbour basin, enclosed by a jetty wall, is still easily recognizable in the landscape when viewed from the surrounding hills. It dates back to building activity in the second century AD. Between 1896 and 1899 three gate structures were found which mark the places where large roads entered the harbour area.

The **Southern Harbour Gate [88]** is dated to the Severan period (around 200 AD) by an inscription stating that it was donated by an Asiarch, and this is confirmed by the architectural decoration. The building gains additional appeal through its successful adaptation to the triangular space between the road and the quay wall running diagonally to it. The **Middle Harbour Gate [87]** stands at the end of the Arcadiane. Three passageways were separated by supports, each consisting of four Ionic columns. It was probably built during the time of Hadrian.

The **Northern Harbour Gate [89]** is only very poorly preserved. The remains of inscriptions permit its interpretation as an arch in honour of a *proconsul Asiae* from the middle of the third century AD. A road, 10 m wide, runs between the gates and the quay. Its course is characterized by straight stretches which meet at hexagonal angles, and by circular sections.

FiE III, 169 - 223; ZABEHLICKY, in: H. MALAY (ed.), Erol Atalay Memorial (1991) 197 - 205; ZABEHLICKY, in: Koester (ed.), Ephesos (Harvard Theol. St. 41, 1995) 201 - 215.

Excavations from 1987 - 1989 on the south side of the harbour basin brought to light a longer stretch of the quay wall. Here it runs in an arc to a pier where the wall turns back to the south before bending to the west. Underwater excavations have determined that the ancient basin was four to six meters deep. This quay was probably erected in the times of Trajan and Hadrian. Sinking of the land with respect to sea-level required that the quay be raised in height by at least 0.80 m in Late Antiquity. To the south, and further towards the city, the quay was paved. Late Roman buildings were also discovered along it closer to the city. HZ

Fig. 1: Harbour gate of the Arcadiane (Reconstruction NIEMANN)

Market buildings at the Harbour [90]

A large, presumably open square stands out between the west of the Harbour Baths [91] and the quay wall, which is bordered to the south and the north by two similar buildings - three-aisled colonnades 25 m wide and 60 or 120 m long. The design of the southern building at the west end of the Arcadiane [82] can still be easily recogniced; the longer northern building now lies outside the fence. The buildings are constructed of four rows of square limestone pillars carrying brick groin vaults, whose fragmentary bases are preserved. Neither building shows signs of walls between the pillars and, apart from their location beside the harbour, there are no characteristic features to suggest that they were warehouses, as they have, up to now, been called. They can, therefore, be designated simply as open porticoes for business and trade.

HT

CHURCH OF MARY AND EPISCOPIUM [95 – 97]

The western part of the south colonnade of the Olympieion [98] was modified in Late Antiquity for the installation of a church complex some 145 m long, and the eastern part was adapted as a palace-like building.

There is no doubt as to the identification with the Church of Mary [95], the Ephesian episcopal church, made famous by the Council of 431 AD; the most recent examination of the ruins have shown, however, that the present Christian buildings are later than this date*; the open sides of the colonnade, dating to Imperial times, were closed with walls of large limestone blocks only around 500 AD, and the colonnade divided into two halves by the large eastern apse.

In its initial phase, the church consisted of the peristyle-like atrium in the west, measuring 43 x 25m (the floor of which is covered with numerous inscriptions from Imperial times), a transverse narthex, and a three-aisled church hall measuring 74 x 29 m. The middle aisle 13 m wide, was supported by forty columns, an age-old expression of magnitude that symbolized divine expectation).

* The problem of the discrepancy in the (much later) Acts of the Council, according to which the Council was held in the "so-called Church of Mary", can only be solved by a philological-archaeological examination of the surviving texts. Although the Council (or a part of it) may have been held in the (adapted) stoa, this was probably not yet a regular Church of Mary.

FiE IV/1, KARWIESE, Die Marienkirche in Ephesos (DenkschrWien 200, 1989); ÖJh 1991 - 92, G8f.; 1993, G16ff.; 1994, G14ff.; 1995, G8 - 15; 1997, G12 - 18; 1998, G13 - 20.

The large apse at the eastern end was entirely built out of stones from the Roman colonnade. The two tall pillars flanking the apse were presumably transferred here from the east chalkidicum of the **colonnade**. Pastophoria for the storage of liturgical offerings were situated on both sides of the apse; from here stairs led to the former upper storey.

The **baptistery [96]** is built on to the north side of the atrium. Its tholos-like baptismal room, clad with marble, is transformed into an octagon by niches (eight symbolizes perfection). The piscina for adult baptism is sunk into the centre of the floor.

Presumably on account of earthquake damage (perhaps 557 AD), the church was rebuilt with extensive alterations. By giving up the columns, the church

Fig. 1: Church of Mary, view to the east (PESENDORFER)

Fig. 2: The sacred ruins served as a burial place in the middle ages

51
50

hall was divided into two parts, whereby the eastern part became a pillar basilica only 23 m long with a narrow narthex. In the presbytery, in front of the apse, originally stood a simple table altar which was later replaced by a marble one. This, in turn, eventually yielded to the semicircular synthronos (bench for the priest). The substructure of the ambo (pulpit) extends from the protruding presbytery, bounded by the templon, into the main body of the church.

In the 2nd phase of building, the western part of the church was erected in an entirely different style. This new brick building, measuring 37 x 29 m, had narrow side aisles and a longitudinal vault supported by massive pillars, as well as a central dome over the nave. This terminated at both sides in an apse with chapel-like pastophories. In the west, an inner narthex was added. In this way, an "ecclesiastical family" came into being with the bishop's residence in the east and the "parish" in the west. The large marble basin in front of the apse of the parish church could well be from one of the large baths and could have been used as a late font (cf. Apsidal building [80]).

It is highly probable that the Church of Mary was detrimentally affected by the Arab assault of 654/5 AD, and its status as episcopal church lost. Nevertheless it continued to function, as is attested by later building projects, such as the connecting door which was broken through the apse of the brick church, or the numerous burials dating at least into the 11th century.

The introduction of **burials** in the interior of the church, from well-sealed tombs to simple graves, most likely began only in the 2nd phase during the 2nd half of the 6th century: Various signs reveal that initially only clergymen could be buried in the eastern part (i.e.,only in the narthex). From then on, a cemetery developed, not only inside, but outside the brick church as well. Apparently for this reason, a small chapel was built onto the southern exterior of the eastern part. Certain clues, such as the presence of glazed pottery, indicate that the northern cemetery in particular can be traced into the 14th century when the Selçuk dynasty of Aydınoğlu ruled here and left the holy places to the Christians.

To the east of the great eastern apse are rooms which seem to have had a public character on account of a bathing basin, a latrine and a well. This could have been a complex for the clergy because the archbishop's residence, the **Episcopium [97]**, might have developed further eastward. Here, living rooms and halls for official purposes, typical of the old Ephesian palaces, surround a central peristyle court which could only be built into the stoa after the architecture of the east chalkidicum of Imperial times had

Fig. 1: Church of Mary, condition before restoration. View into the presbytery and the great apse from the west been removed. A connection with the Church of Mary is strongly suggested by a number of factors: a date around or shortly after 500 AD, its proximity to the church, the shape of individual rooms, and finds which include a censer and glass bottle with the representation of a menorah. To the west, also belonging to this bishop's palace, is a bath complex with the classic bathing rooms in which the frigidarium (cold room) had a marble-lined pool. Judging from the finds, the Episcopium was abandoned in 654/5 AD, when the bishop moved to *Haghios Theologos* (Ayasoluk). The building deteriorated and was filled with rubble. SK

The Church of Mary was extensively renovated between 1984 and 1988 by the Ephesus Museum in Selçuk with the support of the QUATMAN Foundation. In the narthex and nave, and particularly in the area of the presbytery, columns, pillars, door jambs and entire walls were re-erected both to give the visitor the impression of the church and at the same time to afford better protection to the fabric of the building.

MB

OLYMPIEION [98] - TEMPLE OF THE EMPEROR HADRIAN

A temple was built in the Corinthian order after 130 AD in the former coastal swamp. On the basis of dating evidence, its colossal size and other criteria, it could only have been the official provincial temple for Emperor Hadrian as Zeus Olympios. Around 400 AD, the building was levelled down to its foundations.

Coastal-geographical investigations have shown that the area southwest of the acropolis hill was initially a marine and later a coastal swamp, which filled in at the beginning of the 2nd century AD.

The complex built on top of this newly reclaimed land covered an area 350 x 225 m, and thus closely approaches the area of the Temple of Artemis. A temple rose to a presumed height of some 25 m in the middle of an open square which was surrounded on all sides by colonnades. The massive foundations measuring 85 by 57 m show that two large rows of blocks for the columns were first erected on a "floating raft" and then filled with massive amounts of *opus caementitium* (mortared rubble masonry).

The known remains point to a pseudodipteros of 74 columns with a peristasis length of 60 m. The lower part of the only capital found to date, now displayed in the peristasis along with a few other architectural fragments, points to a Corinthian order. The roof appears to have been covered with marble tiles like that of the Temple of Artemis.

Next to the temple, a three-aisled basilican south hall measuring 263 m in length, was important as a monumental entrance into the temenos. In the middle section, across from the northwest gate of the Halls of Verulanus, the side walls were opened by pillars. At both ends were rooms with exedrae (*chalkidica*), which extended beyond the side walls of the Olympieion-temenos. This stoa, as well as additional halls inside the court, indicates much building activity which in turn, points to multiple usage of the complex, presumably in connection with subsequent Imperial cults.

The temple was destroyed around 400 AD, apparently by Christian zealots, and its building components taken down and burned to lime on the site. The halls, however, were left standing. About 100 years later, the block foundations of the temple were completely dismantled, mainly to extract the metal clamps and dowels. SK

Fig. 1: The Olympieion was levelled deep into the foundations

Fig. 2: Part of the entablature of the halls of the Olympieion

Anz 1977, 208f.; 1984, 210f.; 1986, 84f.; ÖJh 1994, G16; 1995, G12 - 15; SCHERRER, in: Steine und Wege, Festschrift D. KNIBBE (1999) 137 - 144.

BYZANTINE PALACE (SO-CALLED SARHOŞ HAMAM) [81]

Approximately 70 m east of the Episcopium stands a somewhat bewildering complex which has up to now been identified as a bath, but is more likely to have been a palace. For although bathing rooms exist, they belong to an older building of the 1st century AD, whose orientation follows that of the nearby Processional Way. This bath was later incorporated into a complex with a somewhat different orientation, which is distinguished by a specific succession of rooms. A double-apsed hall, 45 m long, gives access to a large tetra-conch room, which in turn leads to a small apsed room to the east; a chapel could well have adjoined to the south. Although the structure is by no means yet fully understood, its accentuated, ceremonial character and the existing datable features suggest an interpretation as a palace of the Late Antique *proconsul* or the Byzantine *strategos*, the governor of the military district of Thrakesion, which was established after 610 AD. Thus the spiritual and secular centres would have stood side by side in an Ephesus which was already concentrated on the Coressian quarter.

IONIAN ACROPOLIS [99]

The free-standing hill to the west of the stadium [104] originally protruded like a hook into the bay. Its identification as the Coressus Acropolis, founded about 1000 BC by Greek immigrants under King Androclus, is already probable on the basis of its position and shape, which are typical of early Ionic settlements (cf. the capes from Myonessus to Miletus). In addition to Corressus' association with it, the identification is supported by the fact that the hill is an outcrop of the Panayırdağ, which, with its deep ravines and crevasses, is itself recognisable as the Tracheia ("the jagged") mentioned in the foundation legend. Furthermore, the castle is said to have been joined to the Artemis temple [1] by a cable seven stadia (approx. 1,300 m) long when the Lydians laid siege to it around 565 BC. This also clearly points to the stadium area. The Acropolis was razed under Croesus and building operations carried out here up into Late Antiquity, so that older finds are few, although they date back at least into the 8th century BC.

Byzantine palace: RE Suppl. XII, 1642f.

Ionian Acropolis: KARWIESE, in: Pro Arte Antiqua II. Festschrift H. KENNER (1986) 212ff.; Anz 1979, 253f.

Fig. 1: The heavily overgrown ruins of the so-called Sarhoş Hamam

Fig. 2: Byzantine well house on the slope of the so-called Acropolis hill

Buildings on the Acropolis

The hill plateau, levelled in Roman Imperial times, is occupied by a columned courtyard, measuring 65 m on each side, with a rotunda with twelve radial walls on a rock-hewn base at the centre. Judging from the few remaining architectural fragments, some of which are now stored in front of the stadium, the building stems from about 200 AD. It has always been interpreted as a ***Macellum* [100]** (meat market), but inscriptions say that this was in the Agora [61], so another interpretation is necessary. An **early Byzantine well house [101]** with an entrance hall and open peristyle court lies on the south-eastern shoulder of the hill next to the Plateia [78] leading to the stadium. In addition to the simple relief panels of the water basin showing tendrils and crosses, several marble sculptures still *in situ* (now in the museums in Selçuk and İzmir), were also found here.

Parts of **Hellenistic fortifications [102]** remain on the south-west shoulder of the hill, which, according to the built-in spolia and finds from the soil fill behind the wall, were presumably erected hastily in 191 BC against the approaching Romans. These walls were incorporated into a typical peristyle house with mosaic floors, which was probably built after the severe earthquake of 262 AD. More recent building projects dating to the 6th century were found on the north-western shoulder of the hill. The building remains hewn out of the rock on the north-west flank cannot as yet be interpreted; they were also largely destroyed by a **quarry** in Imperial times or Late Antiquity. The crest of the outcrop towards the north-west bears the remains of a small temple, the substructure of which is almost entirely hewn out of the living rock. Since the structure crosses a deep natural fissure, it is called the **Crevice Temple [103]**. It may be said, with some certainty, to have originally served as an oracular temple of Apollo, which was erected as a prostyle measuring 22 x 15 m around 400 BC (perhaps in gratitude for the victory over the Athenians in the year 409 BC). On the basis of numerous Hellenistic, robed female statuettes found here, and a comment made by Stephanos of Byzantium, Leto, mother of the twins Apollo and Artemis, may also have been worshipped here. SK

So-called Macellum: RE Suppl. XII, 1645.
Well house: JOBST, in: Studien zur spätant. u. byzant. Kunst, Festschrift W. DEICHMANN (MRGZM 10, 1986) 47ff.
Fortifications and Peristyle house: ANZ 1983, 114.
Crevice Temple: ANZ 1978, 9f.; 1979, 130.

Fig. 1: Central Rotunda with twelve radial walls in the so-called Macellum on the plateau of the Acropolis

Fig. 2: Crevice Temple, detail view

BASILICA OF ST. JOHN AND CITADEL ON THE AYASOLUK

Already in the 2nd century AD, a Christian tradition developed which identified the Ephesian *John the Theologian*, as the apostle and author of the gospel and the Apocalypse. In the 5th century, an early Christian church was built over a simple grave on the south slope of the Ayasoluk. This was replaced in the middle of the 6th century, under the patronage of Emperor Justinian, by a monumental domed basilica with a cross-shaped ground plan. When the Ephesians moved to the Ayasoluk, the Basilica of St. John soon assumed the function of the episcopal cathedral and the hill was fortified. The basilica has been extensively renovated and the surrounding area laid out as an archaeological park.

Gate of Persecution and the fortress walls [157]

The fortress walls, which enclose the Basilica of St. John together with its adjoining buildings, have twenty towers and four entrances. The most magnificent and best-preserved is the main entrance at the south side, the so-called Gate of Persecution. The building material used for the gates and fortress walls consisted exclusively of spolia from Ephesus and the Temple of Artemis.

The Gate of Persecution is flanked by two square towers and the gateway is vaulted over. An acanthus frieze adorns the gateway and a sarcophagus relief with grape-gathering cupids is arranged above it. Originally, there were also other sarcophagus slabs showing fleeing girls and armed men representing the discovery by Odysseus of Achilles among the daughters of king Lykomedes on the island of Skiros. The gate received its name when these reliefs were misinterpreted by early European travellers as scenes of persecution. The slabs were carried off to England in the 19th century, and are now displayed in Woburn Abbey.

The exterior walls of the church show two phases of construction. The inner walls, with alternating stone and brick courses, are interrupted by niches, especially in the west around the Atrium [160] and in the south part of the eastern entrance gate.

Fig. 1: The so-called Gate of Persecution. Main entrance to the settlement on the Ayasoluk

Fig. 2: Basilica of St. John, model

These walls from Justinianic and pre-Justinianic times were not erected as fortress walls but as terrace walls, adapted to the requirements of the building site for the Basilica of St. John. At the same time, monotony was avoided by the installation of the niches which accentuated the grandiose character of the complex. No evidence has been found to indicate that the inner walls were strengthened by towers.

The 2.2 m thick outer walls, their outer surfaces built of spolia from the Stadium [104] and other ancient monuments, did serve, however, as actual fortifications. Filled on their inside with mortar and broken stones and strengthened by towers, they were built in great haste against the onslaught of the Arabs in the 8th and 9th centuries. Most of the defence towers have a pentagonal ground plan but square towers are to be found on the south and round towers on the west sides.

The Basilica of St. John [152]

Between the Gate of Persecution and the church lay a propylon, the entrance of which was spanned by three arches, each carried by four columns. It belonged to the church built prior to Justinian. A topographical map of Ephesus can be seen in the left part.

> A topographical map of Ephesus can be seen in the left part of the propylon. A general plan and reconstruction drawings of ancient buildings are mounted on the brick wall of the Basilica of St. John.

The large narthex gate gives access to the church. Five doors lead into the nave and adjacent aisles from the narthex, which was roofed either with five smaller domes or a roof sloping towards the atrium.

Including the atrium, the church was 130 m long and had a cross-shaped ground plan. The cross-shaped nave was roofed with six massive domes. The middle dome, over the site of the alleged grave of the apostle, was higher and larger than the others. Each dome rested on pendentives supported by marble and brick pillars, some of which have been recently restored. Between the pillars stood columns which further subdivided the side aisles and carried the side vaults of the upper storey (see p. 45, fig. 1). These columns, monoliths of blue-veined marble, have been entirely restored. The monograms of Emperor Justinian and his wife Theodora are engraved on the imposts of the early Byzantine capitals, still in Ionic style. This shows that the church was built with imperial sponsorship.

In the middle nave, in front of the bema, lie parts of the great ambo. The connecting path between bema and ambo can also be seen. The bema, lying over the site of the grave, is raised above the church floor by two steps. Four serpentine columns, part of the ciborium, stood in the centre of the bema, the floor of which was paved with coloured marble slabs. Earlier excavations uncovered three graves in the crypt below, one of which is said to be the grave of the apostle. The columns and architraves of the bema date from the middle Byzantine period (10th - 12th centuries AD). Like the synthronos, they have also been partly restored in the last few years.

A topographical map of Ephesus can be seen in the left part of the propylon. A general plan and reconstruction drawings of ancient buildings are mounted on the brick wall of the Basilica of St. John.

Chapel and Treasure House (skeuophylakion) [158]

The building added on to the outside of the church's northern transept, now covered by a wooden roof, was originally planned and built as part of the treasure house, but was converted into a chapel in the 10th - 11th centuries AD. The wall paintings in the apse are very well preserved. In the middle, Christ is shown flanked by John and another saint. The treasure chamber on the left side of the chapel, excavated in 1987, was a two-storey, centrally planned building. It was covered with a dome 6.3 m in diameter. The adjacent parts formed a cross into which chambers were built. Here the valuable possessions of the church and the vessels for the Holy Mass were kept. It can be assumed that there were also niches in the upper storey. The only known counterpart to this building is the treasure house of the Hagia Sophia in Constantinople, modern Istanbul.

Basilica: FiE IV/3; ÖJh 1959, B375ff.; 1960, B66ff.; GÜLTEKİN – SEZER – BARAN, TürkAD 12/1, 1962, 49ff.

Baptistery: IstMitt 32 (1982) 236 - 257.

Baptistery [159]

Crossing the narrow, marble-paved foyer of the treasure house, one passes through a doorway which gives access to the eastern part of the baptistery apse. Prayers were probably said in this room after the baptism. There are mosaics on the floor of the apse, and an altar table which was set up here at the time of the crusades (12th century AD). The door on the west side leads into the central part of the octagonal baptistery, in the centre of which a baptismal font is sunk into the floor. The floors and walls are clad with marble revetment and there are niches and columns. The dome was decorated with glass mosaics as indicated by fragments found during the excavation. Three steps lead down into the baptismal font on both sides. A square basin next to the font served to hold the holy water. This type of baptismal font was used for adult baptism in the 5th and 6th centuries AD. The baptismal ceremony only took place on particular days of the year.

The room on the western side of the apse, symmetrical to the eastern one, was used for preparation and prayers before the baptism. The baptistery was built in the 5th century AD, at the same time as the wood-roofed basilica.

In the Justinianic rebuilding of the church, the old form was retained. The fountain in the aisle between the baptistery and the church was once a Roman sarcophagus, which was brought from Ephesus in the 6th century AD and reworked.

The room on the western side of the baptistery apse leads into the open in front of the western gate of the citadel. The atrium of the church is on the left side of the two towers which flank the entrance.

Atrium of the Basilica of St. John [160]

The atrium, measuring 34 by 47 m, is built on to the west front of the church. When this area was laid out, substructures were erected under the porticoes enclosing the atrium to level the slope of the building site. The inner courtyard is enclosed on three sides by halls with arcades supported by columns. On the outside of these porticoes, there are covered walks, unique in Byzantine architecture, which were closed off by decorated partition panels and offered a view over the harbour of Ephesus. Restoration work on the Corinthian columns and capitals still continues.

Excavations were also carried out in the area between the atrium and the İsa bey Mosque [170]. The architectural debris that can be seen here probably came from a pre-Justinian monastery.

Byzantine Aqueduct [156]

Drinking water from the springs between Belevi and Selçuk was brought by an aqueduct to the Byzantine settlement on Ayasoluk hill and to the Basilica of St. John - the centre of pilgrimage in the Middle Ages. Coming from the north, the conduit passes through the gorge of Şirince, crosses the present day centre of the town of Selçuk, and ends east of the so-called Gate of Persecution. The aqueduct pillars, which are still well-preserved near the railway station, are 15 m high. They were constructed of Ephesian marble spolia which were reshaped for their new use. Among them, and worthy of note, are Ionic capitals of the archaic period (Ephesus Museum Selçuk, large courtyard). The arches spanning them were made of brick. At the end of the water conduit, there is a large water tank which has been excavated and restored in recent years. Fluted columns and composite capitals, from the middle of the 2nd century AD, were brought from Ephesus and reused in the construction of the cistern, which was covered over with arches and barrel vaults.

Fig. 1: The Byzantine aqueduct about 1900

Fig. 2: Appearance of the aqueduct near the railway station in 1995

Hotel
ARTEMİS

The Byzantine-Selçuk Citadel [151]

North of the Basilica of St. John, a well-preserved citadel stands on the highest point of the Ayasoluk hill above the oldest settlement of Ephesus [155]. The encircling walls, built of stone and brick set into a mortar core and fortified with 15 towers, can be traced back to Byzantine, Selçuk, and Ottoman times. Gates in the east and west give direct access to the inner fortress without being connected to the outer stronghold. Narrow stairs on the inside of the enclosing walls lead to the passageways along the battlements and to the embrasures. Inside the citadel are stone-paved streets and several cisterns of varying size. A mosque and a church are built on the hilltop. The apse of the church was turned into a cistern by the Selçuks. In addition, there is, to the west of the mosque, a ruined building which in all probability was the bath (Hamam) of the citadel. MB

Fig. 1: The citadel, view from the archaeological park

THE EPHESUS MUSEUM (EFES MÜZESİ SELÇUK)

The majority of the works displayed in the museum, which is open throughout the year, come from the excavations in Ephesus. The scope of activities, however, also extends to Clarus and other nearby excavations. In terms of exhibits, the number of visitors and cultural activities, the Ephesus Museum is the most important regional museum in Turkey.

The finds from the early excavations in Ephesus are mainly divided among the museums of Istanbul, Izmir, Vienna and London. In 1929, a depot was erected in Ephesus. This formed the basis for the museum which was greatly extended in 1964 and 1976.

The rapidly expanding collection at the Selçuk museum consists of some 50,000 objects. All ages, beginning with the fourth millennium BC, are represented, but there is an emphasis on Classical antiquity through the Middle Ages. The museum is divided into two departments: the archaeological and the ethnographic (Arasta).

This guidebook describes the state of the museum in the spring of 1999. To save space, inventory numbers are often not cited. The comprehensive "Führer durch das Archäologische Museum in Selçuk" (1974; available in archaeological libraries) can be consulted for further information. The description of the rooms follows the advised itinerary, and, as the objects are not numbered, their precise location is given.

Occasional exhibitions of contemporary art are held in the adjoining art gallery, Hikmet Gürçay (Room 10), in an attempt to build a bridge between antique and contemporary art.

DT, ÜY, GT

Fig. 1: Plan of the museum. The arrows show the advised itinerary. The digits 1-10 indicate the room numbers, 11 marks the entrance to the Arasta.

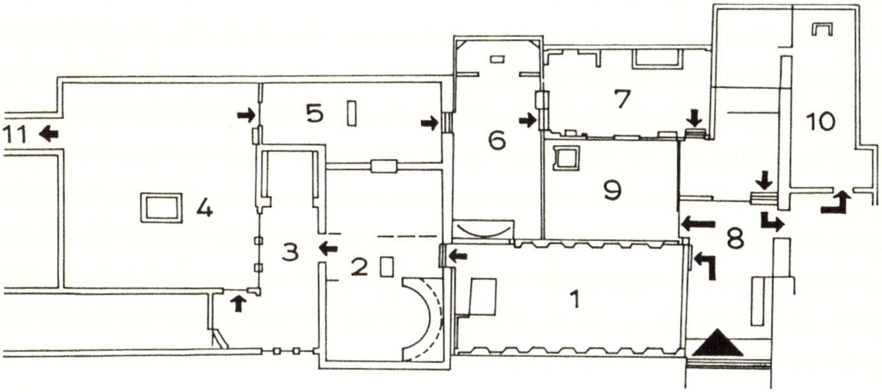

ROOM 1 (ROOM OF THE TERRACE HOUSES)

The room, newly laid out in 1994, mainly displays furnishings, elements of the artistic decoration (sculptures and wall paintings) and small finds from the Terrace Houses (H1 and H2) on Curetes Street.

Wall to the left of the entrance: ground plan of Terrace House 2; next to it, various photos of the excavations.

Left corner: Statue of Hygieia and statuette of male god, most probably Zeus.

Left longitudinal wall, display case 1: head of Aesclepius (H 1), terracotta; little altars with Aesclepian snakes and statuettes of Aesclepius and Hygieia on either side; in addition, medical and cosmetic utensils, scales, pieces of jewellery (burial gifts); a small marble double-basket, various glass vessels, among them - as a rarity - a glass amphora (H 2).

Display case 2: late Hellenistic hero-relief, terracotta (H 1)[1]; small portrait heads and a statuette of fire damaged ivory, 3rd century AD; three bronze statuettes of divinities: Athena, Isis and Serapis, 2nd/3rd century AD (all H 2)[2]; Aphrodite untying her sandals, terracotta (H 1); in the middle, a tray made out of cobalt glass (H 2); two small portrait busts from the 3rd century AD (H 2); small sculptures of gods: two little busts of Dionysus, double Nemesis, small head of Attis made out of calcite, 2nd century AD (H 2)[3]; torso of a Triton, miniature portrait from the 3rd century AD (so-called Plato); to the right, a toy, flutes, knife handles of bone (H 2), spinning whorls and, above, a cosmetic(?) utensil with a figure of Aphrodite carved out of bone (H 2). Table of pavonazetto and a marble vase (H 2).

Left rear corner: reproduction of NW-corner of the so-called Socrates room (H 2/7); with a statuette of Artemis as huntress in the niche in its third (?) usage, and painted layers of various periods on the walls: right, Socrates, 1st century AD; left, the muse Clio, around 400 AD (?)[4].

Rear wall: portrait of Socrates from the 4th/5th century AD (Baths of Scholasticia); altar and thymiaterion (stand for a censer); feet for table and bench (original and cast).

1 Anz 1991, 145; cf. horsemen reliefs in large courtyard (no. 4).

2 İNAN – ALFÖLDI-ROSENBAUM (1979) no. 161. 160. 158; ÖJh 1972 - 75, B461f.

3 İNAN – ALFÖLDI-ROSENBAUM (1979) no. 139. 143; EPRO 68/1 (1978) 329ff. Pl. 77; FiE X/1, no. 103.

4 FiE VIII/1, 93ff.; ÖJh Beih. 2 (1972) 176ff.

Figs. 1 + 2: Emperor Tiberius and his mother Livia (H2)

Fig. 3: Wall painting (H2/7): Socrates

Fig. 4: Late antique portrait of Menander, writer of comedies (SCHIFFLEITNER)

1

2

3

4

Small display case to the left of the entrance to Room 2: bronze statuette of an Egyptian Amun-priest from the 6th century BC (H 2)[5].

Right longitudinal wall: two wall paintings, 4th and 3rd century AD: table-servant and enthroned Demeter (chamber underneath the so-called Temple of Domitian)[6]; relief with two cupids (copy), one grieving while leaning on a torch, the other plucking a lyre; bust of Tiberius in armour, portrait head of Livia and a bronze snake, an ensemble put together in late Roman times (H 2/38)[7]; portrait bust of the poet Menander, 4th/5th century AD (Baths of Scholasticia)[8]; portrait of a priestess of the Imperial cult with crowned bust and another priest's portrait, 3rd century AD[9]; terracotta of a pygmy in the display case; Priapus statue; bust of Emperor Marcus Aurelius in armour, 161 - 180 (H 2)[10]; base of honour for an athlete with victory wreaths (Stairway alley 1).

Room centre: marble table and altar of Zeus (H 2/38); archaistic Artemis statuette, Hadrianic period (H 2); bronze portrait, 3rd century AD (H 1)[11]; bronze oinochoe, around 470 BC (Torbalı)[12]; folding chair-and-table with bronze boxer *protome*, marble bath (H 2); two cupids on dolphins (utensil portion of bronze, fountain figure of marble); small fountain with river god; Eros with hare and dog (H 1); head of Eros, Hadrianic period replica after the *Eros with Bow* by Lysippus[13].

ROOM 2 (ROOM OF THE FOUNTAIN HOUSES)

This room mainly houses the sculptural furnishings of three Ephesian well houses (late 1st and beginning of 2nd century AD).

From entrance area to centre of room: The colossal recumbent figure of a youth in the middle of the room (Inv. 1556) - a personification of the river god Marnas - together with a statue of the river Claseas (fragment in the depot) and a seated statue of Zeus (head: Inv. 1055, left at the entrance to the room) were made for the Fountain of Domitian (built in 92/93 AD) which was erected at the end of the water conduit fed by these rivers. This group of figures was displayed in the fountain niche facing the State Agora. The late Hellenistic

Fig 1: Marble bust of Emperor Marcus Aurelius (H 2)

Fig. 2: Eros and dolphin

Fig. 3: River god Marnas from the Fountain of Domitian

5 WINTER, ZÄS 97, 1971, 146ff.

6 STROCKA, ÖJh 1972 - 75, B469, B471.

7 ÖJh 1983, B105ff.; VETTERS in: Echo, Festschrift J. TRENTINI (1990) 315ff.

8 GOETTE, Studien zu römischen Togadarstellungen (1990) 70.D 11.E 16; FITTSCHEN; AM 106, 1991, 252.

9 İNAN – ROSENBAUM (1966) no. 178 and İNAN – ALFÖLDI-ROSENBAUM (1979) no. 137.

10 ÖJh 1983, 125ff.

11 FULLERTON, The Archaistic Style in Roman Statuary (1990) 17f. P.21. 30.; İNAN – ROSENBAUM (1966) no. 160.

12 VON BOTHMER, in: Studies in Classical Art and Archaeology, Festschrift VON BLANCKENHAGEN (1979) 63ff.

13 FiE X/1, no. 64.

2

1

3

Aphrodite (torso at the room entrance) was found, like the Polyphemus group (see below), near the large niche on Domitian Square[14].

Left entrance wall: The late Hellenistic Polyphemus group was originally set up as a secondary decoration of the large fountain niche facing Domitian Square[15]. The theme of the group is the defeat of Polyphemus (cf. Homer, Odyssey IX pp.318.): left, two companions bringing the wine (wineskin to the left); Polyphemus in the centre, takes a cup from Odysseus; right, sharpening the stake used to blind the giant. In front of Polyphemus lie two Greeks already killed by him. According to the theory of ANDREAE, which has recently been refuted, the group originally decorated the pediment of the temple on the State Agora[16].

Opposite left wall: statues from the façade of the Nymphaeum Traiani (102-114 AD)[17]: reclining satyr (Inv. 754); female portrait statue (Inv. 1404), perhaps a member of the donor's family; a robed Dionysus (Inv. 1405); Androclus (?) with his hunting dog (Inv. 773); Aphrodite or a fountain nymph (Inv. 768) all belonged to the original arrangement. A later rearrangement also included the late Antonine nude Dionysus (Inv. 769) and a work in high relief, approximately one hundred years older, of a man with a coat and shoes carrying a staff (Inv. 1403). The two fragments of grape leaf columns were found at the nymphaeum (Inv. 1727, 1555).

Right half of the room: selection of the sculptural furnishings ($1^{st}/2^{nd}$ century AD) of the fountain (*hydrekdocheion*) of C. Laecanius Bassus and a base for an honorary statue of the donor (Inv. 1986)[18]; on the partition, three tritons of a sea-thiasos (Inv. 1576, 1578, 1579) and the torso of a satyr (Inv. 1577); on the entrance wall and adjoining, a series of female figures: statues of the double Nemesis (?) (Inv. 1580, 1583)[19], an Aphrodite (?) with well preserved head (Inv. 1582); a torso of the *Hera of Ephesus* type (Inv. 1581); two female statues (Inv. 1584, 1585).

Opposite: private portraits and idealized sculpture found at various sites: replica of a classical *strategos* head, late 2nd century AD (Inv. 704); Hellenistic herm busts (Inv. 1833); portrait head of a Hellenistic ruler, so-called Lysimachus (Inv. 1846)[20]. Idealized female heads from early Imperial times: replica of the head of *Artemis Colonna* (Inv. 708); head with bow in its hair (Inv. 1554). Two late republican male portraits (Inv. 1064, 2559) and a Hadrianic female portrait (Inv. 764)[21].

Fig. 1: Polyphemus group, set up in Late Antiquity in the Fountain of Domitian (Schiffleitner)

Fig. 2 + 3: Nymphaeum Traiani: naked Dionysus (Schiffleitner) and so-called Androclus

14 STROCKA, in: Festschrift J. İNAN (1989) 76ff.; Aphrodite: ÖJh Beih. 2 (1972) 165ff.

15 Reconstruction: ANDREAE, in: Festschrift F. BROMMER (1977) 1ff.; Odysseus (1982) 69ff.

16 s. Reconstruction in large courtyard (4); LENZ, IstMitt 48, 1998, 237ff.

17 FLEISCHER, in: Pro Arte Antiqua I, Festschrift H. KENNER (1982) 123f.

18 IvE II 695.; ÖJh 1972-75, B421ff.

19 FLEISCHER, in: Festschrift E. AKURGAL, Anadolu 22, 1981-83 (1989) 132. 136.

20 SMITH, Hellenistic Royal Portraits (1988) 158 no. 19, 67f.

21 İNAN – ROSENBAUM (1966) 136; İNAN – ALFÖLDI-ROSENBAUM (1979) no. 122. 133.

1

2

3

ROOM 3 (ROOM OF THE NEW FINDS AND SMALL FINDS)

On display in this room since 1998 are mainly the new and unpublished finds of the French excavations in Claros, the famous sanctuary of Apollo, some 20 km northwest of Ephesus. In addition, there is a display case with lamps from Ephesus and another showing coins and gold objects (i.g. diadems) found in graves at various locations in western Asia minor. The ivory frieze from Terrace House 2 is another masterpiece of fine art.

Entrance wall, left: lamps found in Ephesus with examples from the 6th century BC to the Byzantine era. The right side of the second row shows lamps produced in Ephesus[22].

Large display case: the ivory frieze[23] which fell down from the upper storey of Terrace House 2, where it was originally used as a lintel decoration, and was found in room H 2/SR 18. It reproduces in miniature form a large frieze portraying three scenes of Trajan's campaigns against barbarians, separated by Victories and personifications of provinces (right, Arabia with the dromedary); in the centre, the emperor himself. Also, parts of small battle friezes, panels and two small friezes with theatre scenes (2nd/3rd century AD). These once decorated a small casket.

22 Concerning the lamps cf. FiE IV/2, 96ff.

23 ÖJh 1972 - 75, pp.B541.; Forschungen und Funde, Festschrift B. NEUTSCH (1980) 95ff.; AA 1983, 539ff.; Papers of the 12th Intern. Congr. of Class. Archaeology in Athens II (1988) 233ff.

Fig. 1: Large ivory frieze from Terrace House 2, detail

Fig. 2: Examples of Ephesian minting: Artemis Ephesia, Gold (121/120 BC); bee-stamp, silver (5th/4th century BC)

LARGE COURTYARD (4)

Especially noteworthy in the large courtyard are pieces of the Hellenistic Belevi mausoleum, the archaic "Kouros of Pamucak", the inscription with the early Imperial customs law of the province of Asia, a collection of capitals and a selection of reliefs.

Near the entrance, right: Side panel of an ambo with the sacrifice of Isaac (Kuşadası, 6th century AD); two slabs from the Meander frieze of the Artemision altar (see Room 6).

Left wall: three inscriptions:[24] inscription of the city Clazomenai honoring Ephesus on the occasion of the first Ephesian Imperial Neocorus(89/90 AD), edict of the proconsul Lucius Antonius Albus about keeping the harbour clean (146/147 AD), Greek-Latin building document about the renewal of street pavement by the proconsul Sextus Appuleius (23/22 BC); adjacent to it, a slab from a Hellenistic weapons frieze at the Magnesian Gate[25].

Front part of the courtyard, right: marbles from the Belevi mausoleum[26]: column, parts of roof decoration (vase, griffin and griffin head) and sarcophagus (coffin from the 1st phase, lid figure from the 2nd phase); in the centre of the courtyard, sundial from the reign of the Emperor Caracalla (212 - 217 AD).

Rear part of the courtyard: under the reconstruction of a pediment with the Polyphemus group[27]: Ephesian capitals, from archaic to Byzantine and Selçuk periods. Behind these, a bridge leads over mosaics from a Roman villa near Yeniköy (south of Selçuk) to the threshold of the ethnographic section. Behind the mosaics are slabs of a weapons frieze from a triumphal monument of early Imperial times and reliefs from the heroon on Curetes Street[28]. In a niche to the left: The unfinished archaic statue of a young male (*Kouros*, 6th century BC), found at the beach of Pamucak; an inscribed stele from Claros and the *Monumentum Ephesinum*, the customs tariff law of the province of Asia (62 AD)[29]; nearby, three statues of robed females: two of these are Roman copies of Hellenistic masterpieces, the *Hera Campana* (Inv. 40) and the *Munich Klio* (Inv. 646). The third is a new find from Clarus (Inv. 2/74/92).

24 IvE II 235. Ia 23. II 459.

25 AntK 25, 1982, 148 fig. 27,3.

26 FiE VI; FLEISCHER, Studien zur seleukidischen Kunst I (1991) 23ff.

27 See Room 2; the original parts of the reconstruction have a yellowish hue.

28 Weapons frieze: TUCHELT, IstMitt Beih. 26 (1979) 113. 117f.; Heroon-Reliefs: ÖJh 1995, 88f.

29 ENGELMANN – KNIBBE, Das Zollgesetz der Provinz Asia. EA 14 (1989).

Fig. 1: Mausoleum at Belevi: sarcophagus and roof decorations
Fig. 2: Androclus heroon: relief showing a horseman fighting against a foot-soldier

Wall opposite the courtyard entrance: Hellenistic votive block with friezes of the gods[30]; grave reliefs[31] of different types from Hellenistic and Imperial times: two gladiator reliefs (left Thrax; right, duel, with referee; from the road to Şirince) - in the centre, a muse sarcophagus[32] of the 3rd century AD from Ephesus; to the left of this a collection of ostotheques; to the right, two inscriptions from the archaic necropolis at the State Agora[33] - further right, stele of a youth (Metropolis, Inv. 7/3/89), donation relief (Inv. 409), horsemen reliefs (Ephesus: Inv. 702 and 253; Metropolis: Inv. 8/3/89)[31]. Near the entrance to Room 5: seated statue of the donor of the East Gymnasium, the so-called Vedia Phaedrina, as well as standing robed female statues from the Nymphaeum Traiani. MA

ROOM 5 (ROOM OF THE GRAVE FINDS)

This room mainly houses finds from graves in Ephesus and its surroundings, together with items consecrated to Cybele.

Entrance area, left, display case 1: late Mycenaean finds of the 14th century BC (LH III A 2) from a grave near the Gate of Persecution[34].

Display case 2: Weapons and other finds from an early Bronze age grave in Didyma.

Last display case, left: a Harpocrates (with finger on the mouth) and a ram from the late archaic necropolis under the State Agora[35] and other clay figurines and vessels from the vicinity of Metropolis (Torbalı).

Entrance area, right: wall text with a description of the methods of burial in Anatolia: to the right, a gravestone of the 1st century BC (Inv. 11/34/84) in the form of a funeral repast from the vicinity of the Church of Mary[36]; left, an unusually richly detailed funeral repast relief from Terrace House 2, dating to the beginning of the 1st century BC (Inv. 1590)[37]; adjacent to it, a wall text telling the story of the Seven Sleepers legend and, below, three ostotheques of the 2nd and 3rd centuries AD from the vicinity of Ephesus (right: Inv. 452;

30 ATALAY, RA 1985/2, 195ff.
31 PFUHL – MÖBIUS, Die ostgriechischen Grabreliefs II (1979) 293ff. and no. 1326. 1358. 1473.
32 KOCH – SICHTERMANN, Römische Sarkophage (1982) 523.
33 IvE II 110. 115
34 GÜLTEKİN – BARAN, TürkAD 13/2, 1964, 122ff.
35 LANGMANN, in: Festschrift F. EICHLER (1967) 103ff.
36 BÜYÜKKOLANCI, TürkAD 27/1, 1988, 73ff.
37 Anz 1963, 55 Pl. 2; PFUHL – MÖBIUS, Die ostgriechischen Grabreliefs II (1979) no. 1867 Pl. 267.

Fig. 1: Mausoleum at Belevi: sarcophagus and roof decorations

Fig. 2: Androclus heroon: relief showing a horseman fighting against a foot-soldier middle: Inv. 1847; left: no number). After the display case with the glass finds, a gravestone portraying a farewell scene of the second half of the 2nd century BC from Selçuk-Abuhayattepe (Inv. 1/22/80)[38]; beside it, a single-figure gravestone depicting Olympias, from Ortaklar (Inv. 422) from the 1st century BC[39]. From the last quarter of the 2nd century BC, the high quality gravestone, to the left of the middle of the room, from the vicinity of the East Gymnasium (Inv. 1845)[40].

Display case with glass finds: an amphoriscus and an alabastron, both cast in a sand mould, from the necropolis under the State Agora again.

Left side of the room: a wall text showing the development of the cult of the Great Mother Goddess of Anatolia; below it, representations and reliefs of Meter from various locations: left, Meter-Cybele of about 470 BC (Inv. 148) from Ephesus (?); in the niche: the enthroned goddess flanked by two lions (Inv. 2256) (late Hellenistic?), found reused in the Saadet-Hatun baths; on either side of the niche, two late Hellenistic reliefs: Inv. 55 and 1858 from the Meter shrine on Panayırdağ as well as Inv. 55/15/74 from Metropolis and Inv. 1629, found near the Basilica of St. John. Meter-Cybele shown in a standard manner, in each case flanked by a youthful Hermes (?) and an older god, probably Zeus[41].

38 ÖJh 1981/82, B13ff.; also see note 36.
39 ÖJh 1913, 178ff.; 1955, B56.
40 AA 1973, 231ff.
41 NAUMANN, Die Ikonographie der Kybele in der phrygischen und griechischen Kunst, IstMitt Beih. 28 (1983); VERMASEREN, CCCAI (EPRO 50/1, 1987); Heinzel, in: Steine und Wege, Festschrift D. KNIBBE (1999) 35-42

ROOM 6 (ROOM OF ARTEMIS EPHESIA)

Figures of Artemis Ephesia and finds from the Artemision are displayed in this room, in addition to finds that have some connection with the temple and cult of Artemis.

ARTEMIS TEMPLE

Wall opposite the entrance to the room: provisional reconstruction of the tendril cyma from the 4th century BC temple, consisting of five small fragments (which do not join together), as well as lion head spouts (Inv. 541); below, fragments of Ionic cyma from the cornice (Inv. 5/23/83; 1626 and 6/23/83 - the one lying on top of the lost denticulation was reworked into a capital of the St. John's Basilica). The head (Inv. 1908), from about 340/330 BC, on the right side of the passage to Room 7, belongs to the relief columns of the temple[42].

THE ALTAR IN THE COURTYARD OF THE ARTEMISION

To the left of the entrance to the room: provisional reconstruction of the 4th century BC altar base, consisting of a orthostate with a relief of a lath-fence (Inv. 7/23/83), meander block (Inv. 8/23/83) and a frieze with a copy of the amazon relief of the *Sciarra-Lansdowne* type (the original is in the Ephesos Museum, Vienna). The original marble head from the second quarter of the 4th century in the display case also belongs to this frieze. The corner capital (Inv. 1/23/83) in the corner of the room has been attributed to the columnar architecture above the altar base. The horse's body (Inv. 2/23/83) and head (Inv. 1959) belong to the akroteria[43]. Next to them, parts of the lead pipe water conduit, most of which is still in situ, from the courtyard altar. Above, a block with a lotus-palmette frieze (Inv. 3/23/83) from the uppermost zone (*epicranitis*) of the oven used for burnt offerings in the interior of the altar[44].

THE ROMAN ARTEMIS EPHESIA

Narrow sides: three statues of Artemis Ephesia from the Prytaneion area are of great significance and considered to be Roman copies of the Artemision cult statue. In the large niche, the so-called Great Artemis (Inv. 712), presumably from the time of Trajan; opposite, the so-called Beautiful Artemis (Inv. 718) from the time of Hadrian; to the left of it, a less than life-size statue from the 2nd century AD, the so-called Small Artemis (Inv. 717)[45].

42 BAMMER, Die Architektur des Jüngeren Artemision (1972); RÜGLER, IstMitt 34 (1988).

43 AA 1968, 400ff.; MUSS, Jb. Kunsthistorische Sammlungen in Wien 80, 1984, 7ff.

44 AA 1972, 714ff.

45 FLEISCHER, Artemis von Ephesos und verwandte Kultstatuen (EPRO 35, 1973); SEITERLE, AW 10, 1979, 3ff.

Fig. 1: Frieze block offering from the burnt offering oven of the altar (4th century BC)

Fig. 2: Marble horse, roof decoration from the altar enclosure

1

2

Display case: small marble torso from the 1st century BC (?), probably also Artemis, but without the so-called breasts or bulls testicles, found near Theatre Street (Inv. 12/34/84)[46].

To the left of the display case: relief (Inv. 457) from the 3rd century AD with representation of Artemis and Serapis, the main Greek-Egyptian god of the city of Alexandria, found south-west of the Ephesian harbour[47].

Opposite the display case: Inscribed round base from the agora in Ephesus, dating to about 200 AD (Inv. 1/5/74) no doubt for an Artemis statuette, with representation of two women at sacrifice flanking an incense holder (thymiaterium)[48].

FINDS FROM THE ARTEMISION

Display case: finds from the geometric period: small bronze peacock, little bell in the shape of a double-duck, large bronze peacock, buffalo (or ram?) and deer (this, perhaps of Hittite inspiration)[49]. Two amber necklaces, and a necklace of glazed clay pearls from the so-called hoard of the geometric peripteros[50].

Finds from the 7th and 6th centuries BC: two bronze griffin trivets; pierced ivory pendant in the shape of a lion's head; bronze omphalos plate; polychrome protomes: female head and bull's head trivet of clay; four Corinthian aryballoi; small Phoenician leg plates, probably from a small casket with the representation of a goddess carrying symbols of the Egyptian gods Bastet and Hathor; ivory pomegranates; four hyperboloid rock crystals which may have served as magnifying glasses.

Among the gold finds, the bull-lion head composition in the shape of a pendant, found in 1986 near the northern cult base, a gold fibula, a gold needle, as well as a gold plate with eyes must be mentioned. The gold statuette of a goddess is a *sphyrelaton* (sheet metal beaten over a wooden core) and comes from the west side of the temple (now to be seen as a copy); the ivory figurine of a goddess in oriental dress, carrying small begging bowls on her head, comes from the northwest corner of the temple; the female ivory figurine of the caryatid type is from the west side of the temple[51]. Next to these, the large lid of a pyxis with carved lotus-palmette decoration, an ivory ram, a small askos for donations, the large white marble lamp, as well as the smaller engraved one made out of green slate. The archaic neocypric limestone head, also displayed in the case, was found in 1970 during the excavation of the altar[52].

UM

46 FLEISCHER (see note 45) 288ff..

47 See p. 155 fig. 3. – Anz 1954, 226ff.; HÖLBL, Zeugnisse ägyptischer Religionsvorstellungen für Ephesus (EPRO 73, 1978) 78f.

48 FLEISCHER, ÖJh 1978 - 80, 63ff.

49 BAMMER, in: Echo, Festschrift J. TRENTINI (1990) 32 fig. 19 (Buffalo).

50 ÖJh 1988, B2ff.; AnatSt 40, 1990, 137ff.

51 ÖJh 1985, 39ff.

52 BREIN, in: Studien zur Religion und Kultur Kleinasiens, Festschrift F. DÖRNER (EPRO 66/1, 1978) 124 Pl. XLI fig. 13.

Fig. 1: So-called Great Artemis, beginning of the 2nd century AD (PESENDORFER)

ROOM 7 (IMPERIAL CULT ROOM)

This room combines excellent examples of Ephesian portraiture from Augustan to Justinianic times with relief friezes from important monuments.

To the right of the entrance: statue of the proconsul Stephanos with sceptre, mappa and scrolls; Curetes Street, 6th century AD[53].

Left wall: frieze panels which were transferred to the portico of the Temple of Hadrian in the 4th century AD. From left to right: scenes of the founding legend with Androclos and the wild boar; sacrifice of the Greeks at an altar; fleeing Amazons; Dionysus procession; assembly of the gods[54].

Next to this: two male portraits of the third century AD[55]; head of Augustus with the oak wreath; private female portrait of Augustan times; portrait of Trajan[56].

behind: portraits of the Emperor Commodus (180 - 192 AD) and a priest of Imperial Cult (around 110 - 130); private portraits of late Severan times (220 - 235)[57].

Adjacent: relief slabs from the altar base of the so-called Temple of Domitian with weapon reliefs and a bull sacrifice in front of an altar (2nd century AD)[58].

Along short wall, opposite the entrance: ensemble of relief panels from the so-called Parthian monument. According to the general opinion of art historians, the monument celebrated the victory of Lucius Verus over the Parthians and was probably erected after his death in 169 AD in the form of a memorial altar[59]; the place where it might originally have been set up, however, has not been determined. Recent research favors a date one generation earlier, and this presents other possibilities of interpretation, such as the representation of a general superiority of the Greco-Roman world to barbarians[60].

From left to right: "adoption scene" (cast of the original slab in Vienna); two fragments from the series of city personifications: armoured figure and amazon bearing standard ("Ephesos", cast); Apollo-Helios on the griffin chariot from the apotheosis series[61]. Below, four of the slabs with bull's-head and garland reliefs.

Figs. 1 + 2: Augustus and Livia, seated statues from the State Agora
Fig. 3: Relief slab from the Parthian Monument, detail: God of the wind

53 FOSS, Essays I. SEVCENKO, Harvard Ukrainian Studies 7 (1983) 196ff.

54 FLEISCHER, Festschrift F. EICHLER (1967) 23ff.

55 İNAN – ROSENBAUM (1966) no. 173 (bust).

56 İNAN – ROSENBAUM (1966) no. 140; İNAN – ALFÖLDI-ROSENBAUM (1979) no. 2. 39.

57 İNAN – ROSENBAUM (1966) no. 55. 163; ÖJh 1983, B133ff.; AURENHAMMER, in: THÜR (ed.), "...Und verschönerte die Stadt..." (SoschrÖAI 27, 1997) 41ff.

58 ÖJh 1932, B55ff.; RE Suppl. XII, 1649f.

59 Most of the slabs are in the Ephesos Museum Vienna: OBERLEITNER in: Funde aus Ephesos und Samothrake (1978) 66ff.; GANSCHOW, AA 1986, 209ff.; STÄHLER, Boreas 10, 1987, 107ff.; KNIBBE, BerMatÖAI 1, 1991, 5ff.

60 Look for the newest discussion in the contributions of ENGEMANN, LIVERANI, OBERLEITNER and LAUBENBERGER, in: FRIESINGER – KRINZINGER, 100 Jahre Österreichische Forschungen in Ephesos. Akten des Symposiums Wien 1995 (DenkschrWien 260, 1999).

61 OBERLEITNER, ÖJh 1995, 39ff.

1

2

3

Right wall: colossal seated statues of Augustus and Livia, head of Augustus with *corona civica*, all found in the area of the Basilica Stoa on the State Agora, with a cross engraved on the forehead[62]; marble pieces (head, left arm) of the colossal acrolithic statue of Titus from the cult-image group of the so-called Temple of Domitian[63].

ROOM 9 (SMALL COURTYARD)

The small courtyard is used as a café; nonetheless, several interesting exhibits can be seen here:

End wall: lion sculpture of the 4th/3rd centuries BC from Tavşantepe near Selçuk[64]; left of this, portrait statue from early Imperial times, reused on Curetes Street in Late Antiquity.

Entrance area: well preserved marble corbel from the Olympieion; various Roman capitals, two altars, reliefs and table feet.

Right wall: Hellenistic milestone, inscribed on two sides, from the Ephesus-Sardis road[65] indicating 410 stadia from Sardis and 90 stadia from Ephesus.

IN FRONT OF THE MUSEUM

Entrance: Eros herm (support figure, spoil near the street fountains).

Front side: two sarcophagi with garlands[66]. MA

62 İNAN – ALFÖLDI-ROSENBAUM (1979) no. 3. 5. 2; BOSCHUNG, Herrscherbild I 2 (1993) Cat. 26. 186.
63 Further fragments in the depot. – KREIKENBOM, 27. Ergh. JdI (1992) 213ff.
64 ERDEMGİL – EVREN, TürkAD 30, 1992, 71ff.
65 IvE VII/2 3601.
66 LIMC III (1986) 855f. no. 5. – Sarcophagus Inv. 261, 4/4/74: IŞIK, in: KOCH (ed.), Grabeskunst der römischen Kaiserzeit (1993) p. 11 Pl. 3,1.4; KOCH – SICHTERMANN, Römische Sarkophage (1982) 521.

Fig. 1: Grave lion from Tavşantepe (4th/3rd centuries BC)

ETHNOGRAPHIC DEPARTMENT

After the restoration of the Turkish bath (*Hamam*) in the western part of the museum building in 1972, its surrounding area was also laid out anew. The area was enclosed in the west and the north with a colonnade while im the south it ends with a wall. In 1995 an ethnographic museum was set up here to include the Turkish bath with exhibits which relate to the arts and crafts up into our times.

Arasta

This is the name given to that part of the retail sales market where, in old Turkish business life, shops were set up in places of busy trade, under covered colonnades on the front of the bazaar facing the street. The arcades in the museum are intended as a latter-day copy of such an *Arasta*.

A **rope walk** with the appropriate equipment is on display in the *Arasta*. The production by hand of hemp rope was an old and flourishing tradition in Anatolia, in particular under Ottoman rule. The processing of hemp and the production of rope on simple looms was based on human labour and was, for a particular group of people, the foundation of their existence. There were well-organized guilds of rope makers in the areas surrounding Tire, Gediz, Burdur and Isparta. Yet general economic problems and new production methods led to a decline in this trade, indeed brought about its almost complete disappearance.

Ropemaking is a family enterprise and the space in front of the house, covered only by a projecting roof, serves as a workshop. The hemp, already beaten and combed, is bundled up and brought to the rope wheel, whereupon the actual rope production begins. The rope master sets up the rope wheel at one end of the rope-walk, and the rope rack with warp bobbin and spinning ring at the other. Then he lays the hemp fibres on the rotating spindles of the rope wheel and twists them into a rope.

Scales are also displayed with their appropriate weights. The size of the scales is in proportion to the load to be weighed.

In regions dominated by agriculture, where tradition, experience and physical strength are of paramount importance, technological methods remain preserved without the slightest alteration right up to our times. The **millstones** in the museum are arranged according to type and are displayed in a chronological series.

Up until 50 years ago there was, in almost every small Anatolian town, a **barber shop**, called *the dear barber* (Cici berber), where a master, a journeyman and an apprentice worked.

The master shaved the local dignitaries, the journeyman saw to the haircuts of the young men and children, and the apprentice swept the shop, brought tea and coffee to the customers and, in his free time, strove to learn the craft from his master. The barbers also performed circumcisions or pulled a painful tooth.

The Rose House and the production of rosewater and roseoil: The Sumerians already knew how to cultivate roses in the third millennium BC. After them, the Assyrians grew this queen of flowers and made from them rosewater and roseoil. Roses have been cultivated in Anatolia since the $12^{th}/13^{th}$ century AD.

The roseoil produced in Turkey is of the world's best quality. Many countries obtain the rosewater and roseoil needed for making essences and cosmetics from Turkey and Bulgaria. The apparatus displayed in the exact copy of a rose house in the *Arasta* can extract 1 kg of roseoil and 1,000 kg of rosewater from 3,500 kg of rose petals. The following can be seen in the rose house:

Fireplace: a simple arrangement for heating the distillation vessel. Cooling basins are built behind these fireplaces which are plastered with clay inside and out.

Kettle or distillation apparatus: a copper vessel with a lid in which the rose petals are boiled in water. The capacity of the vessels, which are tinned on the inside, varies from 24 to 100 litres. The kettle displayed holds 75 kg.

Stills: hemispherical, also of copper, with swan-necks which narrow towards their tips.

Cooling basins: Plastered inside and out, these are of the same size as the fireplaces onto which they are built. The basins are filled with water and the galvanized or copper pipes connected to the stills are led in coils through them.

Glass collecting vessel: The rosewater or roseoil, which has condensed in the pipes passing through the cooling basin, is collected in these glass containers. In a further operation, the roseoil floating on the surface is drawn off with a cannula.

Scimitar display case: *Yatağan* is the name for the 50 - 100 cm long Turkish scimitar which is slightly curved from the hilt to the point. The blade is forged from the finest steel and the hilt made of horn. Worn buckled to a wide belt, the scimitar first made its appearance at the beginning of the 14th century. The places where these scimitars were made were usually also called *Yatağan*. The Yatağan district towns in the provinces of Denizli and Muğla provided the Ottoman

Fig. 1: View into the courtyard of the Arasta

Fig. 2: The rope-walk and ropery

army with scimitars for hundreds of years. Old and new scimitars and sabre hilts of horn are to be seen in the display case.

The coppersmith's workshop: The excavations at Çayönü have demonstrated that copper was already in use in Anatolia in the 7th millennium BC. There are numerous sources of copper ore in Turkey. Nails, door locks and hinges as well as utensils such as kettles, cooking pots, jugs and washbasins were made of copper.

The coppersmith shapes the copper sheet from the factory by hammering it into the desired form in his workshop. In the case of tableware, the poisonous copper is tinned. Sometimes patterns of regional designs are engraved at various places on the vessels. The coppersmith's workshop shown here contains apparatus for tinning, hammering and cutting, welding and soldering. Adjacent to this, a fireplace with bellows has a sand-filled trough in which the copper vessels are cleaned before tinning.

The bead against the evil eye and its production: The glass beads, which were found in large quantities in the excavations of prehistoric Anatolia, can be interpreted as precursors of the *blue beads against the evil eye* as they are made today in the Aegean region in Kemalpaşa and Görece. The glass is melted in a special oven at 900 - 1000 degrees centigrade and coloured; then the required amount of glass is taken up with an iron pipe and shaped into the desired form. Since the beads are primarily used as amulets to ward off the evil eye, blue is the preferred colour. Beads of other colours are also produced for rosaries, key chains and various pieces of jewellery.

The **glass melting oven** displayed in the *Arasta*, which was brought to the museum from the village of Kurudere (district of Kemalpaşa), could be put into operation at any time. The glass beads on display are all new. It should be emphasized that the workshop functioned both as a factory and a place for sale.

Saadet-Hatun-Hamam (Bath)

The 16th century bathhouse, the caravanserai currently being used as a lecture hall, and the temple (Mescit) in Ayasoluk, together form a building complex. The faithfully renovated bathhouse, which was uncovered in 1972, displays all the characteristics of a typical Turkish bath. The cross-shaped ground plan is arranged into a changing room, cold bath, assembly room, warm bath, and sweat room.

Throughout the centuries, the Turkish bath was the place where people cleansed, adorned and enjoyed themselves, observing many a traditional ceremony.

Fig. 1: The collection of old scales

In general it was open during the daytime for women, and at night for men. Women and girls went to the bath in groups. Prior to a wedding, the *bridal bath* was held, where women played for dancing on musical instruments. On their way to the bath, the women carried colourfully embroidered cloths in which the bathing utensils were wrapped. These utensils varied from region to region. A set of bath hand towels consisted of three pieces which were decorated on the edges with fine embroidery. The wooden slippers for the bath were usually inlaid with silver or mother of pearl. The water bowls, which the bathers used to pour water over themselves, and the soap dishes were made of silver, pewter, copper or brass. The soap, a terry-cloth glove made of goat hair, and a sponge were kept in the soap container which was carried by a handle. There were special soaps for the Hamam, decorated, for the most part, with floral motifs.

All the bathing utensils mentioned here can be seen displayed on the models in the wooden bathing cubicles.

Tents

Tents were made by nomads and semi-nomads out of a variety of materials and in different forms. The names are related to their use and the material from which they are made: the round domed tent (yurt), the tent of goat hair blankets, the pasha tent, the ruler tent, the Yörük tent (nomads) etc. The round tent, made of felt blankets on a wooden frame, was already used by the Turks in central Asia. The Yörük tent (goat hair tent) is usually supported by seven or nine posts. Each tent peg has its own designation and function. The tent roof consists of black goat hair blankets. The tent serves as living room and for the storage of articles of daily use. Reed mats are spread out on the floor and carpets, kilims and pillows complete the furnishings. A round tent and a Yörük tent are on exhibition in the museum.

AZ

HISTORY OF THE SELÇUKS AND OTTOMANS

The first Turkish settlement of Izmir and Ephesus began ten years after the battle of Malazgirt (1071). In the year 1081, Caka bey succeeded in uniting the Turks in the region of Izmir and in establishing a partial principality in the coastal area. Invasions by the Byzantines and Catalans occurred in the times following.

Ephesus-Ayasoluk was finally taken by Mehmet bey of the Aydınoğulları dynasty in 1304. Despite the Turkish conquest, the Byzantine bishop's seat in Ephesus remained almost unmolested. After the subjection of the area around Aydın, Gazi Mehmet bey made the town of Birgi his residence. He divided the land under his suzerainty into five parts to which he appointed his sons as princes. He enfeoffed his son Mehmet bey with the principality of Ayasoluk and Sultanhisar. We have several detailed and informative reports on the trade of Ayasoluk under the Aydınoğulları. After the Turks came to power, Ayasoluk was an important centre of trade and one of the most significant harbour towns of the eastern Mediterranean.

The occidental merchants imported textiles, silverware, wine and soap, and exported wine from Kütahya, wheat, rice, beeswax and unspun hemp. At the same time as it gained strength as a city of trade, Ayasoluk developed into an important centre of art and culture.

The relationships between the dynasty of the Aydınoğulları and the Ottoman empire were at first friendly. However, when the Ottoman Beyazit I. Yıldırım (the *Lightening Bolt*) put an end to the unrest in south-east Europe and settled the succession disputes in Byzantium in his favour, he turned his attentions to Asia Minor. During a campaign in the winter of 1389 - 1390 he conquered the principality of the Aydınoğulları. Nevertheless he allowed the prince İsa bey to remain in Ayasoluk. From written sources, we know that the administration of the religious foundations (*vakıf*) was transferred to İsa bey. The prerogative of minting coins, and of being named in the Friday sermon was, however, reserved for Beyazit. After the battle of Ankara in 1402, the Mongol Timur, called *the Lame* (Tamerlane), extended his rule over the whole of Anatolia. He came as far as the region of Aydın and made Ayasoluk his base. During a thirty-day stay he captured the surrounding forts and cities. Timur bequeathed the fief of Aydın to the sons of İsa bey, Musa and Umur II, whereupon Cüneyd and his brother Hasan Ağa, who also belonged to the dynasty of the Aydınoğulları, asserted their rights. Finally Cüneyd captured Izmir and Ayasoluk came under the control of Hasan Ağa. After the death of Umur bey in 1405, Cüneyd bey became sole ruler of the principality. Under Murat II. (1426), Ayasoluk came under lasting Ottoman sovereignty. In the 15th century, Ayasoluk was a city subdivided into sixteen districts and inhabited by Muslims and Christians living in harmony. After the 16th century the place went into decline and Izmir and Kuşadası gained importance as harbour towns.

PB, AZ

İSA BEY MOSQUE [170]

The building inscription on the west portal of the mosque states that the mosque was commissioned by İsa bey of the Aydınoğulları dynasty, and built by the architect Ali from Damascus. The building forms a nearly square rectangle measuring 56.53 x 48.68 m, and has a courtyard surrounded by arcades.

While the east and north walls of the mosque are built of simple ashlar blocks, the west façade is clad with marble slabs. Portal and window frames on the west side are magnificently decorated.

The method of construction of the entrance on the west side is a typical example of Rumselçuk architecture: a highly decorative gate is set within a high niche with pointed arch, the frame of which is artistically decorated with incrustations of white and yellowish stones. The larger building inscription above the gate arch is lost; the smaller one underneath is still preserved.

The portal gives access to a courtyard surrounded on three sides by arcades. The column capitals and the arcade passageways, like the rest of the building material, mainly consist of ancient spolia.

Selçukid Buildings: FiE I, 111-131.

A fountain with a polygonal ground plan stands in the middle of the courtyard for religious ablutions. A triple-arched entrance gives access to the actual prayer hall which is divided into two halves by four massive black granite columns. The middle part of the inner room with the prayer niche (*mihrab*) is vaulted over by two domes decorated with faience. The motifs on the marble panels in the restored prayer niche resemble the ornamentation in the pediment of the Karatay mosque and Alaaddin mosque in Konya. In its original state, the pulpit (*mimber*) was panelled in walnut. The minarets, with patterns of glazed tiles, are built on to the western and eastern corners of the prayer hall.

EÜ

Fig. 1: İsa bey Mosque, view from the atrium of the Basilica of St. John

Fig. 2: Ruins of a Byzantine cloister (?) directly adjoining the mosque

TURKISH BATH HOUSES (HAMAM)

In the town of Ayasoluk, modern Selçuk, there are four still usable bath houses from the time of the Aydınoğulları dynasty and the early Ottoman epoch (1350 - 1450). The walls of all four bath houses are constructed of alternating rows of stone and brick. The dome and vaults are of brick. Ornamentation can be found in the dome and on the squinches.

Apart from these similarities, the bath houses differ in their ground plans. It is clear in all four bath houses where the sweat room was, but the position of the changing rooms has not been clarified. During excavations in the İsa bey hamam, the floors of the splendid changing rooms were uncovered but no trace of the walls or ceiling were found. It is therefore assumed that these rooms were covered with a wooden roof.

The bath houses were erected in close proximity, carefully built and fitted with all the amenities of their time. This suggests that they originated in the heyday of the town of Ayasoluk.

İsa bey Hamam [171]

According to an inscription found near this bath, it was built in the year of the Prophet 766 – that is to say, 1364 AD. Initially it served for the personal hygiene and the prescribed ritual cleansing of the workers involved in the erection of the İsa bey Mosque [170].

Prior to the beginning of excavations, the upper parts of the walls of the sweat room, warm bath and heating room, as well as some of the domes and vaults, were in a semi-ruined condition. The inner rooms were filled to a height of 2.5 m with earth. Excavations have so far shown that this bath had a cross-shaped ground plan consisting of square bath rooms, and that two separate baths (çifte hamam) were created by later additions. The beautiful stucco work of the dome and parts of the ceiling sections are the main focus of attention in the work of restoration. Roman columns were re-used in the forecourt of the bath.

The work of uncovering and restoration which began in 1986 is being continued.

Hamam I

The bath lies to the west of the Byzantine-Selçuk fortress. The special distinguishing features of the building are still easily recognized in the ruins.

In it's present form, it has a symmetrical ground plan consisting of rectangular prism-shaped units. The building is filled with earth up to the height of the squinches.

The domes over the sweat room and warm room, as well as the barrel vault of the heating room, are completely destroyed; the greater part of the other domes are badly damaged.

As decoration for the domes and dome spandrels, the edges of the *Mukarnas* (stalactite vaults) were defined with round mouldings and emphasized by red-ochre colour.

Hamam II

The ground plan of this bath to the west of the İsa bey Hamam shows a central domed room and, on the narrow side, a sweat room with two separate bathing chambers. The *Mukarnas* consist of small painted triangles. AZ

Further buildings from Turkish times

A series of smaller, and art-historically less important buildings, are scattered in and around the old town of Ayasoluk and the area between the İsa bey Mosque and the Artemision. Apart from mosques, they consist of so-called prayer houses (Mescit) and vaulted tombs (Türbe) of especially pious men; one of them belonged to a certain Şahabettin Dede.

These were mainly erected between the middle of the 14th century and the beginning or the middle of the 15th century during the time of the partial principalities. Only seldom have buildings been identified as being from the Ottoman period in the 15th and 16th centuries. EÜ

See p. 222 for details of the Saadet-Hatun-Hamam.

Fig. 1: İsa bey Hamam, condition at the time of the restoration 1995

ROUND TOMB AND POLLIO AQUEDUCT

Outside the town on the road to Tralleis (today's Aydın) and Magnesia, lie the ruins of a round tomb and the impressive, well-preserved aqueduct of Pollio from Augustan times.

The **round tomb** lies 3.8 km outside Selçuk, east of the road in an olive grove opposite the small restaurant on the outskirts of Yeniköy. Originally a tomb monument, it consisted of a socle, some 1.80 m high, with a bench running around it, supporting a monopteros of six columns with Corinthian capitals, in which statues were displayed. It was, no doubt, originally a burial chamber. The richly decorated entablature supported a conical roof, which was crowned by a central acanthus acroterium. The remains of a metrical inscription from the end of the second century AD, strongly suggest that the tomb, as well as a nearby country villa - the mosaic floors of which were cut into during road work - belonged to the leading Ephesian Vedius clan.

The two storey **aqueduct**, with three massive arches in the lower storey and six smaller arches in the upper storey, spans the river and valley of the Dervenddere, presumably called Marnas in antiquity. The river bed still lies under the eastern arch; the ancient road ran through the centre and western arches as is also indicated by the asymmetrical position of the building inscription.

The pillars and arches are built of marble blocks, the imposts and arch fronts offset by simple mouldings. Above the arches lies an architrave course which bears the inscriptions. Remains of a cornice are preserved in the upper storey, above which the water channel ran in an attic zone. The walls laterally adjoining the aqueduct are built up of small stones set with mortar in even courses.

The building inscription on both sides of the aqueduct is written in two lines, above in Latin and below in Greek: C. Sextilius Pollio erected this structure with his wife Ofillia Bassa and his stepson C. Ofillius Proculus from their own funds in honour of Augustus, Tiberius and the Ephesian demos. The mention of Tiberius reveals a building date of 4 - 14 AD.

The aqueduct is part of the *Aqua Throessitica*, named in an inscription and erected by Emperor Augustus to supply Ephesus with water. HT

Round tomb: ÖJh 1930, 46ff.; 1956-58, 58ff.; KÖNIGS – RADT, IstMitt 29, 1979, 317ff.
Pollio aqueduct: FiE III, 256ff.; Aug. Architektur, 21ff.

Fig. 1: Pollio aqueduct: condition in around 1900

Fig. 2: Present day condition after restoration work

0 1 2 3 4 5 6 7M
5.25
2.26
5.16
5.20
1903

FORTIFIED TOWER AND MINING SETTLEMENT ON THE ALADAĞ

East of the House of Mary, on a forested hill 490 m above sea level and 2 km south-east of the fire watch tower of the state forest administration, there is a Hellenistic building (H) around which emergency excavation took place in 1994.

The one-room Hellenistic tower measuring 8.4 x 8.4 m, was probably a part of the outer defences of Ephesus. The walls are built of rusticated blocks of the same type as the Lysimachian city wall and are, today, only preserved to a height of three courses. Further investigations on the north and south side of the tower revealed a floor of irregular stones which may be older than the structure.

In the north-western part of the Hellenistic structure, rooms installed in late Roman times were excavated. Of these, rooms 5 and 6 are of most importance. In the eastern corner of room 5, a cistern with brick walls measuring 1.65 x 1.25 m was installed and the inside plastered with mortar. A sewage pithos, of which only half survives, was let into the middle of a floor made of large, burnt clay slabs and covered with two stone blocks. In the middle of room 5, a large stone measuring 0.9 x 0.9 m was found in situ which could have been used as a mortar. A grain pithos with iron clamps set in lead, half of which was built into and under the north wall, came to light in room 6.The round structure 4 measures 0.75 m in diameter and 0.4 m in depth. There are reasons to believe that this structure served for the storage of clay jugs.

On the north slope of the hill, south of the excavation site, there is a mine in which gold and copper ores were extracted from antiquity until 1890. In view of this, it can be assumed that the settlement sites uncovered in the course of excavations, which in all probability stretch further to the north, served as temporary housing for the people who worked the mines. On the basis of the potsherds, roof tiles and coins found during the excavations, it can be said that the area surrounding the Hellenistic structure was occupied during the Roman and Byzantine eras. SE, DT, GT

FiE I, 81f.; Jobst, in: Studien zur Religion und Kultur Kleinasiens, Festschrift F. Dörner (EPRO 66/1, 1978) 447ff.

Fig. 1: Plan of the excavations on the Aladağ: Hellenistic fortified tower and Late Antique settlement

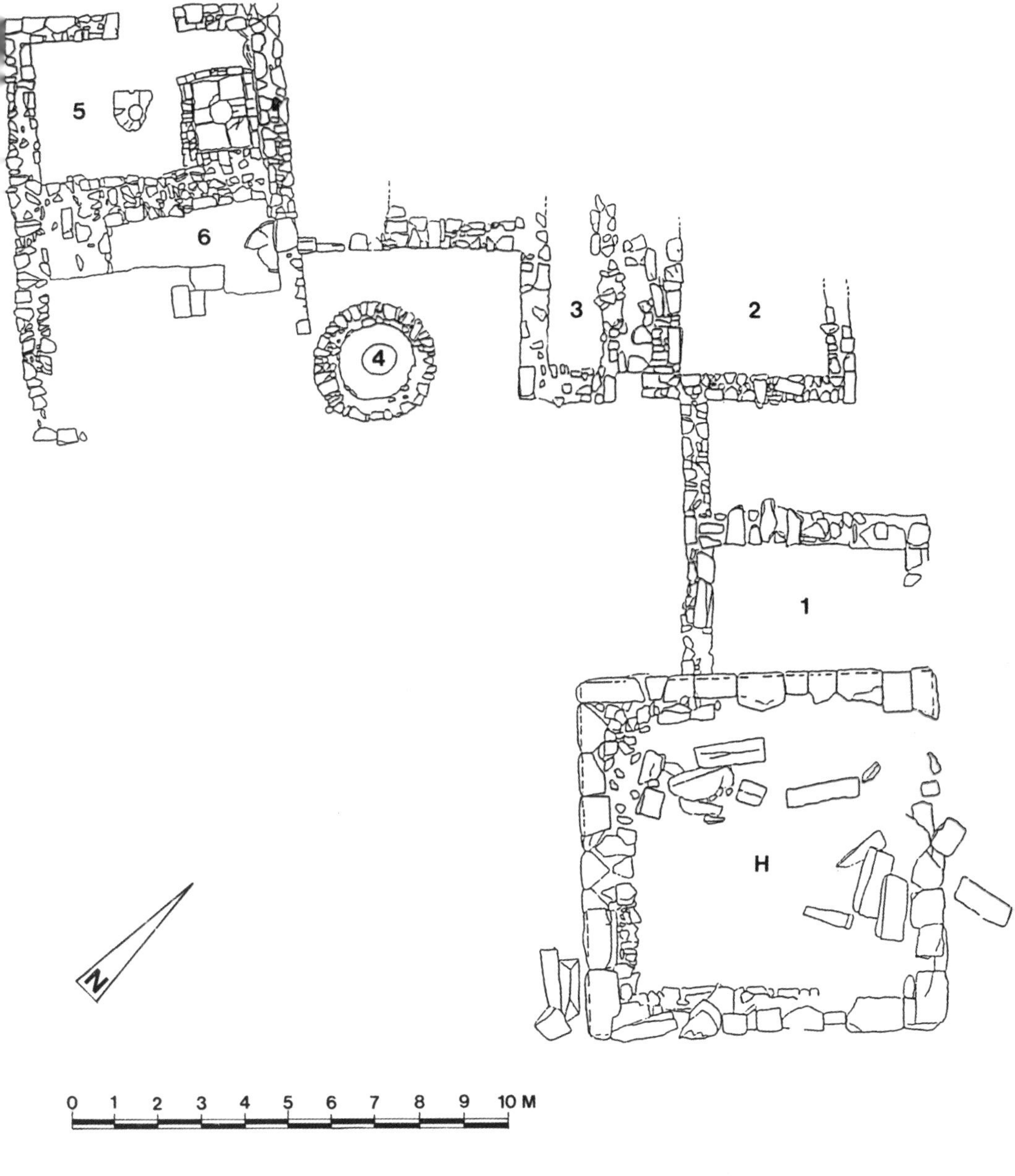
5
6
4
3
2
1
H
N
0 1 2 3 4 5 6 7 8 9 10 M

MERYEMANA EVİ (HOUSE OF THE MOTHER MARY)

This little church, also known as Monastiri üç Kapu (Cloister of the Three Gates), was built in the Byzantine period (perhaps in the 13th century) on the remains of an ancient building on the west slope of the Aladağ, some seven kilometres south of Ephesus. According to a tradition of the Lazarists of Smyrna, the church is built over a house used by Mary, Mother of God, as her last domicile. This local belief can, however, only be traced back to the 19th century and has not, so far, found confirmation in the archaeological investigations.

These were, however, discontinued, although much remains to be discovered in the vicinity. It is hoped that the archaeological exploration of the entire site can be resumed in the near future. The area around the building is laid out like a park and rewards the visitor with a wonderful view. On sunday mornings, catholic services are held in the open air between the little church and an atrium with a cistern.

RP

FiE I, 82f.; A. PRANDI, Ricerche archeologiche a "Meryem Ana Evi" presso Efeso, in: De primordiis cultus Mariani. Acta congressus mariologici-mariani in Lusitania 1967, Roma, Pont. Acc. Mar. 5 (1970) 34 - 42.

Fig. 1: Present day view of the so-called house of the Mother of God

CUSTOMS HOUSE IN PAMUCAK

On a small hill called Kumtepe, sixty metres south of the place where the ancient canal runs into the sea, and approximately 400 m from the beach, are building remains in three distinct phases. The uppermost structure, built directly on the rock, is a columned courtyard with adjoining rooms covering an area of 27 by 30 m. A staircase carved out of the rock gives access to the northern entrance. On the walls of the room, still preserved to a height of 1.5 m, are remains of plaster, and traces of burning are visible. The floor of the atrium exhibits two building phases. Here, an opus sectile pavement, made of eight different types of marble, was laid over a mosaic. Porticos, some three meters wide, line the north and south sides of the atrium. Under the eastern part of the building is a room measuring 5 by 11 m and standing to a height of 5 m. Hewn out of the rock with an east-west orientation, this was built up on the sides with two rows of brick and roofed over with a brick vault.

A barrel-vaulted staircase, only a meter wide, leads to the upper storey. A brick staircase of seven steps leads from the east side of the room into the lower storey of the buildings adjacent to the east. From the entrance to the stairway leading into the northern storey, these structures completely cover the eastern flank of the hill. There is a corridor-like structure, 3.5 m high, which is subdivided into nine rooms measuring 3 - 3.5 m wide and 7 - 8 m long, that are interconnected by doorways. A hewn rock face forms the west wall of the building and the east wall is made out of stone and brick. The roof consists of a flat barrel-vault which is supported in the middle by a column. This vault forms, at the same time, the floor of the second storey, of which little remains. There are, however, in the undisturbed rock, still traces of the pillars which supported the roof. From the 1st to the 7th century, when the building on the hill was in use, this room, situated directly at the entrance of the harbour, was best suited for controlling and inspecting ships entering the port. The existence of dwelling units in the east suggests that this could have been a customs house. The building was presumably devastated and burned down at the time of the Arab invasions. In later years the structure served other purposes; possibly a cloister was installed there.

ÖÖ

THE MAUSOLEUM AT BELEVİ

The Hellenistic burial monument, which possibly resembled, in form, the mausoleum at Halicarnassus, was presumably commissioned by King Lysimachus. Together with the burial chamber, the socle of the two storey structure was carved out of the rock and was clad with marble. There was originally an upper storey encircled by columns.

14 km upstream of Ephesus, near the place called Belevi, the spur of a hill was carved out and levelled to make a tomb and a place for funeral games and other cultic activities in honour of the person to be buried there. The socle of the tomb is carved from a great mass of living rock, 29 m square and 10 m high, into which a burial chamber was carved, utilizing what had probably been a natural crevice on the side towards the mountain. Its entrance was invisible; the blind Doric architecture of the socle only showed a false door at the opposite side facing the plain. The upper storey consisted of a cella and a peristasis with 8 x 8 columns which carried Corinthian capitals of an unusual type. The ambulatory was fitted with a coffered ceiling, the middle fields of which were decorated with mythological scenes. Horse and griffin sculptures as well as vases are all that remains of a rich roof decoration which consisted of antithetic pairs of animals.

The decorative building components, which are of high quality, still exhibited remains of polychrome painting when they were uncovered between 1931 and 1935. In their hypothetical reconstruction of the monument, the excavators suggested a pyramidal roof by analogy with Halicarnassus. More recently, the upper storey has been envisioned as an open courtyard.

The burial monument, most likely planned for Lysimachus, was apparently finished for the Seleucid king Antiochus II. Theos who died in Ephesus in 246 BC.

On the hill above the tomb there is a tumulus which has been interpreted as the grave and heroon for the shepherd Pixadoros who received the honorary name of Euangelos for having discovered a source of the marble needed to build the Artemision. HT

FiE VI; HOEPFNER, AA 1993, 111 -123.
The tomb's peace and quiet is nowadays noticeably disturbed by the new highway to Aydın which runs close by. Parts of the building and its sculpture are spread over three museums: sarcophagai, roof sculptures, and architectural fragments in Selçuk; coffers, servant statues and some capitals in Izmir; and other capitals in Tyre.

Fig. 1: Reconstruction (FOSSEL – THEUER)

Fig. 2: General view of the mausoleum (HOFBAUER)

E. Fossel 63
NACH THEUER

KEÇİ KALESİ (GOATS' CASTLE)

The castle lies 9 km upstream from Selçuk on the hilltop of the Alamandağ, the ancient Mount Gallesion, at an elevation of 300 m.

The crest and slopes of this hill were important to the rulers of this area since the Hellenistic epoch because they are at a strategic point where the main roads from north to south cross the valley of the Küçük Menderes, and a road to Sardis branches off from the road to Izmir.

The fortress, 56.6 x 23 m in plan, consists of an inner stronghold with a rectangular ground plan, and an outer fortification surrounding it on the north and west. A moat, normal for forts of this kind, was not dug - probably because the high position on the hilltop rendered it unnecessary.

Inside the fortress gates are a round and a square tower, and there are buttresses in the castle walls. Deep in the northern part of the inner stronghold are storage rooms some 3 m wide and 5.8 m deep. A small door from the inner courtyard gives access to the round tower which is 6 m in diameter. The square tower in the south, measuring 4.87 x 5.42 m, is not so well-preserved. Its walls are 0.82 m thick.

Two phases can be distinguished in the building history of the structure, but the use of the similar materials and masonry technique suggest a short timespan between them. All the walls are of local broken limestone set in a hard lime mortar. In some places, where the wall projected out to a width of 1.4 - 1.5 m, there were sentry walks along the battlements.

An accurate dating is, at the moment, not possible because there is no building inscription and the fort is not mentioned in the written sources. All fortress installations in the Latmos mountains resemble one another, both in respect of the method of building and in the execution of specific details. For this reason, we can assume that this fort was erected in the Byzantine period under the Lascarides in the 13th century. The Byzantine name of the fort is not known but it is often called Kızılhisar. The ascent takes about an hour. It is most easily made from the northern side, where it follows, for some distance, a medieval road paved with large limestone blocks. There is a Hellenistic fortress on the northern side of Keçi kalesi; the road to it passes by a Hellenistic cistern. AE, Cİ, UM

MÜLLER-WIENER, IstMitt 11, 1961, 85ff.; BAMMER, Ephesos, Stadt an Fluß und Meer (1988) 20f.

Fig. 1: Plan of the goats' castle (MÜLLER-WIENER)

Fig. 2: The ruins of the goats' castle

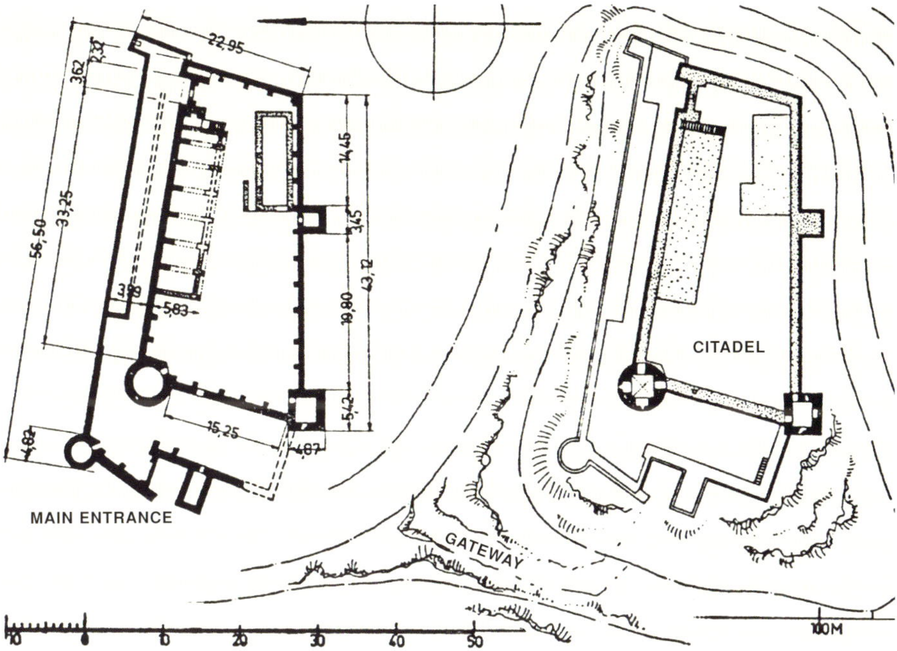
MAIN ENTRANCE
GATEWAY
CITADEL
100M

ŞİRİNCE

The village, inhabited by Greek Orthodox Christians until 1922, lies in the hills some 8 km east of Selçuk. A visit is worthwhile because of the picturesque location and the still relatively numerous houses built in the traditional style. The ruins of a church of Demetrius stand at the edge of the village and, in the centre, there is a domed church consecrated to John the Baptist.

Şirince can be reached either by turning off the main road to Izmir at the signpost, or by taking the dolmuş (collective taxi) which leaves every hour or so from the railway station in Selçuk.

The way up to Şirince (formerly called Kirkindje) follows a creek, which may have been called Claseas in antiquity. In the valley, the road passes by the remains of an ancient aqueduct. Already in the Middle Ages but also in early modern times, the residents of Ephesus fled to here to escape invaders.

A large cave which lies on the side of the valley to the left of the road to Şirince testifies to this. In it, christian symbols have been found together with pottery from the 14th and 15th centuries, as well as the remains of Byzantine frescoes. Further up the road to Şirince, and just to the left, there are large Hellenistic foundations with a church resting on them, which was only recently converted into an agricultural building. About 2 km north of the village are the ruins of a Byzantine cloister, perhaps from the 12th century. In the neighbourhood of the village there are still several very small churches which are now used to shelter livestock.

Up to 1922, Şirince was inhabited by Turkish-speaking Greek Orthodox Christians, who are often viewed as the descendants of the first Ephesian Christians. The village was also called *Orini Efeso* (Ephesus in the hills). The Orthodox Christians made yearly pilgrimages from there on the 15th August to the House of Mary, Meryemana (then called Panayia Kapulu).

Şirince used to be much larger than it is today and had, according to various sources, around 2,000 inhabitants. The village is mentioned in various 19th century travel reports. The lower storeys of the traditional houses are made out of a local green-brown stone laid without mortar; the upper

DEUTSCH, Our Lady of Ephesus (1965); BAMMER, Ephesos, Stadt an Fluß und Meer (1988) 27f.; Archives of the Centre for Asia Minor Studies (CAMS), Athens. Cult cave: ATALAY, ÖJh 1983, 129ff.

storeys consist of half-timbered structures, plastered and often projecting beyond the lower walls. At the entrance to the village, on the right, are the ruins of the Church of St. Demetrius, which formerly had an adjoining cemetery. To the left, in the curve, stands the former village school with a large fountain in the centre of the school yard. The door and window frames are made of rose-coloured andesite. An ethnographic museum is to be set up here. Everywhere in the village there are wells which use ancient ostotheques as collecting troughs. The houses often have ancient worked marbles built into them which may well be from the surroundings of Şirince.

Şirince is the scene of the short novella *Çirkince* by the Turkish writer Sabahattin Ali, which deals with the period of radical change after the first World War. *Farewell Anatolia* (Turkish: Selam söyle Anadolu'ya) by the Greek author Dido Sotiriou a native of Aydın, is also set here. This novel first appeared in Greek in 1962 and has, since then, been reprinted again and again and translated into many languages. This best seller describes, on the basis of the memories of Manolis Axiotis, the co-existence of Turks and Greeks in western Asia Minor before and after the first World War.

The Greeks from Şirince now live in various towns and villages in Greece. Near Katerini in northern Greece there is a village named Nea Ephesos (New Ephesus) in which men and women born in Şirince still live.

After the population exchange, 418 Turkish families from Crete, northern Greece and Bulgaria were settled in Şirince itself. In the meantime many have moved to Selçuk. There were, in 1995, officially 787 village residents who earned their livelihood from agriculture, especially from olive groves and fruit orchards, and, in recent years, also from Turkish and foreign tourists who are frequently given the opportunity to visit the older houses.

UM, ÖÖ

The domed church of John the Baptist in Şirince

The main church of Şirince stands in the western part of the village. The substructure and supporting walls, with exterior measurements of 13.4 by 20.2 m, are well-preserved. The church, measuring 13.4 by 20.2 m on the exterior, is roofed over by two large and six smaller domes, as well as by four barrel-vaults. There is an apse in the east, and the north and south sides each have three windows and a door. The door on the north side, with its richly decorated marble frame, is the main entrance, while the door on the south side leads to the women's gallery. An inscription over the entrance states that the church was consecrated to John the Baptist in 1805. It was perhaps restored in 1832.

Inside the church there are four pillars and six columns which support the domes and the vaults. The columns are of spolia with the missing portions filled in with mortar.

Well preserved wall paintings in the small niches on both sides of the apse and on the southern wall of the church suggest that the walls and the domes were once painted in their entirety. Attachments for wooden beams in the western part indicate that an intermediate storey of wood once existed.

The church was in quite good condition up until about 30 years ago, but deteriorated noticeably when the dome and vaults in the west part collapsed. In 1988, the team for the renovation of the Church of John from the Ephesus Museum in Selçuk began restoration work here with the support of the QUATMAN Foundation. The interior of the church had first to be shovelled free. The pillars and columns were then renovated to provide a strong foundation for the domes and vaults. One of the collapsed domes was covered with modern material in order to allow a better distribution of light. The other domes were restored to their original state and covered with tiles. Frescoes and plaster adhering to walls and domes were restored and conserved. The floor and the wooden intermediate storey in the western part were consolidated, and the wooden roof in front of the entrance was repaired. The area around the church was cleaned up and beautified with flower beds.

In future, this building will provide space for cultural events. MB

Fig. 1: Şirince, village road with free-standing baker's oven

Fig. 2: Paintings in the *prothesis* of the church of St. John the Baptist during the restoration

GLOSSARY

Acanthus	Herbaceous plant with prickly leaves; popular motif in architectural decoration
Acrolithic statue	Statue made of composite materials
Aedicula	Niche framed by columns supporting a pediment, either built into wall or freestanding (see naiskos)
Aediculated facade	Decorative wall with columns arranged in two or three stories and grouped to form projecting pavillions or aediculae normally containing sculpture.
Agora	Open area for informal assembly; market place
Alabastron	Ceramic oil flask, often with white ground recalling its origins as a stone vessel
Ambo	Tribune near the center of the nave in ancient church, for sermons and biblical recitation
Ambulatio	Ambulatory; place for strolling; arcade (especially in apse); cloister
Amphora	Two-handled vessel for transport of wine or oil
Amphoriskos	Small amphora
Analemma walls	Sloping walls bracketing and supporting the curved rows of seats in a theatre auditorium
Anastylosis	Scientific term Physical reconstruction of a building using mainly original architectural elements
Anta (-ae)	Extension(s) of the side walls of a building, especially a temple, which enclose a porch
Apodyterium	Changing room in a Roman bath
Apotheosis	Ascension to haven of the deceased, usually followed by deification
Apotropaic	Having power to avert or turn away evil or bad luck
Apse	Large semicircular or polygonal recess, usually surmounted by a semi-dome, as at eastern end of church
Architrave	Course of long blocks resting on column capitals
Archivolt	Front face of arch; in Roman architecture, usually divided into three fasciae
Aryballos (-oi)	Small, round-bottomed phial(s) for oil, perfume or cosmetics
Asiarch	Highest official of the provincial assembly of Asia
Askos	Sack-shaped vessel originally of leather, later also made in ceramic
Astragal	Bead moulding (in architecture)
Atrium	Small entrance court of Roman house
Attic (-storey)	Half-storey superstructure above the main cornice of a monument
Autochthon	Indigenous person or attitude
Bema	Slightly raised sanctuary in ancient church fronted by marble screen
Blind architecture	Wall articulated by engaged columns (or pilasters) and entablature
Bossed ashlar	A masonry of squared stone blocks with their outer surfaces left unfinished, laid in regular courses
Bucranium	Bull's skull
Caldarium	Hot room in a Roman bath
Caryatid	Human figure, usually female, used as pillar to support entablature
Catagogue feast	Celebration in the cult of Dionysus with an emphasis on fertility and salvation
Cella	Sacred inner room (of temple, tomb, etc.)
Chalcidicum	Annex on the narrow end of a colonnade or stoa
Chaldean Mysterium	Religious movement originating in Syria characterized by notions of salvation
Clazomenaean sarcophagus	Painted clay sarcophagus (named after the city of Clazomenae)
Ciborium	Canopied shrine
Colonnade	Series of columns with entablature along building or street
Concha (-ae)	Shell-like apse(s)
Crater	Bowl for mixing wine and water

Cryptoporticus	Subterranean hall or porch, normally vaulted
Cupid	Minor Roman god of love; usually represented as nude winged boy with double-curved bow and arrows; cherub
Curete(s)	Group of the cult personnel in the Ephesian Prytaneum; originally mythical figures engaged in the birth of Zeus and Artemis
Curvature	Subtle upward curve towards the center of horizontal surfaces in ancient architecture
Cushioned ashlar	A masonry of squared stone blocks with evenly carved convex outer surfaces, laid in even courses
Cybele	Anatolian mother goddes (Greek: Meter Oreia = Mother from the Mountains), also called simply Meter
Cyma	Moulding with double-curved profile terminating the eaves of a temple
Cymation	Moulding decoration with ovals or tri-cusps alternating with lotus flowers
Damnatio memoriae	Damnation of a person's memory; erasure of commemoration
Denticulated cornice	Cornice moulding including at the bottom an even row of small, toothlike rectangular projections
Diodochi	Successors of Alexander the Great
Dipteros	Temple with surrounding double row of columns and at least 8 columns in front. In a pseudo-dipteros the inner row of columns is missing so that the width of peristasis is doubled.
Engaged column	Half-column attached to a wall rather than free-standing
Entablature	The upper portions of a building, usually decorated, situated between the columns and the roof consisting normally of an architrave, frieze and cornice
Epiphany	Manifestation of a deity or superhuman being
Erasure	Effacing of inscriptions (especially in the case of Damnatio memoriae)
Eros (Erotes)	Minor god(s) of love; Roman Cupid(s)
Eustatic	Change of sea level caused by tectonic changes in the earth
Exarch	Governor of certain Byzantine province.
Exedra	A semicircular or rectangular recess off a public space, often provided with benches and statues
Faiance	Decorated tin-glazed earthenware and porcelain
Fasces	Emblem of authority of Roman officials consisting of bundle of rods with projecting axe-blade
Fasciae	Ornamental bands on an architrave or archivolt
Flute	Vertical channel in the surface of a column
Frigidarium	Cold room in Roman bath
Hamam	Turkish bath-house
Harpocrates	Egyptian god (Horus, son of Isis, represented as a child)
Header course	Row of stone blocks or bricks set with long axis perpendicular to wall surface for stronger bond
Herm	Squared pillar or column surmounted by a bust or head (especially Hermes)
Heroon	Cenotaph or funerary monument to a hero or important person
Hippodamian plan	City plan allegedly invented by Hippodamus of Miletus, characterized by regular, parallel streets intersected by other streets at right angles
Hypocaust heating	System first used by the Romans to heat the floors in bath buildings by generating and circulating heated air beneath them
Incrustation (technique)	Decoration of surfaces with inlays of colored stone
In situ	In its original place
Intercolumniation	Space between two columns

Kline	Couch used for reclining at banquets
Koilon	The seating portion of a theatre (Lat.: cavea)
Lekythos	Oil-flask, often used as grave offering
Logeion	Theater stage platform
Lunette	Semicircular field in a wall, often above a door or window
Mappa	Cloth used during sacrifice
Macellum	Meat market
Meander frieze	Ornamental band with continuous meander or spiral pattern
Meter	see Cybele
Middle intercolumniation	Distance between the two center columns of a building front
Monopteros	Open, baldachin-like building with columns but no walls
Naiskos	Little naos (small temple)
Narthex	Shallow entrance hall of ancient Christian/Byzantine basilica or church
Natatio	Swimming pool; cold plunge bath
Necropolis	Burial ground; cemetery
Neocoros	Temple guardian or warden; in Roman Imperial times especially the right to maintain the official Emperor's cult temple in a particular province
Nereid	A daughter of the sea god Nereus; sea-nymph; mermaid
Oinochoe	Spouted pitcher for wine
Oligarchy	Government by a small aristocratic group of persons
Omphalos	Navel; also signifying the center of the earth conceived as a disk
Orthostats	Squared blocks or slabs set on edge to line the base of a wall or socle
Pagan	Unenlightened or irreligious person; especially, non-Christian adherent of Roman cult
Paidiskeion	Educational institution for girls; the term later also used for brothel and latrine
Palaestra	Place of excercise, especially in gymnasium
Pantheon	Entire family of Greco-Roman gods
Passio(n)	Tale of suffering (particularly of Christian martyrs)
Pastophorion (-ia)	Store-room(s) usually adjoining the apse of a church for liturgical implements
Patrocinium	Naming of a church
Pediment	A triangular structure over a building facade, window, niche etc. often containing sculpture
Pendentive	Masonry element designed to carry a dome across the corner of a room, consisting of a spherical triangle with its lower corner rising from a supporting pier at the springing of two adjacent arches
Peripteros	Temple fronted on all four sides with columns
Peristyle	The colonnades surroundinging a building or a courtyard
Phrygian fibula	Phrygian-style clasp similar to a safety-pin
Pilaster	Rectangular column with base and capital projecting from a wall
Piscina	Cold bathing pool in Roman bath; basin, especially for baptisms in ancient Christian baptistery
Pithos	Large storage jar
Plinth	Block supporting statue or column bases
Podium	Rostrum; continuous projecting pedestal around room, house or temple; raised platform around arena of amphitheatre; tall base supporting the lower storey columns in a theatre scaene frons
Polis	City state
Polos	Cylindrical headdress worn by certain divinities
Portico	Colonnade, particularly when attached to a building as a porch
Praefurnium	Heating room in a Roman bath
Presbytery	Part of church reserved for clergy in the vicinity of the altar.
Priapus	A god of fertility

Pronaos	Entrance hall of temple
Propylon	Architecturally developed gate or entrance
Prostyle	Temple with front porch between antae
Protome	Decorative attachments on a vessel serving as handles or spouts
Pseudo-dipteros	see dipteros
Pylon	Gate; often the large entrance gate to a temple or palace, flanked by corner towers
Pyxis	Small box or casket
Returned entablature	Projection of an entablature at right angles to a wall, supported by single or paired columns
Rhyton	Clay cup; drinking horn, sometimes with animal body or head on pointed end
Saw-toothed moulding	Frieze of partially projecting triangular stones sometimes found in Ionic and Corinthian entablatures
Scaenae frons	In theaters, a façade with elaborate columnar display rising behind the stage in two or three stories, normally including aediculae containing sculpture
Solea	Pulpit-like raised platform in front of a presbytery
Sophist	Professional speaker; itinerant teacher who educated youths in science, philosophy and rhetoric
Spolia	Building materials reused from earlier structures
Sphyrelaton	Sheet metal beaten over a wooden core
Stoa	Portico or roofed colonnade or arcade
Strategos	Military general
Stratigraphy	In archaeology, the interrelationship of structures and occupation as well as destruction levels representing the history of a site
Stylobate	Base supporting row of columns
Sudatorium	Hot-air or steam room in Roman baths
Synoicism	Formation of a (new) city out of pre-existing settlements
Taberna	Shop or pub
Temenos	Sacred precinct enclosed by a wall
Templon	Screen or partition separating altar from main body of church
Tendril cyma	Cyma moulding decorated with tendril motif
Tepidarium	Warm room in Roman bath
Terminus ante quem	In history and archaeology, the point in time before which an event must have occurred
Terra sigillata	Modern term for fine Hellenistic-Roman table ware with hard, usually glossy red coating, frequently decorated in relief and stamped by the manufacturer
Tetrarch	Ruler or governor of a fourth of a country or province; in Late Antiquity, one of the four Roman co-emperors
Thiasos	Retinue of Dionysos
Tholos	Circular temple or tomb surmounted by a dome and often encircled by columns
Thrinkos	Altar in enclosed courtyard
Thymiaterium	Incense basin or stand for a censer
Toga (-tus)	Loose outer garment worn by adult Roman males; person so dressed
Torus	Moulding of convex profile; especially as lowest member of base of column
Triclinium	Ancient Roman dining room with couches along three sides
Tropaion	Victory monument consisting of enemy arms and armour
Tubulature	Hollow tile used as a flue
Tumulus tomb	Ancient sepulchral mound
Tyche	Fate, coincidence, luck (and their personification in a goddess)
Tympanum	Triangular space forming center of pediment, often decorated with reliefs
Vine cyma	Cyma decorated with vine-leaf motif

REFERENCES to the Literature

From the very beginning, the results of the Austrian excavations in Ephesus have been regularly published in the form of excavation reports and individual studies in:

ÖJh	Jahreshefte des Österreichischen Archäologischen Instituts
Anz	Anzeiger der Österreichischen Akademie der Wissenschaften
FiE	Forschungen in Ephesos (Band I - XIII)
BerMatÖAI	Berichte und Materialien des Österreichischen Archäologischen Instituts
SoschrÖAI	Sonderschriften des Österreichischen Archäologischen Instituts

Special subjects are dealt with in:

Aug. Architektur	W. ALZINGER, Augusteische Architektur in Ephesos (SoschrÖAI 16, 1974)
IvE	Inschriften von Ephesos I - VIII, in: Inschriften griechischer Städte aus Kleinasien (1979 - 84)

İNAN – ROSENBAUM (1966)
J. İNAN – E. ROSENBAUM, Roman and Early Byzantine Portrait Sculpture in Asia Minor (1966)

İNAN – ALFÖLDI-ROSENBAUM (1979)
J. İNAN – E. ALFÖLDI-ROSENBAUM, Römische und frühbyzantinische Porträtplastiken aus der Türkei, Neue Funde (1966)

For newest research see also:

H. FRIESINGER – F. KRINZINGER, 100 Jahre Österreichische Forschungen in Ephesos. Akten des Symposiums Wien 1995 (Archäologische Forschungen 1 = DenkschrWien 260, 1999)

St. KARWIESE, Groß ist die Artemis der Ephesier (1995)

D. KNIBBE, Ephesus. Geschichte einer bedeutenden antiken Stadt und Portrait einer modernen Großgrabung (1998)

H. KOESTER (ed.), Ephesus, Metropolis of Asia (Harvard theological studies 41, 1995)

G. WIPLINGER – G. WLACH, Ephesus - 100 Years of Austrian Research (1996) [also the German version of 1995 available]

The Ephesus Museum (Efes Müzesi) publishes the series:

EfesHMY	Efes Harabeleri ve Müzesi Yıllığı

The abbreviations of additional literature in this guidebook follow the guidelines of the German Archaeological Institute.

LIST OF CONTRIBUTORS

MA	Maria Aurenhammer	Österreichisches Archäologisches Institut
AB	Anton Bammer	Österreichisches Archäologisches Institut
LB	Lionel Bier	The City University of New York
MB	Mustafa Büyükkolancı	Efes Müzesi Selçuk
PB	Pervin Büyükkolancı	Efes Müzesi Selçuk
SE	Selahattin Erdemgil	Efes Müzesi Selçuk
AE	Adil Evren	Efes Müzesi Selçuk
KH	Karl Herold	Österreichisches Archäologisches Institut
Cİ	Cengiz İçten	Efes Müzesi Selçuk
SK	Stefan Karwiese	Österreichisches Archäologisches Institut
DK	Dieter Knibbe	Österreichisches Archäologisches Institut
FK	Fritz Krinzinger	Österreichisches Archäologisches Institut
CL	Claudia Lang	Österreichische Akademie der Wissenschaften
UM	Ulrike Muss	Österreichisches Archäologisches Institut
UO	Ulrike Outschar	Österreichische Akademie der Wissenschaften
ÖÖ	Öcal Özeren	Efes Müzesi Selçuk
RP	Renate Pillinger	Universität Wien, Archäologisches Institut
AP	Andreas Pülz	Österreichische Akademie der Wissenschaften
PS	Peter Scherrer	Österreichisches Archäologisches Institut
HT	Hilke Thür	Österreichische Akademie der Wissenschaften
BT	Bekir Tuluk	Efes Müzesi Selçuk
GT	Gamze Tuluk	Efes Müzesi Selçuk
DT	Duygu Tüzün	Efes Müzesi Selçuk
EÜ	Enis Üçbaylar	Efes Müzesi Selçuk
GW	Gilbert Wiplinger	Österreichisches Archäologisches Institut
ÜY	Ümran Yüğrük	Efes Müzesi Selçuk
HZ	Heinrich Zabehlicky	Österreichisches Archäologisches Institut
AZ	Ayşe Zülkadiroğlu	Efes Müzesi Selçuk

Illustrations: Unless otherwise stated, all photographs are from the archives of the Österreichisches Archäologisches Institut (Austrian Archaeological Institute), or were supplied by the authors themselves. Many thanks are due to JO PESENDORFER and ANDREAS SCHIFFLEITNER for providing and allowing the publication of many pictures without charge. IRENE DEMBSKI, CLEMENS KNERINGER and NIKI GAIL gave most valuable help in preparing the illustrations for printing.

The overall plan of the ruins at Ephesus was put together by GILBERT WIPLINGER from **drafts (Vorlagen)** from the archives of the institute. FRANZ FICHTINGER undertook the graphic preparation of all plans, and the museum map was drawn by ISABELLA BENDA.

Many thanks are also due to RONALD RISY for diverse forms of support in the fields of editing and organization, in particular in the procurement of the illustrations, as well as to BARBARA BRANDT for editorial work.

ALPHABETICAL INDEX OF MONUMENTS

Numbers correspond to position on the plans of the ruins

(see folder at end of book; detail plans of special sections, at pages 75, 129, 163, 169)

Plan numbers of Monuments

1 Artemision
2 So-called Tribune near the Artemision
3 Coressus Harbour
4 Rock shrine (Meter-Cybele shrine)
5 Byzantine aqueduct
6 Archaic defensive wall (Koressos)
7 Stoa of Damianus
8 Seven Sleepers cemetery
9 Armenian place of worship
10 Magnesian Gate
11 Hellenistic city wall
12 East Gymnasium
13 Basilica in the East Gymnasium
14 St. Luke's Grave (so-called)
15 Street well / fountain
16 Baths on the State Agora
17 Fountain
18 So-called State Agora
19 Doric Gatehouse and South Colonnade of State Agora
20 Temple on the State Agora
21 Basilica Stoa
22 Odeion / Bouleuterion
23 Temenos with Double Monument
24 Prytaneion
25 Banqueting House by the Prytaneion
26 Cathodos of Prytaneion with Embasis
27 Chalcidicum
28 Pollio Monument and Fountain of Domitian
29 Hydrecdocheion of Laecanius Bassus
30 Temple of the Emperors (Temple of Domitian)
31 Niche Monument
32 Memmius Monument
33 Hydreion
34 Round Monument on the Panay_rda_
35 Hercules Gate
36 Curetes Street (Embolos)
37 Trajan's Gatehouse
38 Nymphaeum Traiani
39 Bath Street
40 Temple of Hadrian (Embolos)
41 Varius Bath / Baths of Scholasticia
42 Academy Street
43 Latrine and "House of Pleasure"
44 Alytarchs' Stoa
45 Hellenistic Well
46 Hexagon / Nymphaeum
47 Octagon
48 Androclos Heroon
49 Hadrian's Gate
50 Terrace House 1
51 Terrace House 2
52 Foundations of an Altar
53 Hellenistic Peristyle House
54 So-called "Tube" or Culvert Gate
55 Celsus Library
56 South Gate of the Agora
57 Grave of Dionysius Rhetor
58 Brick vault (Embolos)
59 Circular Monument with Fountain
60 Marble Street
61 Tetragonos Agora (Commercial Market)
62 Hall of Nero
63 West Gate of the Agora
64 North Gate of the Agora
65 West Road
66 Medusa Gate
67 Temple precinct (Serapeion)
70 Round Monument on the Bülbüldağ
71 St. Paul's Grotto (so-called)
72 Theatre Place with fountain
73 Arcadiane east gate
74 Hellenistic Well House (Theatre)
75 Theatre
76 Byzantine Banqueting House (Panayırdağ)
77 Byzantine city wall
78 Theatre Street (Plateia in Coressus)
79 Theatre Gymnasium
80 Apsidal building
81 Byzantine Palace (Sarhoş Hamam)
82 Arcadiane
83 Arcadiane with adjacent Colonnades
84 Four-Column Monument
85 Church on the southern Arcadiane
86 Exedra
87 Middle Harbour Gate
88 Southern Harbour Gate
89 Northern Harbour Gate
90 Market buildings at the Harbour
91 Atrium Thermarum
92 Harbour Baths
93 Harbour Gymnasium
94 Xystoi / Halls of Verulanus
95 Church of Mary
96 Baptistery of the Church of Mary
97 Episcopium of the Church of Mary
98 Olympieion
99 Acropolis
100 Macellum (so-called)
101 Byzantine Well House
102 Late antique Peristyle House / Hellenistic Fortification
103 Crevice Temple
104 Stadium
105 Church in the Stadium
106 Vedius Gymnasium
107 Coressian Gate
110 South Road from the Magnesian Gate
115 Upper Entrance to Ephesus
116 Lower Entrance to Ephesus
151 Fortress (Byzantine - Turkish)
152 Basilica of St. John
153 Mycenaean Grave
154 Classic Grave
155 Prehistoric settlement area
156 Byzantine Aqueduct
157 Gate of Persecution
170 İsa bey Mosque
171 İsa bey Hamam